The Story of
CRAFT

The Craftsman's Role
in Society

Edward Lucie-Smith

Cornell/Phaidon Books
Cornell University Press
Ithaca, New York

First published 1981 by Cornell University Press

International Standard Book Number 0-8014-1428-8
Library of Congress Catalog Card Number 81-65992

Composition in Imprint by
Filmtype Services Limited, Scarborough, North Yorkshire

Printed in the Netherlands by Smeets Offset BV, Weert

Contents

For Lisa Sainsbury

Introduction

This book has a simple but nevertheless ambitious purpose. It is an attempt to see craft — handwork used for making objects — as a practical expression of social life. It concerns itself with the craftsman in his context, not with trying to give an exhaustive history of techniques, which would in any case be impossible in the space at my disposal.

The various forms of crafts are therefore discussed in connection with what I see as my main themes — the functioning of the craftsman as a social animal, and his relationship to our whole view of what a man is. The book examines the development of the idea of individuality and of man's growing sense of his responsibility for his own fate. To these are linked other important, but subsidiary ideas — for example, the development of craft in response to the shaping spirit of taste; and the craftsman's response to the patron, whose demands he either accepts passively, or else tries to modify. I also trace the shift from the unitary idea of craft, where maker and designer are the same, to the moment when the designer comes on the scene as a separate entity. The focus, then, is often on the individuality of the man who invents rather than on the man who creates with his own labour. The designer, as I demonstrate, may easily flourish within a handicraft atmosphere, and his appearance is not solely connected with the rise of industry as it sometimes seems.

Where certain craft activities are concerned, omissions have been made for a variety of reasons. For example, while there is mention of the tin-glazed earthenware which is commonly called faience, there is none of Egyptian faience, a different ware made of sand held together with cement, and covered with a glossy blue or green glaze. Although this was made for a long period — from about 3300 B.C. to around 30 B.C. — it is a dead end. It has had no successors, and few consequences of any kind for the modern crafts.

By contrast, there were areas of activity which seemed to me too sprawling and too enormous to supply me with sufficiently concise and specific illustrations to my arguments. The making of clothes, a craft which involves a large number of different hand skills, is a case in point, despite the fact that it is one of the oldest and most basic of craft occupations, and one which embraces both professional and amateur activity.

There were also kinds of activity which seemed to me somehow alienated from the central notion of craft, elusive though this is when one comes to examine it. All histories of technology, for instance, contain a good deal of information about making coins, as the gradual mechanization of the process pioneered the way for machine production in general. Yet even at its most primitive stage there was always something industrial about coining. The designs the Greek city states stamped on their coins might turn these into great works of art, but the actual process was a purely repetitive one, which aimed to produce a series of objects which were as nearly as possible identical. In fact, it is part of the very nature of a coin that it should deviate as little as possible from the norm which has been chosen — the design itself was originally a guarantee that a norm of weight and value was being adhered to.

The present book's omissions from a technical point of view are more or less easily made good from other books; until now, however, there has been no general view of the evolution of craft, and more particularly of the evolution of the craftsman, psychologically as well as technically. Originally the handcraftsman was a supplier of all man's basic needs. He can never be that again. Today he is more and more both the rival and the ally of the fine artist. The division which the Renaissance created between craft and art is being broken down, but in circumstances very different from those which Renaissance theoreticians would have recognized. If we keep our eyes fixed on techniques only, and do not recognize the mutability of the craftsman's role within society, we shall never understand the true story of craft.

Industry or craft?
Italian silk-
throwing mill.
From an Italian
manuscript of the
14th century.
Milan, Biblioteca
Ambrosiana

1 What is Craft?

The word 'craft' is, like so many important words in English, brief, pungent and ambiguous. The definitions given in the *Shorter Oxford English Dictionary* glide over a whole spectrum of ideas and nuances. In the sixteenth century, for example, craft could be used to mean simply 'strength, power, force'. It could also signify intellectual power, or skill, or, in a pejorative sense, fraud or cunning. (Hence the modern use of 'crafty'.) Additionally, craft could mean occult art, or magic. The sense in which I shall chiefly be using it here, however, is the sixth of the nine basic meanings given by the *Shorter OED*: 'A calling requiring special skill and knowledge; esp. a manual art, a handicraft'. I shall also discuss the meaning which immediately follows — 'the members of a trade or handicraft collectively'. The story of craft is not only the story of man's increasing skill with materials and increasing power over the natural environment; it provides in addition, evidence of the way in which society itself has developed. Men often define themselves through the skills they acquire, and the uses to which they put them.

For my purposes here, craft has three historical stages. First there is the time when everything is craft. All processes of making are hand processes, everything made, whether utilitarian, ritual or merely decorative (and often one cannot separate these functions), is essentially a craft object. Later, at least in Europe, from the Renaissance onwards, it is possible to distinguish two further stages of development. There was an intellectual separation between the idea of craft and that of fine art, which eventually came to be regarded as superior. This development is one of the distinguishing marks of the European Renaissance. Later still, with the Industrial Revolution, there arrived a separation between a craft object and the thing made by a machine — an industrial product.

This separation took place more gradually than is now commonly admitted, especially by those who are ardent partisans of craft. The protests made by John Ruskin and William Morris in the nineteenth century against the evils of the machine — in Ruskin's view it both spoilt what it made and at the same time debased the maker himself — were so effective that what was said and written then have ever since tended to conceal the real complexity of the issues.

If, for example, one looks at the history of textiles from the thirteenth century onwards, one sees how machines gradually came to replace handwork. Highly developed silk-throwing mills already existed in Italy at this time. By the fourteenth century they were

English
18th-century
fly-shuttle loom.
Lancashire, Lewis
Textile Museum

water-powered and enabled two or three operators to do work which had previously required the labour of several hundred. Fulling-mills for woollen cloth also came into use throughout Europe in the thirteenth century. Two heavy wooden mallets powered by a waterwheel reproduced, and thus replaced, the laborious action of physically trampling the cloth with the feet. During the seventeenth century the pace of industrial development in the textile industry quickened still further. The use of automatic looms provoked disturbances at Leiden in Holland in 1620, and ordinances regulating their use were issued in Holland in 1623. An automatic loom was introduced in London as early as 1616, and was the cause of riots there in 1675. It was a ribbon loom, capable of weaving up to six ribbons simultaneously.

This was not, in terms of the time, a large number. Looms capable of weaving up to 24 ribbons at a time were known in Holland as early as 1621, and eventually the number which could be woven simultaneously increased to as many as 50. During the early eighteenth century, before the usual date given for the beginning of the Industrial Revolution, the textile industry became increasingly mechanized. Flax-breaking machines for use in the production of linen were introduced at the end of the 1720s. In 1733 the flying shuttle was invented by John Kay of Bury, and in 1738 Lewis Paul invented a practical spinning machine. Ten years later he invented two carding machines for the treatment of wool; and a more advanced machine which did the same job was introduced simultaneously by Daniel Bourn of Leominster.

A kind of industrialization touched other kinds of manufacture too. In 1389 the first German paper mill was built near Nuremberg by Italian workmen. This, like the slightly earlier fulling mills, was water-powered. In the late sixteenth century wind power began to be more generally exploited — until then it had been used almost solely for grinding corn and (in Holland from 1430 onwards) for drainage operations. 1592 saw the introduction of the first wind-powered saw-mill, once again in Holland.

Fragments of Arretine ware. Roman, 1st century A.D. Arezzo, Museo della Confraternita dei Laici

Mould for Arretine bowl, *c.*30–20 B.C. St Louis Art Museum. Purchase

What this means is that it is mistaken, in many crafts, to talk of an innocent pre-industrial age followed by a corrupt industrial one. If there was ever a departure from a kind of pre-technological Eden, it took place so gradually in many crafts that those who were departing did not notice the fact. It was only later that they began to feel that something had been lost.

People try to distinguish the true craftsman from the artisan not merely through the part machinery plays in the process of production, but through division of labour or the lack of it. In fact, the division of labour in craft activity is something anciently established. It is known, for example, from the signatures, that the decorators of pots in Athenian workshops of the fifth century were not always those who actually made them. Pottery, though now thought of as an extremely personal craft, has frequently been the opposite. Certain wares rely on precision and uniformity for their effect, not on individuality. In Roman times there was a large production of mould-made red gloss pottery at Arezzo in Italy — the so-called Arretine ware. The moulds themselves were not original designs, but were copied from contemporary metalwork. And once the mould-maker's work was done, any pretence at craftsmanlike individuality would have been vain. The aim of the potters was simply to achieve ideal metallic crispness and smoothness, to make each item which came from a particular mould as like its predecessor as possible.

Chinese porcelains, though decorated freehand, offer another

William Hogarth,
English
18th-century
weavers' shop.
London, British
Museum

striking case in point. Porcelain is an intractable material, and requires sophisticated technology and large capital resources if it is to be produced in quantity. In the fifteenth century the Ming emperors centralized production at the large unwalled town of Ching-te-chen, near Nanking, which had good river transportation and was within easy reach of most of the vital raw materials. The manufacture was modelled on the organization of the empire itself, with a director standing in the place of and directly responsible to the emperor. His duty was to see to it that imperial orders were fulfilled, and that production was to the required standard, and in the required quantity. The numbers involved were vast — 159,000 pieces of porcelain were produced in the year 1591 — and there can have been little scope for individual decision at any level below that of the director himself. In addition to this, most of the production was clearly split up on an assembly-line system.

Neither piece-work nor factory conditions were unknown to the European Middle Ages, though the late medieval guild system was so frequently idolized by Ruskin and his disciples. The aim of the guilds often seems to have been to confine men to set tasks, and to make sure that they did not poach in territory belonging to other people. In 1390, the English Parliament passed an act making it illegal for shoemakers to tan leather and for tanners to make shoes. No question here of the craftsman being encouraged to carry out the whole process of manufacture, from first to last, with his own hands. Weaving, always in the forefront of industrial organization because it involved so many repetitive processes, early fell into the hands of men who were entrepreneurs rather than working crafts-men. A book published in 1597 about the early sixteenth-century wool and cloth merchant John Winchcombe offers a telling example of how large some of these entrepreneurial enterprises could be. It describes how Winchcombe had 200 weavers all together in one room, managing 200 looms, with 100 women carding and another 200 women spinning. Once woven the cloth went to 50 clippers and dressers.

Nevertheless, however difficult it may be to define, people today do recognize and respect what seems to them a craft element in most objects produced before the middle of the eighteenth century. They find it again in the artifacts made long after that period by primitive people. And they also find it, though more dubiously, in things made through the use of hand-labour competing with the machine, the sweated products of the so-called Third World.

In addition, there is yet another place where the idea of craft may reasonably be located, and that is in the very heart of modern industry itself, where the artisan with special and superior skills is still commonly described as a craftsman. Often the description is the more exact because it is these industrial craftsmen who create the jigs and tools which guide the machine in its otherwise mindless work — they are important intermediaries between the designer and technologist on the one hand, and the finished industrial product on the other. The uneasiness of their situation sometimes manifests itself in a very common kind of industrial friction, which occurs when the craftsman insists, not merely on being paid a higher wage than the ordinary worker on a production line, but on maintaining the precise differential which he feels to be due to him because of his acknowledged skill.

Finally, we must add to all these the individual artist-craftsmen of our own day, who are the heirs of the Arts and Crafts Movement

Ancient Egyptian gold bracelets, *c*. 940 B.C. London, British Museum

Anglo-Saxon
gold and garnet
purse-lid from
Sutton Hoo,
c. A.D. 625. London,
British Museum

Anglo-Saxon gold,
garnet (mostly
missing) and
enamel brooch,
6th century A.D.
Oxford,
Ashmolean
Museum

which sprang from the protests of Ruskin and the reforming spirit of William Morris. Indeed, it is the interest aroused by their products which has created the need for this book, and one of its major aims is to place them against a wider background.

Because the word craft has to cover so many different categories, our reactions to the concept of craftsmanship are often confused. The aim of this book will be not only to show how the idea of craft has developed, but also to explore how man's attitudes towards it

Japanese black
raku tea-bowl,
Momoyama
period, 16th
century A.D.
Tokyo National
Museum.
Gift of Mr
Matsunaga
Yasuzaemon

Opposite page:
Anglo-Saxon iron
helmet (replica)
from Sutton Hoo,
c. A.D. 625.
London, British
Museum

have changed. For example, it is not merely craft skill itself which has usually commanded respect from those who do not possess it, it is also the ability to control craft, to make it tributary to oneself. Hierarchical ideas have almost invariably tended to express themselves, not in the form of conspicuous wealth alone, but in a parade of precious materials intricately, skilfully and therefore preciously wrought. One of the chief attributes of kingship or chieftainship has always been an ability to exert a monopoly over the work of the best available craftsmen — this tendency appears in the world of the Egyptian pharaohs, in that of Anglo-Saxon chieftains, and also at the court of Louis XIV, the Sun King.

Contrasting with this is the identification of craft with a kind of ideal simplicity. The most sophisticated expression of this attitude probably occurs in Japan, where traditional 'tea taste' — the cult of the tea-ceremony and the articles connected with it — brings with it the idea of a skill which has somehow transcended its own limitations. The roughness and irregularity of a raku tea-bowl is in fact deliberate, yet must at all cost avoid seeming to be so.

Europeans, less poised and subtle in their reactions to what the craftsman makes, have in recent times often seized on his products as a way of rejecting a pervasive materialism, and have thus ironically tended to condemn many creators of the products they admire to a life at, or even below, subsistence level. To patronize the contemporary craftsman has become the expression of values which are partly nostalgic, partly the expression of hope for a better future. To become a professional craftsman is a radical decision, often undertaken as a form of protest against a dehumanizing environment and way of life. Our attitudes towards the people who make this kind of choice are a curious mixture of jealousy, envy and honest admiration. Here, too, the context within which the craftsman works is almost, if not quite, as important as the skills he has so laboriously acquired and the objects he produces.

2 The Beginnings

It was Benjamin Franklin who said that 'Man is a tool-making animal.' Every consideration of craft, before it examines what is made, or the processes used, must look first at the materials and implements employed.

Certain birds and animals, notably apes and monkeys, use improvised tools — objects found by chance in the environment. The human use of tools clearly began at the same stage, and it was only when a suitable natural object could not be immediately found that a less suitable one was roughly shaped to serve the immediate purpose. This in turn was followed by a period when tools were regularly made, but when there was little or no standardization. Then came the regular creation of more-or-less standardized tools, such as stone hand-axes, but with little specialization of function. These processes took a long time. To quote the prehistorian Gordon Childe: 'Every tool embodies the collective experience of countless generations.'

Sometimes, indeed, experience actually suggested that it was easier not to specialize, once a certain level of dexterity had been reached. For example, North American Indian women used the same stone hammer for a multitude of purposes: to break dry wood for fires, to crush bones in order to extract the marrow, to pound dried meat for pemmican, to drive tent pegs into the ground and to beat hides in order to make them pliable.

There is also the fact that tools, though they do evolve and alter, do not always do so in logical fashion. Tool-types persisted long after they should have been superseded, simply because people had got used to using them, or were too poor to obtain better. Even at the close of the nineteenth century, certain prehistoric stone tools were still in regular use in Ireland. Social and ritual needs also played a part, sometimes being pushed so far as to rob a particular tool of all its original utility. In New Guinea, stone axes became symbols of wealth, and grew in size until they were too cumbersome to be practical. The stone adze of Oceania became a god, and in doing so developed a handle too large, too elaborate and too weak to be used.

It was not until about A.D. 500 that most ordinary hand-tools achieved their present form, though of course many of them came near to it long before that date. But until then the story is one, not only of differentiation, but also of continuous evolution. It is no accident that we still name the various stages in the evolution of prehistoric society after the materials from which their tools were made — the Stone Age, the Bronze Age, and finally the Iron Age.

Early 19th-century ceremonial axe from Tahiti. Munich, Museum für Völkerkunde

The earliest stone tools, made of flint, are so primitive that it is sometimes difficult for even the trained archaeologist to differentiate between what is man-made and what is the product of nature. The oldest tools are simple pebbles, flaked so as to make an edge equally suitable for cutting, chopping or scraping. Worked pebbles of this kind have been found in the Olduvai Valley Gorge in Tanzania, in the lowest of a series of sedimentary layers. They are believed to be about 1.75 million years old.

The next stage is represented by the evolution of stone hand-axes, which in Europe were almost invariably made of flint. Such axes were the first fully standardized, general-purpose tools.

Flint tools from the Olduvai Valley Gorge, Tanzania, *c.* 3–2 million B.C. to 500,000 B.C. London, British Museum

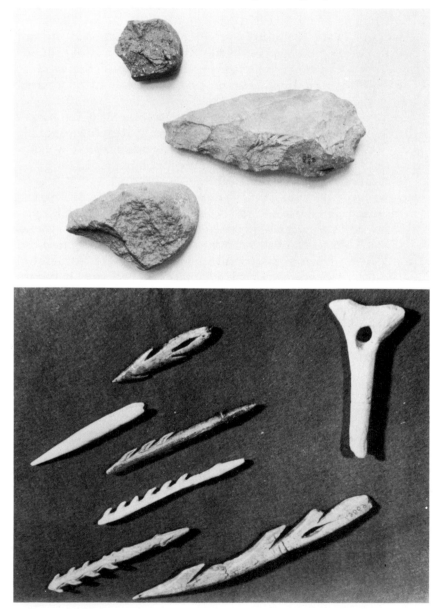

Bone and reindeer horn spearheads, Upper Paleolithic, *c.* 10,000 B.C. St Germain, Musée des Antiquités Nationales

The earliest makers of flint implements thought in terms of shaping a pebble or nodule for the particular purpose they had in mind. But because of the physical characteristics of their material, they at some stage began to approach the task differently and to think of the flint implement as a blade struck from a core which was afterwards discarded. It was only a short step from this to the idea of preparing the core itself first, in such a way that the flakes could be struck from it more certainly and evenly. Flake-culture may have replaced hand-axe culture partly for climatic reasons, as the flakes were especially suitable for use as skinning-knives and skin-scrapers, which would be needed when men began to prepare the skins of the animals they killed as a protection against wet or cold weather.

Gradually flint tools grew more and more elegant and sophisticated in form, until in the Late Paleolithic period one finds beautiful laurel-leaf-shaped blades and neat barbed arrow-heads shaped by striking off a multitude of small flakes until the desired form was achieved.

Stone was not the only material used for tools. In certain cultures, with ready access to the seashore, shells were almost equally important, especially as ready-made scrapers. And everywhere much use was made of bone, ivory and reindeer antler. The Magdalenians, who belong to the last phase of the Paleolithic, used these for barbed spear-heads, loose points for harpoons, spear-throwers and the so-called *bâtons de commandement* which most archaeologists now think were intended for straightening spear and arrow shafts which had first been softened in water or steam. They also made antler hammers and chisels and bone needles with eyes. Much of their technology resembled that of the modern Eskimos, as they lived under much the same sort of conditions.

The aesthetic sense which Late Paleolithic flints seem to express is shown more emphatically and unmistakably in the more ambitious of these bone and antler objects, especially in the spear-throwers and arrow-straighteners, which are sometimes adorned with carved and engraved representations of animals. It is, how-

Reindeer carved from mammoth tusk found at Bruniquel, France, *c.* 10,500 B.C. London, British Museum

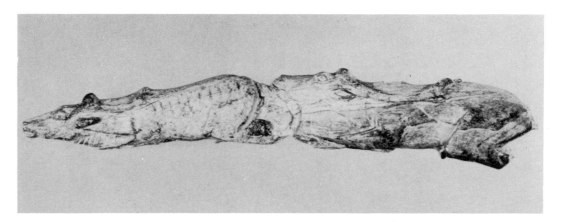

ever, a fact that the most elaborate and beautiful flint objects of all were not produced until after the introduction of metal. Apparently they were made simply as artistic *tours de force*.

The evolution of stone tools and weapons — for it must always be remembered that a weapon is itself a kind of tool, an instrument for killing with — gives a first glimpse of the complexity of the craft aesthetic, which demands at its highest a union of the beautiful and the useful, of what is practical and what is psychologically satisfying.

The ability to work stone, and to turn it into tools, was the first craft skill, but to these were gradually added others. The order in which they came was related to the way in which man himself evolved from hunter into settler, from villager to townsman. Although, for example, pottery is generally thought of as the first of the crafts, next to the making of tools, perhaps because of its inevitable association with the soil itself, it does not actually deserve to be given this primacy. Before man learned to make true pots, he had learned many other skills. Among the earliest must have been the ability to prepare and sew together skins and to make baskets, both of which are associated with a society of hunters and gatherers, rather than with one which roots itself in one place and cultivates the soil.

The ability to prepare and use skins is associated with a tendency to move northwards, into regions which man had previously been unable to inhabit because of the severity of the climate. Clearly these skins were at first used in their raw state. Later, they were probably salted. Both flints and salt were traded over long distances from an early date, and the need for salt may have been connected with leather-craft as well as with diet. The first true tanning process made use of alum — the white-tawing or Cordovan process — and this may have been discovered when alum was used in mistake for common salt. Since leather is a perishable material, very little concrete evidence is available. The earliest literary reference to making leather seems to be the one in *The Iliad*, when the poet describes the fight for Patroclus's corpse:

As when the slaughter'd bull's yet reeking hide,
Strain'd with full force, and tugged from side to side
The brawny curriers stretch and labour o'er
The extended surface, drunk with fat and gore.
(Alexander Pope's translation)

It does at least give a splendidly barbarous impression of the beginnings of the craft.

Baskets seem to have been invented as a result of the practice of harvesting wild seeds and berries, and also perhaps because of the need to transport possessions from place to place. The North American Indians, before the coming of the Europeans, used baskets for every conceivable domestic purpose, and the ability to produce a beautiful basket was considered the highest merit in a woman.

Fragment of a
Neolithic fishing
basket from
Nidløse,
Denmark,
c. 30,000 B.C.
Copenhagen
National Museum

This humble craft is interesting for more than one reason. First, it seems to have achieved near-perfection very early. Finds made in Egypt indicate that excellent baskets were being made there around 5000 B.C. Secondly, because it achieved a high standard so easily, it stabilized itself and became almost static. Baskets very like the Predynastic ones I have just mentioned are still being made in Egypt today. It seems probable that Neolithic basketry made use of all the techniques still commonly employed by basket-weavers throughout the world — coiling, plaiting, twining and so forth, according to the kind of material available.

But baskets have a deeper fascination than this. While it is true that the first baskets may have been simple *ad hoc* containers, made of whatever grass or leafage was available, wrapped round a particular object, and destined to be destroyed when what was being carried was unwrapped again, they do represent, far more than the chipping of flint in a predetermined pattern, the first logical, orderly and systematic use of materials, where the final shape completely expressed the nature of the processes that had been used. Most of the basic techniques required for both weaving and knitting are already present in basket-work.

Perhaps because it is the most elaborate and beautiful known (the decorated baskets made by the Pomo Indians of Southern California have been described as 'feathered jewels'), a good deal of scholar-ship has been devoted to North American Indian basketry. One thing which emerges is the degree of poetic meaning attached by the Indians to their baskets. It was not merely that baskets were full of social symbolism — when the Choctaw Indians sent a gift of fruit it was in a heart-shaped basket to denote sincerity — it was also that the patterns of decoration spoke an elaborate symbolic language. On a Washington basket a particular design represented not just ripples upon water, but the subtle movements of the underwaters of a certain lake upon a particular occasion.

Since making a basket is largely repetitive work, it easily becomes ritualized. The best ways of using traditional materials were for the North American Indian basket-weavers immutable and long deter-mined.

There is a beautiful description, not from the United States but from the Aleutian Islands of *c*.1900, which gives some idea of the spirit in which baskets were made. Here, too, the work was done by women, and the materials used were strand wheat or wild rye. Though the tribe lived on the shore, the basket-weavers went inland to gather what they wanted, taking only two or three young blades from every stalk. The selected blades were then taken back to the village, spread on the ground, and watched and turned for two weeks while being kept away from sunlight. They were then sorted into three grades — fine, medium and coarse. The coarse and medium stalks were split with the fingernails, then the sorted and split grasses were put into bundles, which were hung out on foggy and cloudy days while being handled with a twisting motion in order to make the grasses pliable and tough. Finally the material was brought indoors to complete the drying process, and the stalks were further split. Only then were they considered fit for the actual basket-weaving, which took place indoors during the winter months.

Obviously what this description implies is a completely organic,

19th-century North American Indian basket — Chumaz, from Santa Inez, California. New York, Museum of the American Indian, Heye Foundation

Pomo Indian woman weaving a latticed twine basket.

Early 19th-century Pomo basket, decorated with shells and feathers, from California. New York, Museum of the American Indian, Heye Foundation

non-commercial economy, with craft skills acquired instinctively and handed down from generation to generation so that the business of making a basket acquired a ceremonial quality, putting the maker at one with nature and its seasons. It represents the pre-lapsarian ideal towards which many modern craftsmen aspire. Yet if one looks at the evolution of more central crafts one soon begins to realize how early such notions began to be challenged by quite different notions about the maker of objects and his or her place in the community.

Both pottery and weaving may have evolved out of basketry — the first from the custom of covering a basket with clay in order to make it waterproof, the second from the technique itself. Another way in which pottery originated may have been with the clay-lined pits which were used for cooking. Examples have been found at Jericho, and also at a site in Kurdistan. Though making pots is now in many ways the most central of the crafts, its evolution was surprisingly slow. Men soon learned that clay itself was pliable, and would take many forms. Unfired clay models are known from the Mesolithic period, 120,000 years ago. But pottery was unknown throughout the Stone Age, even to people who could shape stone and bone, make baskets and produce a kind of leatherwork. In part this slowness to develop was due to social patterns. Societies of hunters and gatherers are nomadic, and because of this naturally preferred unbreakable materials. It was only when men settled more or less permanently on the land that they began to see much advantage in using pots. Even so, the development of agriculture and the development of pottery do not necessarily coincide. Men already lived in fortified towns before vessels of fire-hardened clay made their appearance. This seems to have happened within a

Potter's wheel from
Ur, *c.* 3200 B.C.
London, British
Museum

Ancient Egyptian
painted wood
tomb-model of a
potters' workshop.
From Saqqara,
6th Dynasty
(*c.* 2323–2151 B.C.).
Cairo Museum

century or two of the year 6000 B.C., in an area extending from
modern Iraq to the eastern part of the Mediterranean basin.

The first pots were formed entirely by hand, and it is probable
that they, like baskets, were the work of women. Each woman made
them for her own domestic use, just as she performed other
household tasks. Indeed, like many of these tasks, the earliest
pot-bakings were probably seasonal rituals, performed at a particular time of year and hedged about with tabus. Today, in the
Kabylia, the women still make pottery only once a year. Further
south in Africa, many Bantu tribes will not fire pots when the moon
is on the wane, as this, they believe, will inevitably make the pots
crack.

There soon arose a distinction between fine ware, valued for its
aesthetic qualities, and rough, or purely utilitarian pottery, but the
potter's wheel, which enabled potters to achieve complete regularity of shape, was not invented until the second half of the fourth
millennium B.C. Very primitive examples have been found at Ur in
Sumer. They consist of two flat round slabs, generally made of
stone but sometimes of baked clay. One of these slabs has a hole in
the centre, and the other a pivot. Probably a further slab of wood
was set on top of the whole mechanism to enlarge the area the potter
worked on. These early wheels needed two people to work them.
The potter threw, while the wheel was turned by an apprentice.
The foot wheel was probably not known before the second century
B.C.

The use of the potter's wheel meant a great change in the attitude
towards craft. A means of rapid production implies the presence of
a specialist. Men, family bread-winners, in many communities
tended to replace women as the makers of pots. One such specialist

could now easily supply the needs of a village of a couple of hundred inhabitants, exchanging his skill and labour for what others produced. Indeed, he could probably produce more pots than his own community required. This led, almost immediately, to the establishment of a market, and one soon finds evidence of pots being traded, though at first only locally because of their fragility. Soon, however, they began to travel farther. In the late Bronze Age, fine Mycenaean wares were exported to all areas of the eastern Mediterranean, and, because of the quality of the work itself, one can be sure that it was the pots themselves which were traded, and not just what they contained.

Minoan pottery cup from Phaistos, imitating wooden stave construction. Bronze Age. Heraklion Archaeological Museum

The decoration and shapes of early pottery were of course influenced by the progress of technique. For example, narrow-necked vessels only made their appearance when craftsmen had discovered that pots could be made in two parts, which were then luted together. But there was also a constant interchange of forms with other crafts. The tractability of clay, and its cheapness, meant that pots were often made in imitation of vessels in rarer and more expensive materials, particularly metal. Yet the desire to produce a cheap imitation was not always the criterion. There are also imitations of basketry and leather, and even of the gourds which were used as containers. In Early Minoan Crete, potters reproduced the staved wooden chalices produced by contemporary

Boldly decorated Late Neolithic pot from Dimini, Thessaly, *c.* 2500 B.C. Athens, National Archaeological Museum

woodworkers, and even imitated the grain of the wood with painted decoration.

In fact, there is something unexpected about the development of decoration in general, not only because it so often involves imitating something else but because it seems to take precedence of the desire to make a pot useful and functional. Slipping and burnishing techniques have an extremely practical result — they make a pot more waterproof. Nevertheless, archaeological investigation has made it clear that these additional processes were first developed for purely aesthetic reasons, to make the pot more pleasing to the eye. On the same sites were found good quality wares, with slipping and burnishing in evidence, and undecorated domestic pottery of much poorer make, such as water-jugs and cooking pots, where extra waterproofing might have been useful but is nevertheless not present.

Though pottery provides a good example of craft specialization, it is by no means certain that early potters were universally respected for their skill. In part, this may have been due to their primary material. The anthropologist George M. Forster, investigating the status of the potter in a contemporary Mexican village, found that those who practised the craft both deprecated themselves and were looked down upon by non-potters. 'Here you find us in all this dirt,' one of his potter-interviewees said to him. Some archaeologists have maintained that agricultural Semitic societies invariably despised artisans specializing in any kind of craft and regarded agriculture as a more central and therefore more prestigious occupation. Potters are sometimes outsiders or actual outcasts in primitive societies. Today in Ethiopia, the Faleshas, a sect of black Jews, serve as travelling potters for a predominantly Christian population. The depressed status of the craftsman-potter is not, however, universal. In western Tibet, potters used to be

Mycenaean vase,
15th century B.C.
Athens, National
Archaeological
Museum

considered high-caste, and occupied a higher social and economic position than comparable groups.

One reason why histories of craft tend to put such emphasis on pottery is purely adventitious. A pot, though fragile, is essentially almost indestructible. Its form re-appears when it is reconstructed, and most techniques for decorating pots are also relatively durable. The result is that pots, once they appear, are the best means the archaeologist has of measuring both continuity and change in a particular culture. Survival of a particular class of pottery will, for example, often demonstrate essential cultural continuity despite superficially drastic political change. Marked alteration in the types of pots being made at a particular site implies either the massive influx of a new population group or the entire destruction of one culture and its replacement by another and rival one.

Weaving, like pottery, is commonly accorded a central position in craft histories, but more because of its importance in social development than thanks to its prominence in archaeology. Despite the fact that woven materials are so much more perishable than pots, there is evidence that structures made of intersecting threads were known in the Mesolithic age. The first evidence of true weaving dates from the sixth, or even perhaps the seventh millennium B.C. Textile remains have been found at the Neolithic site of Çatal Hüyük and in the oldest layers at Jericho. The earliest known representation of a loom occurs on the inside of a Predynastic dish from Badari in Egypt, which dates from about 4400 B.C.

Predynastic dish from Badari, Egypt, showing a loom, *c.* 5000 B.C. London, University College, Petrie Collection

All the chief natural fibre groups appear in early archaeological remains, vegetable fibres, such as bast and cotton, being found earlier than wool or silk. Cotton, for instance, is first found around 3000 B.C. in India. Wool first appears in profusion in Scandinavia around 1000 B.C., and silk about the same time in China. Silk supplies a good example of the way in which a particular craft skill might remain exclusive to one area for a considerable time, rather than being rapidly disseminated. It was first exported to the West under the Han Dynasty (202 B.C.–A.D. 220), and its shine and softness caused a sensation among people who had never seen anything of this nature before. The demand for it was such that it led to the establishment of the overland Silk Road, a network of caravan routes which brought the precious fabric from its place of origin to Syrian markets. But raw silk was not actually produced in Europe itself until the sixth century A.D.

China was also probably the source of certain important innovations in weaving technique, notably the treadle loom, which became the basis of the medieval European textile industry. It travelled from China via the Near East and did not appear in the West until the rise of an organized woollen industry in the Low Countries in the eleventh and twelfth centuries A.D.

The development of weaving in ancient times is easiest to trace in Egypt where, thanks to the dry climate, many well-preserved specimens have been found. From these we know that very fine linen cloths were being produced as early as Dynasty I, *c.*3000 B.C.,

Opposite above: Ancient Egyptian painted wood tomb-model of a weavers' shop. From Thebes, *c.* 2000 B.C. Cairo Museum

Opposite below: Dalmatic with tapestry border from Tutankhamun's tomb. Oxford, Ashmolean Museum, Griffith Institute

with no fewer than 160 to 120 threads per inch. By Dynasty XI, *c*. 2100 B.C., looped techniques were being used to produce towels similar to modern Turkish towels. Pattern weaves are not found in Egypt until Dynasty XVIII. The tombs of the pharaohs Tuthmosis IV and Tutankhamun have yielded examples of true tapestry weaving.

For its full effect, pattern depends not only on more complex weaving techniques, but on dye for colouring the threads. Dyeing always had something alchemical about it — recipes and methods were closely guarded secrets, and certain dyestuffs had very real prestige. In the ancient world the most prestigious of all were the red and purple dyes made from the *purpura murex*, which seem to have been developed by the Phoenicians during the first millennium B.C. Large quantities of shellfish were needed to dye even small amounts of wool, and purple became the Roman imperial colour, reserved for the ruler himself and for the great officers of

state, whose ceremonial dress was the *toga praetexta*, a white cloak adorned with a purple stripe.

Dyed and pattern-woven fabrics were rivalled by embroidery, which allowed greater flexibility in making designs. Embroidery has been found on Egyptian mummy cloths, and it is of course mentioned by Homer, who describes Helen of Troy embroidering a picture representing the Trojan Wars. This, together with the description in *The Odyssey* of Penelope weaving by day and unpicking what she had done by night, so as to hold her importunate suitors at bay, supplies an early example of textile craft as an aristocratic pastime, a tradition which was to be taken over and further developed by the noble households of the Middle Ages.

Wood, another perishable material, also survives best in dry climates, and most of our surviving specimens of ancient carpentry, like our specimens of ancient weaving, have been found in Egypt. Shortage of material gave the Ancient Egyptians a particular impetus to perfect piecing and joining techniques at an early date. Egyptian wooden coffins of the Old Kingdom illustrate how wide was the contemporary woodworker's repertoire. There is a variety of different sorts of joints — the plain butt joint, the mitre joint fixed by dowels, shoulder-mitres, double shoulder-mitres and dovetails. The only basic woodworking tool which the Egyptians lacked was the lathe, credited by the Roman writer Pliny the Elder to the seventh century B.C.

The most striking characteristics of Ancient Egyptian furniture, however, are sophistication and elaboration. Though there is little

Ancient Egyptian painted wood tomb-model of a carpenters' shop. From Saqqara, 6th Dynasty (*c.* 2323–2151 B.C.). Cairo Museum

Highly decorated
Ancient Egyptian
chair, *c*. 1333–
1323 B.C.
From
Tutankhamun's
tomb. Cairo
Museum

complete furniture surviving from the Early Dynastic period (*c*.3100–*c*.2700 B.C.), there are enough fragments to indicate a high standard of luxury. For example, there is a series of carved ivory bull's legs, which were obviously used as supports for stools, couches and small chests. Just a little later is the funerary furniture of Queen Hetepheres, wife of Sneferu, the first pharaoh of the Fourth Dynasty, and mother of Cheops, builder of the Great Pyramid at Giza. This ensemble includes an armchair, a carrying-chair, a bed, a headrest and a large collapsible canopy. All of these have most of the wooden elements sheathed in thick gold plating.

Tutankhamun's furniture is less massively valuable, but even more artistic and elaborate. Particularly striking is a series of elegant chairs. One, the most formal of all, has a base made like an X-shaped folding stool. The seat, deeply curved, is made of ebony and inlaid with irregular pieces of ivory to imitate goatskin. The back is panelled, in a pattern which resembles the wall-decoration of contemporary buildings. With the chair goes a matching foot-stool, which is inlaid with nine bound figures who represent the traditional enemies of Egypt. In terms of craftsmanship this chair, which dates from *c*.1361–*c*.1352 B.C., is fully the equal of anything produced by the great French *ébénistes* of the eighteenth century.

Two decorated Ancient Egyptian chairs from a tomb at Bibou el Molrek. 18th Dynasty. Cairo Museum

Its irrational structure (the back is a completely separate element from the seat), and the use of one material to imitate another place it very far from the ideals of the nineteenth-century Arts and Crafts Movement.

In most regions the development of building techniques must have been allied to increasing expertise in carpentry. Among primitive peoples, for example, building and carpentry are usually one and the same activity. Among the Bakonde in Africa there is a traditional division of labour between males and females — the man cuts the trees for the hut; builds it; thatches it, and also makes the door and the bed within it. The woman fetches the grass for the thatch, and also mud-plasters the walls and the floor. Simple building of this type also demonstrates the importance of using the materials closest to hand. This, indeed, was a situation which long persisted. In the Middle Ages, transporting a load of stone from the quarry to the workshop cost at least as much as buying the stone at the quarry itself. In order to get rid of excess weight building stone was invariably dressed where it was found, and not at the site of construction.

Characteristic building technologies developed according to region and the materials available. In the ancient Near East, where good stone was scarce, moulds for making unbaked mud bricks long predated the invention of pottery. Often, as the supply of materials and the ability to handle them improved, an idiom learned from one medium would be transferred to another. The Classical Greek column evolved from the simple tree-trunk, and, though it was made of stone, its use was originally suggested by techniques of building with timber. The forms of early Egyptian stone buildings owe something to the papyrus reed — in particular, Zoser's buildings at Saqqara are copies in limestone of the primitive houses and temples in reed, clay and mud brick which immediately preceded them.

The capacity to bring building materials from a long distance and to muster a large workforce to deal with them was a conspicuous sign of a centralized state and a powerful ruler. The Great Pyramid at Giza attested the power of the pharaoh who built it. King Solomon's temple in Jerusalem, so vividly described in the First Book of Kings, was built in part of cedar and fir brought from the Lebanon:

> Now therefore command thou that they hew me cedar trees out of Lebanon; and my servants shall be with thy servants: and unto thee will I give hire for thy servants according to all that thou shalt appoint: for thou knowest there is not among us any that can skill to hew timber like unto the Sidonians.

The ancient Egyptians also traded precious woods — chiefly cedar and ebony — over long distances. The famous Amherst Papyrus recounts the story of one such voyage — to Lebanon for cedar-wood, and disastrous as it turned out.

Detail of the Parthenon showing how the method of construction derives from wooden prototypes

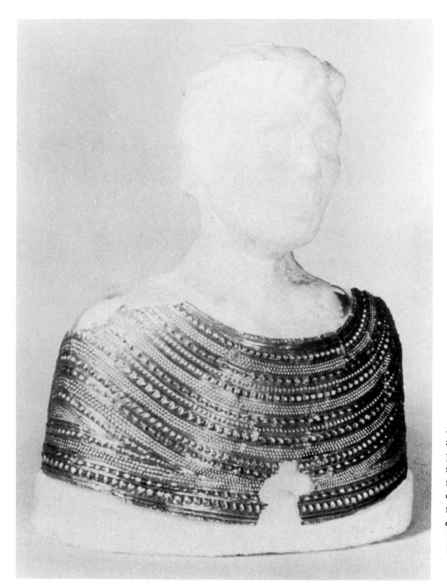

A symbol of
authority:
prehistoric gold
sheet ceremonial
mould cape,
decorated in
repoussé,
c. 1400–1200 B.C.
London, British
Museum

The ability to do precise and accurate stonework and carpentry
obviously depended to a large extent on the replacement of stone
tools, however skilfully made, with metal ones. It is impossible, for
example, to make a spoked wheel without a metal saw. The
appearance of metal, and its surprisingly slow permeation of man's
material culture, is of the greatest importance to almost all the
issues treated in this book.

The first metals to make their appearance were copper and gold,
the reason being that both of these can be found uncombined in
nature. During the Chalcolithic period, which intervened between
the end of the Neolithic or New Stone Age and the beginning of the
regular use of metals, men discovered that metal could be shaped
by hammering, and that this process actually served to harden

copper. But metals were first used more for ornamental than for useful purposes.

The next stage was the deliberate search for metals beneath the ground. The practice of actually mining for gold seems to have begun around 3000 B.C. Rare, malleable, untarnishable, it had from the beginning unique prestige as a repository of value and a symbol of authority. Its technological role was subtle. It was the ancient jeweller who discovered new methods in the management of metals, simply because his favoured material was so reluctant to unite with others as a compound, if not as an amalgam. All soldering techniques, for example, stem finally from experiments made in jewellers' workshops.

The discovery that it was possible to smelt copper was probably connected, on the other hand, with the making of pottery, and particularly with the introduction of glazes. Alkaline glazes based on soda found in a natural state in the desert were known in Egypt as early as the fifth millennium B.C. Malachite, a compound of copper, was used as a colouring agent. Since copper is a much commoner metal than gold, and a harder one, it rapidly acquired a practical as well as a decorative role as a material for tools. Lewis Mumford remarks that 'The tool brought man into closer harmony with his environment, not merely because it enabled him to reshape it, but because it made him realize the limits of his capacities.' This paradoxical statement really takes on its fullest force when we consider the precision of the metal tool, rather than the more uncertain nature of a stone one.

Etruscan gold fibula with lions, showing intricate soldering techniques, 7th century B.C. Rome, Vatican Museum

The next step was to combine copper with tin, to produce bronze, a harder and more practical material for tools of all kinds. Since tin is much less widespread than copper, the production of bronze tended to be confined to a few localities. Bronze was most likely to be produced where tin and copper were found together. The copper smelting process, turning malachite, which appears to be stone, into shining metal, made those associated with it seem to have magical powers. The fashioning of bronze tools and weapons, especially the latter, thanks to their association with ideas of manhood, power and death, was a further decisive step towards turning the craftsman into a man apart.

Nevertheless one must not exaggerate the immediate impact of the use of metals on human civilization. Throughout the Copper and Bronze Ages the consumption of metal was very small. It has been estimated, for instance, that the consumption of copper in the ancient world between 2800 B.C. and 1300 B.C. only amounted to about 10,000 tons. The precision of metal tools was valued the more because they were scarce and expensive. In fact, one of the things which long after the introduction of iron held back the development of anything resembling industrialism was the fact that any large and ambitious mechanical device tended to be made of wood, as sufficient metal was not available for such purposes.

As a rarity, man-made iron, as opposed to naturally occurring iron from meteorites, may go back as far as 1800 B.C., but it was certainly not produced on a regular basis until some four hundred years later. Miniature tools made of iron were found in the tomb of Tutankhamun. At this point it was probably still thought of as a precious, rather than a common metal. We know that, in the Egyptian New Kingdom, it was five times more valuable than gold and twenty times dearer than silver.

The first people to produce iron on something like a commercial scale were probably the Hittites, in Asia Minor, and they succeeded in keeping the process a secret until the power of the Hittite Empire

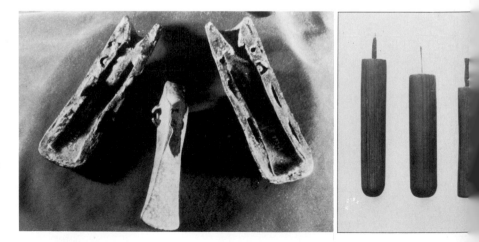

Prehistoric mould with a bronze axe of the type made from it, *c*. 4000–3000 B.C. St Germain, Musée des Antiquités Nationales

weakened around 1200 B.C. The knowledge of how to obtain it spread to Palestine, and by the tenth century B.C. iron was already cheap enough to be used on some occasions for making agricultural implements. As knowledge of iron spread, so did the tendency to explore its properties and see if they could be improved by new processes. Quench-hardening of iron seems to have been known around 900 B.C., and tools made from hardened iron are known in both Assyria and Egypt between 800 and 700 B.C.

The difficulty of producing iron set blacksmiths apart from the communities they served even more than the coppersmiths who preceded them. Among primitive tribesmen all kinds of superstitions still attach to the blacksmith's profession. For example, the Ila-speaking peoples of Zambia believe it would be impossible to smelt iron without using the proper medicines which transform the ore. The most important person in connection with the blacksmith's craft is here the 'iron-doctor', who has knowledge of the substances required. The work itself is carried on only in the spring, and when smelting is to be done a temporary hut is built where the smelters live in a state of ritual tabu. They are not allowed to enter their own homes; their wives, who remain in the village, are treated like those recently widowed, and may not wash, anoint themselves, or wear ornaments which might attract male attention. The men, while building the kiln for smelting, are not allowed to drink water.

Blacksmiths, like potters, are regarded in primitive communities with an uneasy and uneven mixture of contempt (sometimes even fear) and respect — the exact formula varying widely from one place to another. Even more than potters, they are culturally isolated from the rest of the community, a fact which is sometimes symbolized by their connection with tribal secret societies, as in West Africa, and by their reputation as magicians. Some African tribes actually worship the smith's tools, whereas others — always nomads — make him a despised pariah. The reason, in both cases, seems to be the way in which the possession of skill singles a man out, and at the same time removes him from the prevailing hierarchical structure, and also the connection in this case between the workman and his admittedly dangerous, though at the same time benificent material. The link between smiths and the occult is consistent, whatever their status. The Masai think they bring death and disease. The Wachagga, another African tribe, both fear and venerate them, but think they are particularly undesirable as sons-in-law, since in case of divorce they are reputed to be able to make their wives sterile. In Java, on the other hand, the blacksmith is considered theoretically equal to the prince, his 'brother', and smiths' genealogies are traced back to the gods.

Primitive craft of whatever type cannot be fully understood unless one sees it as part of a much larger system of customs, ideas and beliefs. Sometimes, in special cases, ritual considerations might completely freeze technological development. The Romans con-

Miniature iron tools (in modern handles) found in Tutankhamun's tomb.
Oxford, Ashmolean Museum

tinued to use stone knives for sacrificial purposes, just as the Hebrews used them for circumcision. As men discovered new craft processes, they consistently linked them to mythical archetypes. In Tanzania one finds creation myths which relate to not one but three different crafts — blacksmithing, pottery and weaving. Both blacksmithing and pottery had a particular appeal to the primitive imagination because they make use of the transforming and mysterious powers of fire.

At a more mundane level, however, one does see certain important strands of development. Craft in primitive societies is highly ritualized. Among the Maori, for example, only men of rank were employed to make canoes and every stage in the building of a canoe was accompanied by appropriate ceremonies — one at the felling of the tree, one to give power to the axe to shape the vessel, one when it was drawn out of the bush, and so forth. Equally often a particular craft remained the province of one sex. If domestic, it was the work of women, with men being called in only where superior physical strength was required, where the work involved going some distance from home, or where it was concerned with weaponry. In addition to being divided between the sexes, crafts were often hereditary, in the case of women's skills passing from mother to daughter. Yet when a particular craft left the purely domestic environment, and became a means of earning a living for an entire family, it often passed from female into male hands — I have noted that this seems to have happened to pottery with the introduction of the wheel. Herodotus notes that in Classical Greece it was still the duty of the housewife to weave, whereas in contemporary Egypt the husband worked the loom. The reason is clear: in Greece, weaving was still done to supply the needs of the household; in Egypt it was done commercially.

Minoan faience statuettes of the mother goddess. From Knossos, *c*. 1600–1550 B.C. Kandia Museum

Carved prow of
Maori war-canoe,
early 19th century.
London, Museum
of Mankind

The growth of cities had an immense impact both on the development of craft and on attitudes towards craft. It was large communities which could afford to support the specialized handi-craftsman. Already by 2500 B.C. the larger settlements in Mesopotamia contained between 8,000 and 12,000 inhabitants. Wherever we find cities rather than villages we also find a finer subdivision of labour. In Minoan Knossos there was gem-cutting, ivory carving, faience manufacture, jewellery-making, silversmithing and the craft of making stone vessels — nearly all of them luxury trades. At Chanhu-daro, one of the cities of the Indus Valley civilization, the bead-makers occupied a quarter of their own.

It is often assumed that in slave-owning societies craftsmen must have been slaves. In early civilizations this was not the case. In the ancient Near East, where the fully recognizable professional crafts-man first appeared, he was typically a free-born man. He might — indeed he usually did — work for a master rather than for himself, but he possessed his own tools and laboured only for a definite period — a day, a month or a season — in the house of his employer. Such free craftsmen very soon organized themselves into guilds or fraternities. A clay tablet from Ras Shamra dating from the fourteenth century B.C. provides a list of the guilds of that city.

In general, basic craft skills soon reached an advanced stage in many areas of activity, and then remained for a long time unaltered. Even less subject to change, once it had been established, was the basic pattern of the professional craftsman's existence. For instance, at the present day the skilled craftsman — carpenters are a case in point — is quite typically a man who owns his own tools, and who hires himself out for a specific job. His special knowledge, as well as the implements he holds in his hands, give him at least partial independence of the prevailing industrial system.

3 The Ancient World

It is easiest to summarize the place of craft and craftsmen in the ancient world by looking at the ancient crafts in their most fully developed form, under the Roman Empire. The Empire embraced such a vast territory that it brought together many craft traditions — Eastern and Western, Syrian, Greek, Egyptian and Celtic. Its excellent system of communications made possible not only an active trade in fabricated objects — the Roman dramatist Terence speaks of British and Pictish baskets being taken to Rome — but also a constant interchange of ideas among those who produced them.

Yet, in considering Roman craft, one immediately encounters two paradoxes. The actual status of the craftsman had on the whole declined from the position he had occupied in the cities of the ancient Near East; while the Classical ideal, which was the intellectual matrix within which all craftsman worked, was actually hostile to what most of us would consider the true essence of craft, if we look at it from a twentieth-century point of view.

The decline in status predated the rise of the Empire itself. In fifth-century Athens, for example, the potters who produced the marvellous red-figure wares, which were exported all over the Mediterranean, were aliens, without citizenship rights. The orator Isocrates (436–338 B.C.) speaks of the 'insolence' of saying that the great painters Zeuxis and Parrhasius ranked with the painters of pots. We know that the production of red-figure was pretty much factory work — a prosperous Athenian workshop of this type might employ as many as seventy men.

In free Greek cities the status of the craftsman seems to have been depressed by two things in particular. One was continuing competition from household handicrafts. The other was the way in which the institution of slavery tended to reduce the free craftsman to the level of those who were not free. In the craft workshops free men and slaves worked side by side, and the rate of pay for all was equal. The Greek system spread to Italy after 350 B.C., and was then disseminated by the Romans. Because so many skilled craftsmen were, if not slaves, then freedmen, and still bore in Roman eyes the mark of slavery, there developed a prejudice against artisans in general.

The craftsmen's custom of banding themselves together in guilds, and of their occupying a special quarter of a particular city, nevertheless continued. At Metz, in Roman Gaul, there was a sandal-makers' quarter. At Rome itself there was a carpenters' quarter, and a *collegium*, or guild, of workers in wood. At Arles, in Provence, there was a *collegium* which included both builders and

Roman relief of the Praetorian Guard. Roman armour and weapons were made in state factories. Paris, Musée du Louvre carpenters among its members, some of them evidently of superior class. The inscription of his coffin tells us that Q. Candidus Benignus, who belonged to this guild, was a student of building theory and also a specialist in waterworks and road-building. We are further told that he was sweet-tempered, gentle, studious and a good host.

If Benignus stood at one end of the social scale, employees in the Imperial workshops stood at the other. In the third century A.D. these included slaves, freedmen, free citizens and also people condemned for some crime. What they had in common was the fact that they found it increasingly difficult to leave their employment. As the Empire aged and its frontiers began to contract, the labour-shortage grew ever more acute. This led eventually to a first, tentative attempt at true industrialization — the development of the watermills with which Benignus was probably concerned. Then, as for many centuries, such machines were largely constructed from wood. The labour shortage also led to a tendency to try and bind artisans to their tasks by draconian legal measures.

Certain jobs had in any case always been subjected to strict state control. Rome lived by arms; and she lived by money. Large-scale armour factories were already being established by the Romans before 100 B.C. — they existed at Pozzuoli, Syracuse, Populonia, Reggio and Volterra. Later they were transferred to the provinces, near the mines that produced the necessary metal. The efficient, standardized equipment of the Roman legionary was produced under equally efficient, standardized conditions.

The money supply was of even more vital concern to those who ruled Rome. Moneyers were public slaves (the lowest category), and sometimes the authorities had a hard job to hold them down. Under the emperor Aurelian they revolted, and the battle which followed is said to have cost the lives of 7,000 legionaries.

The spectrum of Roman crafts was broader than anything we have so far encountered. In metal, there was a new emphasis on three materials — brass, which first became important in the closing years of the Roman Republic; pewter — an early mention is in a comedy by Plautus (254–184 B.C.) and iron, which had remained almost a curiosity in Europe, if not in the Near East, until the Classical period in Greece, and which only attained its full importance with the rise of the Romans. It must always be remembered, however, that the Romans, as much as their Greek predecessors, were not nearly as dependent on iron as we are today. Copper and bronze were only very slowly being displaced.

One can comprehend this if one looks at what the Roman smith could and could not do with his material. Basically he could forge it, but not cast it. He knew something about the properties of steel, but not how to make it reliably. Because he did not have full control of the carbon content of his material, he could never be quite sure how it would behave when the crucial moment came — the punch he was using, for example, would sometimes, and disconcertingly,

turn out to be softer than what he intended to pierce.

The fuel used by the Roman blacksmith was mostly charcoal, and his anvil was usually still primitive — a roughly shaped block of iron. His other basic tools, little changed from Roman times to our own, were tongs and hammers. The heaviest hammer — the sledge-hammer — has not changed at all, but the form of small hammers is now somewhat different. The ball-pene hammer, with a flat face at one end and a ball at the other, was still unknown, and instead the Romans used a cross-pene, with the head balanced by a shape like a blunt chisel.

The most advanced form of craft technology was in weaponry. From the second century A.D. onwards Roman blacksmiths were able to make pattern-welded blades. This was an elaboration of the process known as case-hardening. Iron worked in the presence of charcoal, which is almost pure carbon, acquires a thin layer of carbon alloy — in other words steel. Such a piece of iron, repeatedly folded and hammered out, is streaked through with thin bands of steel — it has both resilience and strength. For pattern-welded blades a number of case-hardened iron rods were welded together, to make sword blades which, when etched, revealed

Roman ceremonial
bronze helmet
from Newstead.
3rd century A.D.
London, British
Museum

intricately watered patterns — the visible evidence of a wonderfully
complex structure.

The pattern-welding technique was inherited by the Viking
smiths of the Dark Ages, a number of whom proudly signed their
work. Swords made by Ingebri, who apparently worked in the
tenth century, have been found in Norway, Sweden, France and
Denmark, as well as in the Thames at London. But the technique
remained somewhat hit-and-miss, just as it had been in Roman
times. Smiths who could produce reliable swords remained rare,
and even in the reign of Charlemagne the simplest kind of
unadorned sword-blade was worth as much as three cows. Charlemagne's own legendary sword Joyeuse was confidently attributed to
the demi-god Wayland the Smith, despite the fact that the Emperor
himself was a Christian.

Roman smiths could also occasionally produce elaborate pieces of
embossed armour. One of the most spectacular surviving examples
is the parade helmet with a naturalistic face-mask which was found
at Newstead, a Roman fort near Melrose.

The other base metals presented the Romans with many fewer
problems. Pewter, used for domestic utensils, was invariably cast,
in re-usable moulds made from clay mixed with calves' hair. After
casting, pewter objects were turned and trimmed on a type of lathe.
Bronze, too, was commonly cast — in this case the alloy was always
given an additional percentage of lead, which made the molten

metal flow more easily. Various casting techniques were used —
lost wax, with or without a clay core according to size, was one of
the commonest methods. The Romans also seem to have employed
re-usable two-piece clay moulds for mass-production purposes; and
stone moulds, for casting open vessels. Cast vessels, such as those
made of pewter, would be finished on a lathe, often very elaborately
and with a good deal of wastage of material. Another way of making
bronze vessels was to raise them from metal sheet, but the lathe was
attuned to the Classical taste for absolutely regular geometrical
forms. Plato himself praises it for this quality.

Though the more elaborate bronze vessels and mounts give a
good idea of the Roman aesthetic, this is conveyed yet more vividly
by work in precious metals, and particularly by the considerable
quantities of Roman silver plate which have survived. Elaborate
silver table services were in no sense a novelty. Greek craftsmen of
the Classical period had made particularly impressive examples for
barbarian clients in Thrace and in the Crimea. The relief decoration echoed exactly the sculptural style of the time. This Classical
style, now somewhat drier and more linear, is still to be seen in the
massive pieces of Roman silver which have survived from the
troubled fourth century — perhaps the most spectacular example of
all is the Oceanus dish, the largest item from the Mildenhall
Treasure.

Oceanus dish from
the Mildenhall
Treasure. Roman,
4th century A.D.
London, British
Museum

Etruscan gold bracelets showing elaborate granulation. From Cerveteri, 2nd half of the 7th century B.C. Rome, Vatican Museum

Right:
One of the David plates: Samuel anoints David, Byzantine, A.D. 628. Cyprus Museum

Far right:
Roman silver cup with decoration in repoussé. From the Boscoreale Treasure, 1st century B.C. Paris, Musée du Louvre

In modified form, the style seen in the Oceanus dish persisted well into the Byzantine period. The nine 'David Plates' discovered in Cyprus in 1902 carry control stamps of the Emperor Heraclius (A.D. 610–41), and the Old Testament subject-matter is related to illuminations in Byzantine manuscripts of the Psalms dating from the ninth to the twelfth century. But one can also see in them surviving traces of Roman Classicism — David slaying the bear strikes the precise attitude of Mithras slaying the bull, or Hercules fighting the lion.

The essential feature of silverwork in this style is its desire to suppress all traces of the maker's hand. Everything is as impersonal and smoothly finished as possible. Good technique here implies a control over the material so complete as almost to deprive it of its essential character. One meets the same thing, in even more exaggerated form, in the silver produced by leading French and English Neoclassical silversmiths.

Roman goldwork, especially the jewellery, does not reach the heights attained by the best Roman silver plate. More colourful than Greek work, it is also more careless and usually a great deal more vulgar. Nevertheless there is a wide variety of different techniques. The fine Etruscan use of granulation — a lost secret until quite recently — no longer appears in Roman work, but there is repoussé work (decoration hammered from behind in a piece of sheet metal), engraving, enamel (of which more in a moment), and niello (engraved decoration filled with a blackened, easily fusible compound of silver), which now makes its appearance for the first time. Jewels are often surprisingly fragile. Rings, instead of being made in low grade alloy, are made of thin sheet gold round a composition core.

Arretine pottery imitating metalwork. Roman, 1st–2nd century A.D. St Germain, Musée des Antiquités Nationales

An interesting feature of Roman jewellery is its marked regional variation — or, rather, the fact that one finds a completely Classical style existing side by side with others which contain distinctly anti-Classical elements. Romano-British jewellery, for example, provides a number of types which do not occur elsewhere. One such type is the 'dragonesque' brooch, usually made in bronze and enamelled, which represents a survival of a style which had developed in Britain before Claudius's invasion of A.D. 43, and which lasted well into the second century.

The distinction between 'central' and 'fringe' styles appears yet more clearly in pottery. One kind of Roman norm is represented by the Arretine pottery already mentioned in Chapter One. These moulded wares with relief decorations were a continuation of a Hellenistic fashion. Arretine pottery was mould-made, in imitation of silver, but was seldom or never moulded directly from an original in precious metal. The mould was made of clay, and the decoration was stamped upon its inner surface by means of punches, often with freehand additions of decorative garlands etc. Once the mould was complete it was fired in a kiln. The pot or bowl was then made of clay, which was worked into the mould with the fingers, and afterwards the mould and its filling were allowed to dry. The drying process, with much moisture being taken up by the porous mould itself, caused the piece to shrink within the matrix, so that it could be removed without damage. It was then coated with the glossing agent, consisting of fine clay particles held in suspension in liquid. Rainwater can activate clay in this way, so can potash made by pouring water over wood ash. The red colouring so typical of Arretine comes from iron oxides in the clay itself — no additional colouring is needed.

The best Arretine is cool, impersonal, as much an industrial product as jasper-ware by Wedgwood. The whole object of the various processes employed, as with Roman silverware, is to remove all traces of the craftsman's labour. Essentially, once the mould itself was made, technical expertise was all that was required, and any number of identical pots could be produced from a single mould by different operatives.

There is, however, a kind of pottery typical of Gaul and Britain which in one sense derives from Arretine, yet which produces a completely different aesthetic effect. These are the hunt cups with freehand barbotine decoration. Barbotine is clay in a very soft, almost liquid state and is used to make freehand relief designs in a technique analogous to icing a cake. The hunt cups are strongly Celtic in spirit. Everything about them is wonderfully free and impulsive. Their makers may indeed have been trying to produce a version of the metropolitan pottery they knew and no doubt admired, but their failure to equal its precision produced quite different qualities.

The Romans also made glazed pottery, though it was always much less common than the red gloss wares. The glazes they used

Romano-British lead-glazed flagon, 1st century A.D. London, British Museum

Romano-British
Castor ware hunt
cup with barbotine
decoration. From
Verulamium,
2nd–3rd century
A.D.

were chemically quite different from the alkali silicate glazes known
to the Ancient Egyptians, which continued to be employed on the
Eastern fringes of the Roman Empire, on the border with Parthia.
Elsewhere Roman glazes were lead silicate, coloured green with
cupric oxide, or honey brown with ferric oxide. The technique
seems to have appeared during the first century B.C. in Asia Minor
or northern Syria, and many of the best pieces have moulded
decoration which relates them to pottery in the Arretine style.

Glazed pottery has connections with two other forms of craftwork which have not so far been discussed in this book — glass and
enamel. Glass has, in its earliest days, a strangely intermittent
history. Glass beads are known from about the middle of the third
millennium B.C., hollow vessels in glass are first found around 1500
B.C., but the craft died out almost completely after three centuries.
It was then revived in Mesopotamia and Syria in the ninth century,
and slowly spread westward and northward. Glass-making arrived
in Alexandria soon after the foundation of the city in 332 B.C. and
this was soon the most important centre of production, as it was for
many luxury crafts during the Hellenistic age.

Glass could be treated in various ways. It could be, and
sometimes was, treated like a lump of semi-precious stone, and

shaped by grinding. It could also be cast in a mould, or applied in a molten state to a core which was afterwards removed — the so-called 'sand-core' technique, whereby vessels were made of glass threads or rods wound round and round a core of mud and vegetable fibre while they were still in a semi-liquid state. The vessel, once formed, was reheated and then rolled backwards and forwards across a flat surface to make it smooth — what glass-makers call marvering.

Moulded glass allowed the glass-maker to produce rich and elaborate effects by arranging slices of polychrome glass canes in patterns, and then fusing them all together in a mould. It has sometimes been thought that polychrome bowls of this type were the 'murrhine' vessels so much valued by wealthy Roman collectors.

During the first century B.C. the glass industry was completely transformed by the invention of glass-blowing, which has the same importance to the glass-maker as the wheel has to the potter. It very much extended the range of possible forms, and it made glass production not only much easier, but also much cheaper. Syria, the place of origin of so many inventions, was in all likelihood the place where glass-blowing also got its start.

Roman glass was a mixture of silica, soda and lime. Its principal constituent was sand, carefully chosen for its freedom from impurities. It was the presence of a nearby deposit of suitable sand which made Cologne an important glass-making centre under the Roman

Gallo-Roman blown glass vessels, 2nd century A.D. Paris, Musée du Louvre

The Lycurgus Cup. Cage-decoration cut from thick glass. Roman, 4th century A.D. London, British Museum

Empire. Soda came from various sources — in many cases from burnt seaweed. The glass-makers of the period were able to produce quite a wide range of colours at will, using copper oxide under different firing conditions for dark blue, dark green and ruby red, cobalt for deep blue, manganese for yellow and purple, antimony for opaque yellow, and iron for pale blue, bottle-green, amber and black. The actual technique of blowing the glass was clearly much the same as it is today, and vessels were sometimes blown into moulds to achieve particular forms — slab-sided vessels for instance, as well as little bottles shaped like heads or like bunches of grapes.

Much Roman glass was elaborately decorated; a few pieces are astonishing technical *tours de force*. First, the glass could be shaped and manipulated while hot, and trails and blobs of glass, often in a contrasting colour, could be added to it. Secondly, it could be decorated when it had cooled. The Romans made painted glasses, and they also understood the technique of wheelcutting and engraving. While most cutting and carving of glass was fairly simple, there are exceptions. One of the most famous is the Portland Vase in the British Museum, a blue amphora cased with white, where the white layer is cut away to make cameo figures in low relief. This deserves to be compared to the finest Roman cameo work in hardstone, such as the Gemma Augustea in the Kunsthistorisches Museum, Vienna, and the Grand Camée de France in

The Portland Vase. Cameo-cut glass in two layers. Roman, 1st century B.C. London, British Museum

The Gemma
Augustea.
Cameo-carving in
sardonyx. Roman,
1st century A.D.
Vienna,
Kunsthistorisches
Museum

the Cabinet des Médailles in Paris. Both of these are allegorical celebrations of the Augustan House, and the Portland Vase shows the same restrained Classical style, typical of the reign of Augustus and his immediate successors. So magnificent an object is likely to have been an imperial commission.

A later style of virtuoso glass-cutting is represented by the Lycurgus Cup, also in the British Museum. This is a so-called 'cage-cup', where the vessel is surrounded by almost free-standing decoration, joined to the cup itself by little bridges. Recent research has proved that such cups were made by laboriously cutting away a blank of very thick glass. They date from the fourth century A.D.

Enamelling is a method of fusing vitreous material to metal for decorative purposes. The earliest known specimens of the technique are Mycenaean, and date from about 1200 B.C. It was not, however, much developed until the Roman period, when it was used as a cheap and rapid substitute for glass and hardstone inlays. Glass inlays, as opposed to actual enamel, are lavishly used in some Ancient Egyptian jewellery, including spectacular jewels found in the tomb of Tutankhamun, and were later popular with Celtic goldsmiths, who apparently used glass as a substitute for coral.

Under the Romans, enamelling remained a favourite 'barbarian' technique, particularly popular among the Britons and the Gauls, and used, since methods were still uncertain in their results, for decorating small objects. Its employment, like that made of barbotine in British and Gaulish hunt cups, was very much an example of the way in which one cultural tradition survived within the embrace of another. The one reference made to enamelling in ancient literature illustrates the point very neatly. It comes from the

Roman moulded
glass cup from
Colchester, 1st
century A.D.
London, British
Museum

Imagines of Philostratus, written in the third century A.D., and refers to 'silver bridles and many-coloured and golden disks. These colours the barbarians who live by the Ocean cast of glowing ore. The colours run and become hard as stone and preserve what is painted with them.'

In contrast to techniques such as glass-making and enamelling, which developed a fresh impetus under the Romans, others remained more or less static. Though the basic materials were organic and therefore perishable, a fair amount of evidence survives concerning Roman weaving and leatherwork. What we know of Roman weaving suggests that it was the product of two different traditions — woollen fabrics in the northern and western Roman provinces; and finer fabrics in a greater variety of materials in Egypt and the Roman East. There was even a difference in the way yarns were spun — in the North and West they were usually spun clockwise; in the East almost invariably anticlockwise. At least three types of loom were in use. The oldest and simplest was the warp-weighted vertical loom, but this met with increasing competition from the two-beam loom, which was sometimes used to produce tapestry. Very late in the history of the Empire, probably in the fourth century, the horizontal loom was introduced on the Eastern borders of Roman territory. It has been suggested that it was taken over and adapted from the looms used by the nomads of Central Asia. Horizontal looms seem to have been used chiefly for complex weaves, particularly in silk.

Leatherwork was a curious mixture of the sophisticated and the primitive. Leatherworkers were capable of extremely intricate and accurate cutting. Fancy shoes and boots had uppers in complex network patterns, all cut without a slip from a single piece of hide. But shoe and boot-soles remained clumsy, however elegant the rest of the design, with three or more layers of thick leather joined by iron nails.

The craft area in which the Romans made greatest progress, compared to what had existed before the Empire was founded, was

Roman leather
shoe with punched
decoration, from
London. Museum
of London

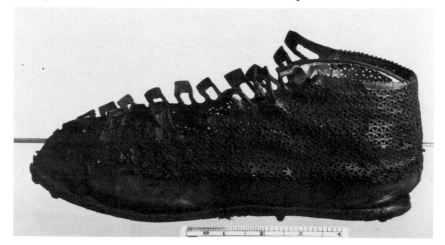

Roman pictorial mosaic of Meleager, 4th century A.D. London, British Museum

undoubtedly building. Roman genius revolutionized almost every aspect of construction, and revolutionized ideas about architecture at the same time.

While the Romans employed all the building materials hitherto traditional in the Mediterranean area — chiefly wood, cut stone and stone rubble — they introduced a very important new one. This was concrete, a mixture of clay, lime, grit, water and rubble, which could be shaped while wet in wooden moulds or forms, and which afterwards hardened into a solid mass. Concrete came into use from the second century B.C. onwards, and soon made post-and-beam systems of construction obsolete. Walls and ceilings could now be moulded in any way the builder wished, and space itself became a plastic element.

Concrete had another and less desirable characteristic. This was the fact that it was vulnerable to moisture. The Romans therefore developed a wide variety of facing techniques, using random bits of stone, regular blocks, bricks, and eventually carefully matched sheets of marble and pictorial mosaics where these seemed appro-

priate. The less expensive and luxurious facings were themselves
often covered with plaster, and this in turn could be painted. As a
result, illusion played a large part in Roman architecture —
buildings were made of one substance, but seemed to be made of
another. When the Emperor Augustus boasted that he had turned
Rome from a city of brick into one of marble, he was really claiming
to have exchanged one form of surface finish for another and more
glamorous one.

Another popular Roman building material shared the plasticity,
and also something of the chameleon quality, of concrete. This was
terracotta, which was moulded into gutters, waterspouts and other
decorative features, and was also used for floor and roof tiles.

The nature of Roman building materials wrought profound
changes in attitudes towards the builder's craft. A Greek temple,
such as the Parthenon, essentially made its effect when looked at
from outside. Roman buildings were enclosed spaces, best appreciated from within. Their complexity meant that the architect — the
man who drew plans, measured, calculated stresses — became a
different person from the builder, who carried someone else's ideas
into effect. Roman building is conceptual in its origins, and
industrial in the method of construction used.

The separation between idea and execution, visible in so many of
the Roman crafts, in pottery as much as in building, also manifests
itself in the fine arts. One of the reasons why people now find it so
difficult to get to grips with the Roman achievement in the arts is
that they are baffled and distracted by the Roman love of copies.
Very often a work of art executed in one medium is copied in
another. A famous Greek painting will be translated into terms of
mosaic, a Greek sculpture in bronze will be remade in marble.

The copying of masterpieces of Greek sculpture became a craft in
itself, and the Romans seem, indeed, to have made little distinction
between sculptors in stone and ordinary masons, calling both
marmorarii. Sculptors — often either slaves or freedmen and
almost invariably Greeks rather than Roman citizens — were
organized in workshops, and copies were made not from the
originals themselves, but from plaster casts.

From about 100 B.C. onwards the pointing technique was used.
Points marked on the plaster cast were transferred to the block of
stone to be carved. Once the figure had been roughed out, more
fixed points were set, and secondary measurements made with
compasses. Each point was marked by what is now called a
puntello, a small dome-shaped protuberance, with a small depres-
sion in the centre to take the compass. These *puntelli* have
occasionally survived on unfinished Roman statues, and they
supply positive proof that the work was carried out in this way.

Translation from bronze into marble often meant that the
copyists had to introduce unsightly struts to support extended
limbs. Even where they managed to avoid this, they usually had to
put in a tree-trunk or something of the kind to give additional

strength and stability to a standing figure. In these copies one sees in extreme form what one also encounters elsewhere in the Roman crafts — a disregard for the true nature of the material. It is tempting to link this disregard for the nature of materials with the generally low status of the artisan, who was there chiefly to carry out ideas and concepts dictated to him from above. It is only on the barbarian fringes of the Empire — in Britain and Gaul, and in some of the easternmost provinces, that one finds a freer and more organic relationship between the maker and what is made.

Paradoxically enough, however, the work of the Roman *marmorarii* can also show how the material dictates its own terms, even in unfavourable circumstances. Pressure to produce carved marble rapidly and in quantity meant that the masons increasingly began to look for short cuts. Most of these came from the use of the bow-drill, a tool which probably goes back to Paleolithic times, which speeded up the process of getting rid of large areas of unwanted stone. A series of vertical holes was made, and the surplus material was then neatly knocked away. In the early Empire great efforts were made to remove all traces of drill work. Later the craftsmen were more careless. In addition, they had discovered the use of the so-called running-drill — the drill held at an angle so as to make a continuous channel in the surface of the stone. This greatly simplified the undercutting of drapery, and made possible dramatic contrasts of light and shade. The Baroque quality of much Roman sculpture, from the second century A.D. onwards, is due to the increasingly unconcealed employment of running-drill techniques.

Roman marble
statue of
Abundance,
showing use of
struts. Rome,
Vatican Museum

4 The Eastern World

Steatite seals from Mohenjodaro. Indian, 3rd–2nd millennium B.C. London, British Museum

The Middle East, India and the Far East made their own distinctive contributions to the development of craft, and there were indeed epochs when their technology was much ahead of anything known in the West. But eventually they fell into a kind of stagnation, from which they only recently began to emerge. For this reason, they have to be treated separately from the main story, even though it would be unintelligible without them.

India, China and Japan have distinctive craft-specialities of their own, but each learned and borrowed from the others, and this confuses the historical pattern. After the turmoil and the decay of ancient civilization which they suffered in the nineteenth century, they have emerged with perhaps even greater differences than before, which also conditions the European reaction to their respective achievements in the crafts. Where craft in India has remained upon a traditional basis, and hand-production is still the essential thing in large sectors of the Indian economy, Japan by contrast has become a highly industrialized society with a romantic cult of craft and the craftsman.

Of the three regions I have named, it is India which presents the greatest problems to the historian. Indian village crafts of the present day have been much studied, but the story of the development of craft is still full of gaps. The earliest-known phase of Indian civilization was revealed as recently as 1924, when the ancient cities of the Indus valley began to be excavated. Here, in the third millennium B.C., there existed an urban civilization very like that which flourished at the same period in Mesopotamia. The population lived in regularly planned cities made of fire-baked rather than sun-dried brick. Their most characteristic products are engraved seal-stones and pottery storage jars covered with red-ochre slip and elaborately patterned in black before firing. It is an indication of the static nature of Indian rural culture that pottery of much the same sort is still made today in some villages of western India.

India, however, has never been celebrated for ceramics, nor for building in brick. Indian architecture shows a command of stone which began very early. In some cases, as for example at Ellora in the Deccan, which dates from the third quarter of the eighth century A.D., the builders preferred to carve the structure out of the living rock, rather than pile it up stone by stone. Ellora shares one characteristic with many other Hindu temples: it is almost as much sculpture as it is architecture, and the elaborate exterior decoration counts for far more than the minuscule interior spaces. The mosques and tombs of Mogul India, superficially very different in

Indian printed cotton panel with Tree of Life design, 18th century. Detroit Institute of Arts

style from the Hindu buildings and dedicated to a totally different religion, also show a tremendous mastery of stone-carving. The relief patterns and inlays of the Taj Mahal are so obsessively detailed and precise that they seem in some ways closer to jewellery than to architecture.

Rock cut temple at Ellora, 8th century A.D.

So far as the world outside was concerned, India was famous for two things — in early days for skill in working metal; and later for textiles, particularly cotton. Indian iron is mentioned as an object of commerce in a Greek text of the first century A.D., the *Periplous of the Erythraean Sea*. One remarkable monument to Indian skill with iron survives near Delhi — the famous Iron Pillar beside the Qutub Minar. This, more than 16 inches in diameter and 23 feet 8 inches high, dates from the fourth century A.D. and is made of wrought iron of the finest quality, with a minimal sulphur content.

Indian cottons, especially very fine muslins, were known to the Romans, who called them 'woven winds' and paid very high prices for them. Later the Arabs were the entrepreneurs in a lively trade with Europe, shipping both finished cotton fabric and the raw material, which became important for use in candlewicks. The Arabs were later displaced by Portuguese and British merchant-adventurers, one of the chief sources of goods being Bengal. Already in the sixteenth century Indian craftsmen were beginning to adapt themselves to the taste of these new European customers.

Carved and inlaid
decoration: the
Taj Mahal, Agra,
17th century

The Iron Pillar,
Qutub Minar,
Delhi, 8th century
A.D.

The 'Bengalla' or 'Sutgonge' (Satgaon) quilts exported to Europe have a medley of assorted motifs — the gods and heroes of the Classical world together with characters from the Old Testament, Portuguese soldiers and purely Indian monsters. The quilts are embroidered in yellow silk on a background of cotton or jute.

It is only after the middle of the eighteenth century that the surviving records of the English East India Company enable one to discover under what conditions these Indian export goods were made. The weavers worked in nearly all the towns and villages of

Detail of a painting by a Calcutta artist showing a European household and the type of Indian carpet also made for export, *c*. 1782. London, Victoria and Albert Museum

Bengal, and the unit was the extended family — several brothers, perhaps, with wives, children and more distant relatives. For the most part (there were a few exceptions according to caste) it was the men who did the actual weaving, while women spun and did other tasks connected with the making of cloth. Export goods were for the most part medium-grade, neither the very finest weaves (reserved for court use in Delhi or Murshidabad), nor the coarsest. There were often based on models supplied from Europe, and some of these were in turn *chinoiseries*, inspired by imported Chinese

Detail of Bengali white cotton coverlet embroidered in yellow silk, 19th century. London, Victoria and Albert Museum

particular, *Tanti* and *Kayashta*, and because it was caste-oriented the craft was also largely hereditary. Muslims, though not usually weavers, were often commercial embroiderers — here males did the work destined for Europe, while women specialized in embroidered cloths destined for export to Arab countries.

After the breakdown of Mogul rule following the Battle of Plassey in 1757, the organization of the textile industry was taken over more or less directly by the East India Company itself. The qualification is necessary because the Company in fact worked through brokers. Its factors advanced the bulk of the finished price to these brokers, so that they in turn could make advances to the weavers. An independent valuer assessed the finished product and the balance was then paid. Since the advance often covered the work of more than a year the Company was able to create a monopoly of the Bengali weaving industry.

Printed and painted cottons formed an important element in the Indian export trade, being shipped from the Gujerat and Coromandel coasts (in the west and south-west respectively), as well as from Bengal. The story of these exotic calico designs — once thought to be typical of India itself — is in fact very complex. The designs were often based on models supplied from Europe, and some of these were in turn *chinoiseries*, inspired by imported Chinese

Detail of
18th-century
Mogul miniature
showing women
wearing finely
woven cotton
garments. Private
Collection

works of art. Indian versions of European *chinoiseries* were in due
course exported to China, as the Indian textile industry did not
confine itself to supplying Europe alone. In China, such Indian
cottons sometimes served as the inspiration for embroideries on
silk, and these in turn were exported to Europe.

   The success of the Indian textile industry, which was entirely
craft-based, had curious economic and other consequences. Sir
Dudley North, author of *Considerations upon the East India
Trade*, published in England in 1701, pointed out that the compe-

Green jade Mogul
vase set with
rubies and
emeralds,
18th–19th
century. London,
Victoria and
Albert Museum

tition of cheap East India goods would in the end force Europeans to invent machines for making things. It was in fact precisely the competition of Indian textiles which sparked off the industrialization of the European cloth-making industry, already briefly described in Chapter One, which spearheaded the European Industrial Revolution as a whole.

As a result of the new industrial techniques, the Indian textile industry slumped at the end of the eighteenth century. Dacca, which had been one of the chief weaving towns, dwindled from 200,000 inhabitants to 68,000 between the years 1800 and 1838. By the 1880s the great Indian enterprises were virtually defunct. What survived were the two extreme ends of the market. Very fine weaving continued to be produced, though now as handkerchiefs for memsahibs rather than saris for princesses. Some of these muslins were just as fine as they had been in Roman times. The puritanical Emperor Aurangzeb (1658–1707) once rebuked his daughter for being too scantily clad, and received the reply that she was wearing seven layers of cloth. What also lived on was the part of the weaving trade which catered for the very poor. Coarse handmade materials were still used, because they were even cheaper than the new European imports.

The division between luxury craft goods and the products of what is in fact sweated labour is still visible in India today — on the one hand wonderfully fine cashmeres and magnificent gold brocades, both made in an absolutely traditional way; and on the other cheap and careless hand-weaving in shoddy materials.

In India, luxury textiles have in fact survived more successfully than any of the other luxury crafts except the making of jewellery. Under the Mogul emperors the best craftsmen tended to follow the court wherever it transported itself — whether it was in Delhi, Agra, Fatepur Sikri or Arungabad. Particular specialities, in addition to jewellery and fine textiles, were carved hardstones and carpets. The hardstone, usually jade, was often itself inlaid with jewels held in gold cloisons, and these marvellous jade objects are

Jade scent bottle set with rubies. Mogul, 17th century. London, Victoria and Albert Museum

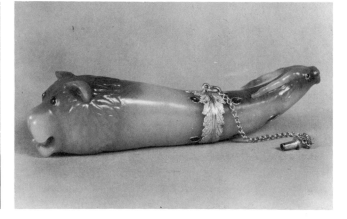

Chair and footstool in European style, from Berhampur, Bengal. Ebony and ivory, mid-19th century. London, Victoria and Albert Museum

the equivalent of the masterpieces produced slightly earlier by the goldsmiths of the Renaissance in Europe. Indian carpets were strongly influenced by Persian exemplars, but often abandoned the symmetry and repetition which give Persian carpets their character. Indian carpets were large-scale woven pictures, and experts have speculated that some of the designs may have been supplied by court artists, such as the famous animal painter Mansūr.

This would not be the only example of Indian craftsmen going outside what might seem to be the real boundaries of their discipline. Among the most curious products of the Indian artisan are pieces of furniture constructed of ivory and ivory veneer.

These, inspired by English pattern books such as that issued by George Hepplewhite, were made for European patrons, especially rich East India Company officials stationed in and around Murshidabad. The clash of cultures is eloquently expressed in these splendid and slightly improbable objects.

Indian jewellery, as opposed to larger luxury items, was and remained a special case. The market here was largely confined to native patrons, as indeed it still is today. For these, jewellery had a twofold significance. It was portable wealth, in a society which had no satisfactory banking system. In addition, jewels had a complex magical and astrological significance. Precious stones, according to colour, were the expression of different cosmic energies, and had to be set in particular patterns if their fullest virtue was to be passed on to the wearer. Indian goldsmiths became particularly adroit, not only in following these magical conventions, but in making the greatest possible show with the available material. Like the jewellery made in ancient times, Indian jewels are seldom made of

Indian canopy in ebony and ivory, 17th century. Private Collection

adulterated metal, but the metal is beaten out to the thinnest and finest point. The filigree-work typical of some Indian jewellery is more than simply decorative. It is a device for making a small amount of gold go a long way.

Jewellery, like the most delicate weaving, is an example of a craft which resists industrialization by its very nature, not because of any particular cult of hand-work. Anyone who visits the Zaveri Bazaar, the goldsmiths' and silversmiths' quarter in contemporary Bombay, will be aware of the continuing vitality of at least one set of traditional craft skills in India. The jewellers are supported by both good and bad traits in Indian society — the impulse to hoard wealth and at the same time to flaunt it; and respect for the workman's skills and knowledge of what he can be expected to do. In India it is still customary to commission a piece of jewellery rather than to buy it ready-made; and in this case, as once in medieval Europe, it is also customary to pay two separate sums — so much for materials, and so much for the labour.

Today the crafts in India survive in two ways — as enterprises, largely government-supported, which are directed at the export trade and at tourists; and as less self-conscious hand-work for a native Indian clientele. In many ways the basic divisions are no different from those established at the end of the eighteenth century: what the tourist buys, or what is exported, is in the middle range of quality; while the finest and the roughest work are both for local consumption. Work for foreigners shows two kinds of distortion. First, there is the temptation to use slightly inferior or

Below left:
Indian head-ornament set with pearls, rubies, turquoises and emeralds. Delhi, 18th century. London, Victoria and Albert Museum

Below right:
Indian neck-ornament set with rubies and emeralds in gold filigree. Delhi, 19th century. London, Victoria and Albert Museum

Indian ornament in silver filigree. Cuttack, 19th century. London, Victoria and Albert Museum

non-traditional materials — modern dyes, paints and fibres for example — to bring goods within the desired price-range. Secondly, there is the need to adapt traditional skills to non-traditional ends. The marble workshops at Agra now produce cigarette-boxes and coffee-table tops, using the inlay technique once used to decorate the Taj Mahal. But this process of adaptation is not novel. It has been going on, as the history of the Bengal textile-trade demonstrates, at least since the sixteenth century.

Nor is European fascination with the universality of handicraft in India anything new. Indian artists, themselves often more artisans than independent creators in the European sense, were forced to find a new market among Europeans when Britain became the dominant political power upon the subcontinent. Indian painting for the British became a special sub-style, equipped with its own particular range of subject-matter. An important part of this subject-matter was the Indian craftsman at work. British patrons, with an industrial revolution newly under way at home, were struck by the diversity, and also one suspects by the primitiveness, of Indian craft techniques. Sets of pictures, often very large in number, depict the various Indian crafts and métiers, and very

often what they seem to emphasize is the crudity of the means used to achieve a particular end. European draughtsmen also recorded the informal nature of Indian craft; for example, prisoners squatting at a makeshift horizontal loom made of trimmed logs. One already senses, from images of this sort, the huge gap between the two societies — that to which the artist himself belonged, and that which had produced his patron.

Similar sets of pictures were produced in China, especially in and around Canton, for sale to Europeans, though these are generally more poised, more sophisticated and a good deal less lively than their Indian counterparts. Their existence confirms the fact that, certainly in the seventeenth, eighteenth and nineteenth centuries, the relationship between the Chinese handicraft industries and European markets was very similar to that which existed between Indian craftsmen and European customers. One very important similarity was the fact that craft and industry could be spoken of in one breath. China, like India, relied upon cheap and abundant labour, endowed with craft skills which were often hereditary, to produce goods which in Europe would have required a much greater degree of mechanization.

But there are important differences as well as similarities. On the whole, China has made a far more decisive and important contribution to European technology than India, and the products of Chinese craftsmen breathe a very different atmosphere. Early

J.L. Kipling, loom for weaving dhurries, Amritsar gaol, 1870. London, Victoria and Albert Museum

Chinese potters
applying glaze.
Anonymous.
Gouache on paper,
late 18th century.
London, British
Museum

Chinese porcelain
factory, showing
the kilns and bowls
being glazed and
packed.
Anonymous.
Gouache on paper,
late 18th century.
London, British
Museum

Chinese bronze
vessels, Shang
Dynasty:
Left; a *Huo,*

Washington, Freer
Gallery of Art,
Right: a *Chüeh.*
Private Collection

Chinese civilization developed with remarkable independence. Once it reached the Bronze Age, which happened with much greater abruptness than was the case in the Mediterranean basin, Chinese metalsmiths started producing the bronze ritual vessels which are amongst the most impressive specimens of bronze-work made anywhere, at any period. They imply the existence of a hierarchical society, in which great wealth had accumulated in the hands of a few people. The earliest of these elaborate ritual vessels date from the beginning of the Shang Dynasty, around 1500 B.C.

What the vessels imply, taken in the general context of Chinese craft production, is the existence of a hieratic not to say hermetic element. The bronze sacrificial vessels of the Shang are foci for spiritual forces, and the dense abstract and semi-abstract patterns that cover them are an expression of those forces. At a later period, but one which is still remarkably early by European standards, the bronze ritual vessels made under the Shang and Chou Dynasties became much sought-after antiques, and an elaborate connoisseurship developed in connection with them. This antiquarian interest was typical of the latter part of the Northern Sung Dynasty, and particularly of the reign of the Emperor Hui Tsung (A.D. 1100 –25), a painter and scholar who presided over the collapse of the regime. Hui Tsung decreed that ancient bronze vessels should be collected and imitated, and in 1092 a publication entitled *Illustra-*

Liu Sung Nien,
*Appreciating
Antiques*. Painting
on silk. Sung
Dynasty,
960–1279.
Collection of the
National Palace
Museum, Taiwan

tions for the Study of Antiquity was issued as a guide to those who
wished to imitate ancient styles.

Imperial interest in the crafts and intervention in their development is also illustrated by the making of lacquer, which has an
Indian name (derived from the Sanskrit) but is a Chinese invention
originally used for painting on the walls of Shang tombs. By the
Han Dynasty (206 B.C. – A.D. 220) small objects covered in lacquer
were being produced in official ateliers. As the archaeological
evidence shows, wine cups and boxes for medicines, ointments and
sweets were supplied to army officers serving on the north-western
frontier of the Chinese empire, and also to a military colony in
North Korea. Made in the last century B.C. and the first century
A.D., these were already, in line with imperial policy, imitating
objects in earlier styles. Even at this date it seems to have been the
practice to supply imperial workshops with antique objects to be
copied.

Court patronage was also important to the development of
ceramics, and particularly so to that of porcelain, one of the most
important Chinese contributions to technological development
taken as a whole, and one which remained a Chinese monopoly
even longer than the production of silk. What we should now
recognize as true porcelain was first made under the T'ang Dynasty
(A.D. 618–906), though curiously enough the Chinese themselves
never made an absolutely rigid distinction between true porcelain
— white and vitrified — and the best grades of stoneware. During
the Sung Dynasty (A.D. 960–1279), when porcelain first became
comparatively common, high-quality ceramics were made in a wide
variety of regional types, but after the fall of the Northern Sung
(A.D. 1126), when the Chinese court and government fled south of
the Yangtze River, official kilns were established on the outskirts of
the new capital, Hangchow. Later, under the first Ming Emperor,

Lacquer box from
a Han tomb near
Pyongyang, North
Korea. Central
History Museum,
Pyongyang

Hung Wu (A.D. 1368–98), the official kilns were moved to Ching-te-chen in Kiansi, rather than being kept in the vicinity of the palace. An imperial commissioner with the rank of Secretary of the Board of Works was sent to the new centre of production 'in order that the imperial wares might be in larger numbers and of finer quality'. Under the Ming, and later under the Ch'ing, Ching-te-chen became the centre of an enormous industry, many of whose products went, not to the palace in Peking, but for export.

The Sung stonewares and porcelains were monochromes, and relied for their effect on strength and purity of form. Despite their refinement and subtlety of curvature, the best wares of this period are essentially impersonal, and many were mould-made rather than thrown. With the introduction of underglaze blue decoration in the fourteenth century, and later of polychrome enamels, decoration became important but remained anonymous. A single piece might be the work of several hands.

Chinese porcelain-makers responded to the needs of growing export markets just as the makers of printed and embroidered stuffs did in India, and certain shapes and certain types of decoration were made in response to the tastes and needs of particular foreign

Chinese white porcelain vase. T'ang Dynasty, 618–906. London, Victoria and Albert Museum

Chinese grey porcellanous stoneware vase with a crackled glaze. Southern Kuan ware from Hangchow. Sung Dynasty, 960–1279. London, Victoria and Albert Museum

Chinese white porcelain dish with moulded designs. Ting ware. Sung dynasty, 960–1279. London, Victoria and Albert Museum

Above: Chinese blue-and-white porcelain flower-holder with a Persian inscription. Ming Dynasty, Cheng Te, 1506–21. Collection of the National Palace Museum, Taiwan

Above right: Chinese blue-and-white porcelain plate with a European coat of arms, 17th century. London, Victoria and Albert Museum

customers. Under the Ming, porcelains were made especially for export to Islamic countries, and the Ottoman sultans built up the large collection of Ming blue-and-whites which still survives in the Topkapi Museum in Istanbul. As trade with Europe increased, a distinction grew up between the private factories, which catered to it, and those which made 'Chinese taste' wares for internal, chiefly palace consumption. Once again the parallel with the Indian textile industry is close, since this became a difference of actual quality as well as of style. What was made for home use was of consistently finer quality — better potted, better decorated and altogether more refined. Yet the importance of the export trade could not be denied — when the Ming Dynasty collapsed in a series of political convulsions during the first half of the seventeenth century it was certainly European demand which kept Ching-te-chen in full production.

Already towards the close of that century, there was in China increasing interest in and response to foreign styles of decoration. The Chinese reacted to growing European enthusiasm for Japanese Imari wares by producing their own version of Imari patterns. Later there were experiments with European subject-matter, sometimes specially ordered by European entrepreneurs. Particularly interesting are the armorial porcelains for the European market which began to be produced at Canton in southern China during the second quarter of the eighteenth century.

Chinese porcelain, in all its guises, was pre-eminently a product made for a market. It did not vary according to the whim of the potter, but according to what the customer demanded, be he a

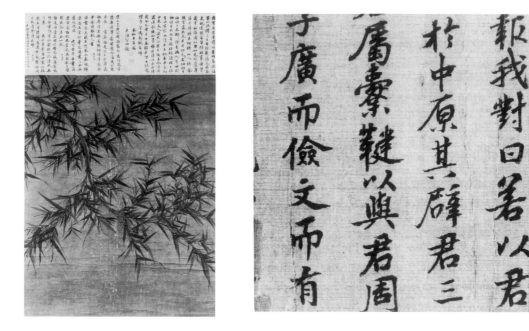

gentleman-scholar of Sung times, or an eighteenth-century European merchant. One can scarcely talk of individual expression, since it is clear that the making and decorating of fine porcelains was a complex operation in which many hands were involved, the aim being to achieve a consistent product.

If we compare the history of Chinese porcelain with that of Chinese painting we see that the distinction between the artist and the artisan was drawn very early. Painting, in Chinese terms, was closely connected to the art of writing — the same materials were used, and the images grew from the strokes used to form Chinese ideograms. Some branches of painting — for instance, the depiction of bamboo — became quasi-abstract exercises. What mattered was the rhythm of the brushstroke, not what was actually depicted. Though there were professional painters, the assumption was that making paintings, like writing poems, was a perfectly suitable and even creditable occupation for a high official or a gentleman of leisure. Though manual dexterity was the very essence of Chinese brushwork, to be an artist was in no way to occupy oneself with one of the demeaning manual occupations. The Emperor Hui Tsung, already mentioned, was the most celebrated bird-and-flower painter of his time. Unlike the craftsman, the painter was concerned with seizing the very essence of things — a few masterly strokes were enough, when made by one of the great Sung masters of landscape, to conjure up a mood, an atmosphere, indeed the whole spirit of the universe. However refined his productions, the Chinese craftsman did not make nearly such exalted claims. Perhaps the closest he came to it was in providing the artist with the best materials available — the finest brushes, rubbing stones, ink, silk and paper.

Above left: Wen T'ung, *Bamboo*. Hanging scroll. Ink on paper. Sung Dynasty, 960–1279. Collection of the National Palace Museum, Taiwan

Above: Detail of calligraphy by the Emperor Kao-tsung, *c.* 1120–40. Southern Sung Dynasty. London, British Museum

The mention of paper brings me to what was, in addition to silk and porcelain, China's great gift to technology — the invention of printing. Paper, which everywhere precedes printing, had been known for a long time in China. The earliest known specimens were discovered by archaeological expeditions in Central Asia, and date from the end of the first century A.D. Printing appeared in response to religious needs — both Buddhists and Taoists thought it meritorious to multiply religious images and religious texts. Block-print images seem in fact to have preceded religious texts — the earliest well-defined example dates from A.D. 770 and comes from Japan. The earliest printed text is all but a century later. It is a copy of the Buddhist Diamond Sutra, and was printed in 868. The fact that the Chinese language does not consist of alphabetical characters but of ideograms both helped and hindered the development of printing. Block-printing, where the whole page is printed from an integral block, is particularly suited to a language of this sort — just as painting was an extension of the act of writing, so the printing of a sheet of ideograms was a small step from printing a single woodcut image. What defeated the Chinese printer, though he did make efforts to solve it, was the problem of movable type. Chinese writing has more than seven thousand characters in common use.

In Southern Sung times there was a passion for catalogues, encyclopaedias and treatises of all kinds. These, often illustrated,

The Diamond Sutra, printed in 868. London, British Museum

helped to spread and codify antiquarian taste, and brought working craftsmen still further under the influence of scholars, at least when their efforts were directed at a Chinese clientele. Printing had a closely similar impact on the decorative arts of the European Renaissance, as will appear in due course.

At a first, superficial glance, the craft aesthetic in Japan is very close to that which prevailed in China — not surprisingly, when the whole of Japanese culture is so much in debt to Chinese models. A closer examination, however, reveals that there are in reality vast differences of attitude. In fact, the crafts have been given a place in Japanese life which is unique; and in many respects it is Japan which has supplied the model now followed by European and American artist-craftsmen of the present day. In the Japanese crafts there is an admiration of simplicity and rusticity, a cult of spontaneity, which in turn is based on the teachings of Zen Buddhism. At the same time, there is a feeling for virtuoso use of materials and extreme refinement of technique. One feature of the Japanese attitude which has perhaps been insufficiently noticed is the seamless unity between what we should call the fine arts on the one hand and the decorative arts on the other. For example, Japanese 'flung ink' painting, which clearly derives from Sung models, is by no means at odds with the sensibility expressed in the more spontaneous kinds of Japanese pottery. Similarly, the more splendid decorative wares have a recognizable kinship with the splendid Japanese screens of the seventeenth and eighteenth centuries, which are as near as Japan has come in recent times to major mural painting.

The Japanese crafts can essentially be put in four different categories, though the first two have close relationships with one another. There are the folk crafts, the tea-ceremony and samurai crafts, the luxury crafts and objects made for export. The fourth group is easily disposed of. The Japanese, like the Chinese, built up a considerable export trade with Europe, in spite of the fact that Japan was even more tightly closed against foreigners than the Celestial Empire. The chief article of commerce was porcelain, and here the Japanese benefited from the disturbances which brought the Ming Dynasty to an end, and which tended to interrupt supplies to European markets. Though the kilns were organized on a much less rigid and centralized basis, the Japanese, like the Chinese, were not averse to meeting the demands of overseas customers.

Japanese folk crafts covered a wide spectrum — wickerwork, woodwork, pottery and the cruder forms of lacquer. Essentially, however, these were admired within the framework of Zen and its visible expression the tea-ceremony, which promoted a self-conscious cult of simplicity and rusticity. Tea-ceremony taste embraced all the implements connected with the ceremony itself and the construction and decoration of the tea-house or tea-room in which it was held. The standards were set by the leading tea-

Japanese
blue-and-white
Imari ware jar,
imitating a
Chinese original,
17th century.
Tokyo National
Museum

masters, and often, especially in the beginning, what they selected was taken directly from the surrounding environment — imported wares from China and especially from Korea, plus the vital but slapdash products of native folk-kilns. It was the man who chose from a multitude of possible utensils, not the actual maker, who set the standard.

As the cult of the tea-ceremony spread, chance-found objects were no longer enough to supply the new demand, and certain kinds of pottery began to be made especially for the purpose. The Raku wares, made by a family of Kyoto potters, are typical of tea-ceremony taste, which has been described by a Japanese expert as being 'an aesthetics of actual living, and one in which utility is the first principle of beauty.' Yet this aesthetics was full of arcane lore — Japanese experts on the crafts speak often of *hiden*, the secret traditions passed from master to pupil, of *okugi*, or inner mysteries, of *hijutsu*, or secret art. This, rather than mere social inertia as in India, was the reason why family continuity remained so powerful a force in many branches of the Japanese crafts. The first major Raku potter, Chojiro, was the son of a Korean immigrant and a Japanese woman. He lived from 1515 to 1594. The thirteenth Raku, still a maker of tea-ceremony wares, died as recently as 1944.

From the moment of its appearance, Raku was associated with the Way of Tea, and with fine tea-bowls in particular. But fineness, by a typical Zen paradox, meant irregularity, apparent lack of finish, and deliberate absence of technical virtuosity. What the Raku potters sought to embody was the quality the Japanese call *wabi* — the spirit of restraint and lack of ostentation which is the essence of the tea-ceremony itself. At the same time, however, the Japanese soon began to find in certain craft objects, not merely good taste and usefulness, but the expression of moral qualities. A celebrated Japanese craft potter of the present day, Kei Fujiwara, once said: 'It is refinement and character that distinguish the true potter from the man who merely works at making pots. He must be someone who experiences and recognises what is good, whether in music, painting, literature or philosophy. By absorbing these into his being, he can put strength and character into what he makes out of clay.' This is not a modern set of attitudes, as it would be in the West, but can be traced back directly to the sixteenth century, and perhaps to an earlier epoch still.

Such attitudes were not confined to the makers of tea-ceremony wares, or even to Japanese potters in general. For example, the classic native treatise on Japanese sword furniture remarks of one craftsman that the traces of his chisel 'so bold and yet so delicate, betray such an elevation of tone, such a distinction of character, that the work cannot be looked at without emotion.' The mystique of the Japanese sword paralleled that of the Way of Tea, and the tea-ceremony was often a favourite form of relaxation with leading samurai. Though Japanese swordsmiths learned comparatively

early how to produce reliable and effective blades, finer perhaps than the work of even the best European or Islamic craftsmen, their approach to the task was still governed by the typical Japanese cult of spontaneity. Describing his craft, the best swordsmith of present-day Japan, Akahira Miyairi, heir to centuries of accumulated lore, said: 'Remember, our work is not done by measuring and talking. The hammering, the forging, all the processes are performed by intuition. It's the split-second intuitive decision to remove the iron from the fire, when and how to bring up the flame, to immerse the blade in the water now — it is these acts of intuition that produce a sword.'

Yet there is quite another aspect of Japanese craft, work which shows, not a rough spontaneity, but incredible finesse in the

Detail of a gold ground screen by Nonomura Sotatsu. Japanese, early 17th century. Washington, Freer Gallery of Art

Japanese sword (*tachi*), Kamakura, 12th century. Tokyo National Museum

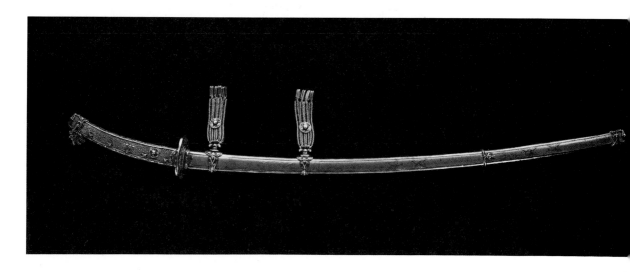

Japanese lacquer document box, 17th century. London, Victoria and Albert Museum

handling of difficult materials. Japanese tea-taste pottery stands in violent contrast to the fine porcelains of Arita, and in particular to the delicate *kakiemon* wares which became so popular in eighteenth-century Europe and which were slavishly imitated by leading European porcelain factories, especially Meissen.

For the most impressive combination of luxury and laboriousness, however, one must turn to Japanese lacquer. A huge variety of different techniques were used, each with its own descriptive name. A typical one is *makie* — layer upon layer of transparent lacquer, each thickly sprinkled with minute flecks of gold. When the work is finally polished, it acquires deep, lustrous colour-tones ranging from gold to brown or reddish-brown, depending on the number of layers of lacquer which have been applied.

Lid of Japanese lacquer treasure box in *makie* technique. Late Heian to Early Kamakura. Seattle Art Museum

Japanese Imari bottle showing a geisha and her attendant. Japanese, 18th century. The extravagantly dressed geishas encouraged extravagant decoration in general. Kyoto, Matsur Collection

Yet even lacquer was not immune from the influence of Zen philosophy. There is a series of extraordinary lacquers associated with the names of celebrated Japanese artists of the seventeenth and eighteenth centuries — Sotatsu, Koetsu, Korin and Kenzan. Among the materials they used to supplement the actual lacquer itself are sheet lead, pewter, mother-of-pearl and carefully selected grainy wood. The effects they achieved were bold in the extreme. In fact, these lacquers often repeat compositions also found on screens attributed to the same artists. Wonderfully decorative as these pieces are, it sometimes shocks European taste to find apparent spontaneity being achieved by such patently unspontaneous means. This is a superficial reaction. What is more important is the practical demonstration of the lack of boundaries between art and craft in Japanese culture. Two of the artists I have just named, Koetsu and Kenzan, are also extremely celebrated as potters. Even granted the fact that their pottery, marvellous as it is,

Japanese Imari
porcelain bowl
decorated in
underglaze blue
and overglaze
enamels.
18th century.
Tokyo National
Museum

Earthenware pitcher
with decoration by
Kenzan. Japanese,
18th century.
Osaka, Itsuo Art
Museum

Earthenware dish
with decoration by
Kenzan showing
autumn grasses
and running
water. Japanese,
18th century.

Harunobu, woodblock print of a geisha and her lover admiring the autumn moon. The sentiment is typically Japanese in its desire to identify with nature, and the eating utensils reflect the impact of 'tea-taste'. Japanese, *c.* 1768. London, British Museum

forms a kind of eddy or backwater in the main line of development in Japanese ceramics, one is bound to be impressed by the unity of sensibility to be discovered in their work, no matter what medium they were employing, and by their complete freedom to move from one method of expression to another.

One reason for this freedom was the fact that Japanese art, taken as a whole, was a view of nature and of natural forces, and not of man alone. While there is plenty of human interest — the Japanese have a liking for narrative and a strong sense of caricature — man, whether grotesque or noble, is only an expression of things which are also to be found elsewhere. The craftsman is respected as a channel through which these natural forces express themselves. He succeeds to the extent to which he makes himself a conduit for their flow.

It was not accidental that the rise of the Arts and Crafts Movement in Europe during the 1880s coincided with a strong renewal of interest in Japan. From that moment onwards, Europeans began to think of the craftsman not merely as the possessor of a particular kind of skill, but as a man who presented alternative and perhaps superior answers to the questions traditionally asked only of the fine artist.

Japanese culture was perhaps the first to see craftwork as having a moral value as an activity, quite apart from what was actually produced; just as it was the first to see craft as expressing the moral condition of those who practised it. In this sense, the whole modern theory of craft has Japanese roots.

5 The Islamic World

Islamic crafts have to be thought about and discussed in a different way from those of India, China and Japan, and this for a simple reason. Islam is a religion, not a geographical area or an ethnic group. The creed which burst out of the Arabian peninsula after the death of the prophet Mohammed in A.D. 632 spread in less than eighty years as far as Central Asia in the East and Spain and North Africa in the West. People became Moslems by conversion, forcible or otherwise, and brought with them, into the service of a new religion and a new way of life, the long-established traditions of the regions where they lived. In particular, Islam brought together the cultures which had once lain on either side of Rome's eastern frontier — that of Sassanian Persia on the one hand, and of the Roman Near East on the other. Despite centuries of enmity, these cultures were already close to one another in many important respects.

The Sassanians, whom Islam completely swallowed up, left behind them a legacy of sumptuous court crafts, meant to bolster the prestige of an absolute ruler. Amongst the most characteristic Sassanian products are superb pieces of silver, evidently meant for use at court banquets. There are also textiles woven in rich patterns, though of these only fragments remain. East Rome, its

Detail of a silk cloth woven with elephants and inscription. Persian, 10th century. Paris, Musée du Louvre

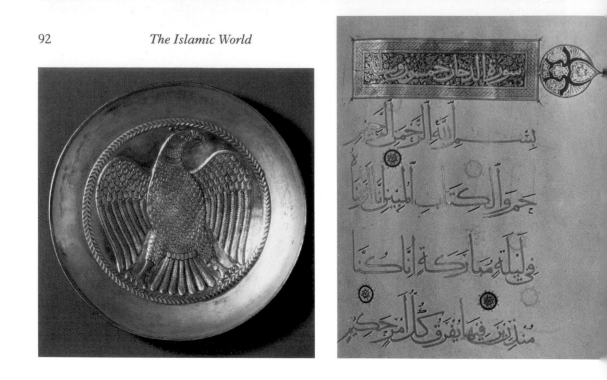

territories truncated, survived until 1453, transformed into Byzantium. There is no sharp dividing line between the Byzantine style and its Classical predecessor. In the eastern part of the Roman empire, Classical norms of shape, decoration and proportion had gradually been superseded by something more intense and more recognizably Oriental in its ideas about both decoration and proportion. The Islamic invaders, when they took over formerly Byzantine provinces in Syria and Egypt, found there many artefacts which were already to their taste. Much Islamic glass develops naturally and gradually out of what was already being made in the glass houses of Syria: just as some of the rest makes use of identifiably Sassanian techniques, such as the use of wheelcut facets on vessels of thick glass. Early Islamic silks, more particularly those with magnificent monsters, birds or animals paired in roundels, are also clearly the descendants of what had been woven previously in both Sassanian and East Roman workshops.

Islam did, however, bring with it some important changes. Even more than Christianity, it was the religion of a book. It put great emphasis on calligraphy, as writing was the vehicle through which the Prophet's word was made manifest. Islamic objects, and even the textiles, are often inscribed; and in many cases, for example the bowls decorated in black and white or black and brown made at the Nishapur potteries during the tenth century, the entire decoration of the object consists of magnificent Cufic script.

Islamic teaching was puritanical in its attitudes towards the representation of living beings, something which it inherited from Judaism. Yet Islamic art is not entirely abstract — the human impulse to reflect the joys of the visible world was too strong to be repressed by religion. Indeed, even human figures appear many

Above left:
Sassanian silver dish with eagle relief. Persian, 5th–6th century. Washington, Freer Gallery of Art

Above:
Islamic calligraphy, from the Koran. London, British Museum

Sassanian silver flask with embossed decoration. Persian, 5th–6th century. London, British Museum

times. There is, for example, a whole class of magnificent velvets, made in Persia during the seventeenth century, where the decoration consists of large-scale human figures with a few tufts of flowers scattered between them. But one always senses a feeling of reserve in the Islamic approach to representation. Artists avoid total realism, even in narrative book-illustration. They prefer to use what is represented as a component in some elaborate pattern, and where this is not possible they are still careful to stress the decorative quality of what is shown, rather than its truth to nature. As in Japan, there is no hard-and-fast dividing line between the fine and the applied arts.

Another thing one has to understand is that Islamic society enshrined a paradox, and that the crafts reflected this fact. Islam was originally a religion of poor nomads. Later, there were great Islamic cities, some of them new and highly successful foundations. Yet, since so much of the territory within which the new religion

Fatimid Hedwig glass with wheelcut decoration. Egyptian, 11th century. Kunstsammlungen der Veste, Coburg

prevailed was arid, the nomadic way of life was never entirely abandoned, and indeed as the source from which Islam had sprung it retained a prestige which was felt even by rulers comfortably established in great cities. One of the most important of the Islamic crafts, indeed the one which in many ways sums up most of the rest, was building. This might seem to reflect the desire to be settled, to establish something permanent. Yet one notes how, time after time, Islamic rulers abandoned cities which had been strenuously created. Fatepur Sikri and Aurungabad in India are two out of many examples. Other crafts, notably textiles, remained positively linked to the nomadic way of life, and in a sense have become identified with it — sometimes wrongly, as it happens.

Islamic architecture, especially after the Ottoman conquest of Constantinople, owed a great deal to the Roman tradition of building, which Byzantium had further developed. It was not merely that Justinian's great domed cathedral of Saint Sophia was turned into a mosque, but that it provided a model for the other mosques built in Ottoman territory from the sixteenth century onwards. There were, however, differences. Saint Sophia had mosaic decoration which was executed at different periods and did not form a completely coherent or harmonious scheme. Many Ottoman mosques of the sixteenth and seventeenth centuries were ornamented instead with splendid tilework. The pretence that structure and surface were the same thing, still precariously maintained in Roman architecture by the use of facing materials, such as marble and brick, which might conceivably be fully structural, is here completely abandoned, and almost the whole of the building is covered with magnificent patterns. The visitor passes from the experience of space, subtly manipulated, to an even more intense experience of surface.

Wonderful tilework is also found in Iran, but in the Islamic buildings of India there is a shift to marble, carved or inlaid in patterns with stones of contrasting colour. The jewel-like nature of this decoration has already been described.

The emphasis on intricate surface pattern is in fact characteristic of a broad spectrum of Islamic crafts, and nowhere more so than in textiles, themselves the chiefest glory of Islamic workshops, at least insofar as Europeans were concerned. Yet European admiration for Islamic weavers has long been mingled with ignorance of what they actually produced, under what conditions, and with what intentions.

From the point of view of their impact upon Europe, Islamic textiles can be divided into three groups. There are luxurious patterned materials woven in silk — at first flat weaves, and later velvets. There are pile carpets; and lastly there are the heavy-grade tapestry-woven stuffs, both carpets and hangings, which are called kelims.

It was the luxury silks which first deeply impressed the European mind, but the story of their development is extremely complex and

far from purely Islamic. Patterned silks, like silk in general, were first produced in China. Later, as has been noted, the craft of silk-weaving spread to Byzantium. Byzantine silks, or certainly the best of them, were made for imperial use in strictly controlled court workshops, by weavers originally recruited from Syria and Iran. The workshops themselves contained men of many different trades — dyers, different kinds of weavers and even tailors, who made up the finished stuffs. Both raw material and the finished products were carefully stockpiled. Luxurious silk clothing was a frequent form of official gift, and an important distinguishing mark in the governmental hierarchy. There were regular imperial distributions to court functionaries, and the Byzantine emperors also used the products of their court workshops as an aid to diplomacy, making presents to visiting ambassadors and other distinguished strangers. Part of the production was sold rather than given away. There was at one time a permanent exhibition building in Constantinople called 'The House of Lamps', because it was illuminated at night.

Silk panel in Isfahan style. Persian, 17th century. Lisbon, Gulbenkian Foundation

Persian 17th-century tilework on the Jomeh (Friday) Mosque, Isfahan

Suleymaniye Mosque, Istanbul, 16th century. Built by Sinan for Sultan Suleyman the Magnificent as a rival to Santa Sophia

14th-century
Italian silk
brocade with
griffins and eagles
in medallions,
pomegranates and
pseudo-Arabic
lettering. Lyons,
Musée de
l'Histoire des
Tissus

Left: 8th-10th century Byzantine silk cloth. Berlin, Kunstgeverben Museum

Right: 10th-century Byzantine silk brocade. Aachen Cathedral

Foreigners, however, were only allowed to buy inferior weavings, fabrics of narrow loom-widths, and without the huge patterns (two or three repeats at most in a single garment) which were considered the finest.

In addition to the silks woven in the court workshops, others, of perhaps equal quality, were brought to Constantinople from Syria, even after it fell to Islam, but the distribution of these, too, was carefully controlled by the ruler.

As Byzantine power weakened, patterned silks were more and more freely exported to the West, especially after Constantinople fell to the crusaders in 1204. In the thirteenth and fourteenth centuries the Italian trading republics began to establish native silk-industries of their own. Patterns which had long remained relatively conservative — that is to say static and symmetrical — started to change more rapidly. At the start of the fourteenth century a new style, asymetrical and full of movement, appeared in the silks then being produced in Italian workshops. One feature of these patterns was the use of bands of illegible pseudo-Arabic lettering, but taken as a whole the new freedom was undoubtedly the product of influence from China. Thanks to the savage military genius of Genghis Khan, a new trading-route had been established in the wake of the Mongols, stretching all the way across Asia.

Islamic silks were thus not *sui generis*. Produced in a region which lay between China on the one hand and Europe on the other, they reflected the influence of both, while sometimes making their own kind of mark upon other cultures. Much of their tradition was inherited directly from Byzantium. Like Byzantine silks, Islamic

weavings in this precious material remained very much a court craft, and even after the Turkish conquest of Constantinople in 1453, the silk workshops seem to have been organized in very much the same fashion as they had been previously. Stylistically, however, the earliest Ottoman silks are less Byzantine than Western. In Europe, the 'wild style' of the fourteenth century had been replaced by formal pomegranate patterns built on a diagonal lattice, and these were also popular in Ottoman workshops — so popular, indeed, that they influenced other crafts, such as decorative tilework. But there is another strain as well. In Ottoman work it is easy to perceive the continuing seduction of Iran, which reveals itself through the use of naturalistically drawn flowers — tulips, carnations and hyacinths — and also through the presence of

White earthenware wall tiles painted in underglaze blue and green. Syrian, *c*. 1425. London, Victoria and Albert Museum

Right and below: Details of a pile carpet found in a Scythian tomb at Pazyryk Altai, Siberia. 5th-4th century B.C. Leningrad, Hermitage Museum

Islamic heraldic emblems — the crescent, and also the tiger-stripes and the three crystal balls associated with Timur.

By the beginning of the seventeenth century Ottoman textile design had acquired a very distinct character of its own, with tremendously bold floral patterns, which are nevertheless cunningly diversified in scale, small motifs being superimposed upon larger ones, to create a movement of pattern on pattern which now seems quintessentially Islamic. At the same period the Iranian court-workshops were producing the velvets with large-scale human figures which have already been mentioned — flouting strict Islamic law but creating through broad rhythms something very typical of Islamic taste as a whole.

The Islamic flavour is as all-pervasive in designs for pile carpets, as it is in Iranian and Ottoman silk weaving, yet its precise

character is just as hard to pin down. Contrary to popular belief, pile carpets are not an Islamic invention, though they are now so closely identified with Islamic culture. The fact that they are much more ancient than the birth of Islam was conclusively proved in 1949 by the discovery of a well-preserved pile carpet dating from the fifth or fourth century B.C., at Pazyryk, in the grave of a Siberian chieftain. The carpet is of high technical quality. Its design relates it to Assyrian and Achaemenid art; and from the evidence offered by this discovery alone, it seems certain that carpets were being made in Iran long before the word of the Prophet arrived there; and that the new Islamic rulers inherited workshops specializing in this particular weaving technique from the Sassanians, whom they displaced. There is also literary evidence to support this suggestion. In A.D. 637, for example, the

Roman army sacked the royal Sassanian palace at Ctesiphon; and it is on record that they discovered there a carpet known as 'The Spring of Chosroes', said to have been worked 'of gold and silver and set with innumerable precious stones'. The seasonal name suggests that it may have resembled the later garden carpets, some of which are worked with gold and silver thread.

Recognizably Oriental carpets, with stylized animals in octagons, appear in European painting from the mid-fourteenth century onwards, and one or two surviving specimens can be dated to the fifteenth century. This particular design is a good instance of the essential conservatism of the craft of carpet-making, as it appears in different forms over a span of several hundred years. In many cases the weavers obviously used patterns which had been handed down orally and by example, and which could be learned by heart.

Carpet-production in Iran and the Near East was not, however, completely unified. It can be split into a number of overlapping divisions. There is, for example, a division between the small pieces produced by nomads, who were restricted to easily portable looms, and the larger ones made by settled farmers and townsmen. Town

Ottoman Turkish red velvet cushion cover patterned in gold and silver thread and green velvet. 17th century. London, Colnaghi Fine Arts Ltd

workshops can in turn be divided into those whose production went to the court, and which came under the direct influence of the ruler; and those which worked for middlemen or private clients. The latter did less sophisticated work, often relying on standardized elements. When one sees a pattern-unit broken off arbitrarily, as often happens in Oriental carpets, one can be sure that the piece has been produced in a commercial workshop of this type.

For the very finest carpets, Mogul and Iranian ones in particular, designs seem to have been produced by specially commissioned court artists, rather than by the weavers themselves. Yet it seems likely that these designs were not fully worked out, full-scale cartoons of the type used for European tapestries, but relatively slight sketches which allowed considerable liberty of interpretation.

Many carpet designs were profoundly influenced by the Islamic way of life. Prayer rugs, with an arched design which could be pointed towards Mecca, are an obvious example. So too are the garden carpets reflecting the Iranian notion of paradise — a fertile garden with flowers, trees, streams, birds and animals, which offers a contrast to the harshness of desert landscape. On the other hand it was also customary, from a very early date, to make carpets never intended for local use. The splendid silk and gold *'polonaise'* carpets woven in Isfahan and Kashan in the early seventeenth century seem all to have been intended as gifts for important foreigners. They take their name from the fact that so many of them were discovered in Polish collections during the nineteenth century.

Kelims, the flat tapestry-weave carpets and hangings, which have only recently come to be appreciated in the West, are, unlike pile

Nomads weaving a kelim, Kiz Kalesi, Turkey

Persian kelim from
Shiraz, 19th
century. London,
Benardout and
Benardout Ltd

carpets, made for purely local consumption. Indeed, the majority were not articles of trade, but were made within families for their own use. Whereas pile carpets were generally the work of men, these were the responsibility of women and often formed an important part of the dowry a bride brought to her husband. The bold patterns of these kelims, often identified with a particular district, show even more clearly than other textiles the conservative, folk basis of much Islamic craftwork.

Craft-activities with a recognizably Islamic character also include carving in hardstone, ivory and wood, glass-making, metalworking and distinctive types of pottery. The use of hardstones was intermittent. There was a short-lived industry using rock crystal in Fatimid Egypt during the tenth and eleventh centuries; and another, using jade, in Transoxania during the fifteenth century and later in Mogul India. It also seems likely, from a few surviving pieces, that jade was carved in the Ottoman court workshops in Istanbul. Whereas Chinese jade-carving often stresses the ritual importance of the material, or seeks to discover the form lying hidden within a particular pebble or even boulder of the precious material, Mogul and Turkish pieces make a direct appeal to the sense of luxury. They are often inlaid with gold and encrusted with jewels, and give a good idea of the sumptuousness of Oriental court life.

Islamic wood and ivory carving are closely related to one another, not least because wood was often inlaid with ivory or bone. Both crafts show a typical love of intricacy and control of elaborate surface pattern, as if the ban on representation built up extra stores of imagination and energy which could only be released by taking decoration as far as it would go. Inscriptions often play an important part in the design. Objects in metal, especially those made of bronze or brass, are stylistically related to those made of other materials. Engraving, inlay, overlay and repoussé techniques

Persian brass ewer damascened in silver, Seljuk, *c.* 1250. New York, Metropolitan Museum of Art, Rogers Fund, 1944

Opposite page: Rock crystal ewer from Cairo, 10th century. Venice, San Marco Treasure

Islamic brass bowl damascened in silver, 14th century. Berlin, Staatliche Museen

Enamelled and
gilded Islamic
mosque lamp,
13th century.
Washington, Freer
Gallery of Art

Enamelled and
gilded glass bowl
with Arabic
inscriptions.
Syrian, c. 1325.
The Hague,
Gemeentemuseum

Persian Seljuk *minai* ware bowl, 13th century. Detroit Institute of Arts

are all used to provide the required density of pattern. One technique, damascening or *kúftgari*, is especially typical of Islamic metalwork of post-fifteenth century date. Here an iron or steel base is scored all over with closely cross-hatched lines, and gold or silver wires adhere to this background when hammered on to make a design. The technique was particularly favoured for the decoration of armour and weapons.

The technology of working metal, as opposed to simple craft technique, was for long better understood in Islamic territories than it was in the West. It was from Islam that the Western metalsmiths of the Middle Ages learned to exert a greater degree of control over their material. Part of this knowledge was gained during the crusades; part of it came from contact between the Moors of Spain and the Christian enemies who were eventually to drive them out of the Iberian peninsula. During the ninth century Toledo was already the chief centre for the production of Moorish blades, and when the Moorish rulers left, their craftsmen often remained and were at least nominally converted to the opposing religion.

Islamic glass developed directly from the Roman and Sassanian glass industries which preceded it. Syria and Egypt were the chief centres of production, just as they had been in Hellenistic and Roman times, and the technical range of the glass-maker was now extended to include not only painting in fired pigments (already

Toledo dagger, with damascened decoration, showing Islamic influence, 16th century. New York, Metropolitan Museum of Art

known in the ancient world) but also gilding. Gilded and enamelled glasses were produced in Aleppo and Damascus, and as many as eight different colours were sometimes used on a single piece. The forms, as opposed to the decoration, of Islamic glass were often influenced by contemporary metalwork, which perhaps demonstrates the higher standing of the latter. Glass-production in Aleppo probably lasted until the Mongol invasion of 1260. In Damascus it continued until Timur captured the city in 1400, carrying off many of its skilled craftsmen to Samarkand. Leadership in glass-making then passed to the Venetian workshops at Murano.

Islamic ceramics show the same genius for decoration as other Islamic crafts. The use of gilding as a means of decorating glass is matched by the use of metallic lustre on pottery, and it is probable that the technique was originally acquired from the glass-makers. In fact, lustre decoration is just one aspect of the flexible interchange of ideas between different craft disciplines which took place in the Islamic world, and the lustre-painters themselves probably took ideas not only from glass, but from metalwork, carved wood, textiles and stucco, all of which seem to have contributed to their repertoire of designs.

Yet Islamic pottery was not merely imitative. There was an important series of technological innovations, full of promise for the future. Admiration for the Sung porcelains imported from China inspired a search for a finer and harder body. The solution found was not true porcelain, of the kind the Chinese produced, but frit — clay mixed with ground quartz which provided a true fusion of body and glaze when the piece was fired. The Islamic potters were also responsible for the discovery of underglaze painting, which did not run in the kiln. This was soon combined with overglaze enamel painting in order to produce the elaborately pictorial '*minai*' wares. The Islamic contribution to the decoration of ceramics is absolutely fundamental, and it is these wares, not the

Islamic carved wooden door, 14th century, from the tomb of Mahmoud, Agra Fort

Far left: Parade helmet made for the Duke of Alba. Toledo, 1580. New York, Metropolitan Museum of Art

Left: Tin-enamelled pottery bowl with lustre decoration. Persian, mid-13th century. New York, Metropolitan Museum of Art, Fletcher Fund, 1932

pottery produced in antiquity, which are the direct ancestors of most of the ceramics produced in the West from the late Middle Ages until the belated introduction of true porcelain in the early eighteenth century.

Because of the Islamic respect for the written word the arts of the book were inevitably very important in Islamic culture. But at this point one encounters a paradox. Islamic book-making was very ready to absorb certain technological advances. The craft of paper-making, for instance, was transmitted from China to the Arab world without meeting much resistance, arriving there in the middle of the eighth century. Significantly, Islam in turn became the means of transmitting knowledge of paper-making to Europe. The earliest known European document on paper dates from the year A.D. 1109, and was issued by King Roger of Sicily. It is written in both Latin and Arabic. On the other hand printing, though so closely linked to paper-making, met with religious opposition, as to the devout it seemed a sacrilegious means of transmitting the word of the Prophet. Medieval Arabic block-printed texts have indeed been discovered in Egypt, but generally the invention made no headway. This means that, despite a high level of literary culture, technological progress in any fundamental sense was slow, since knowledge could not be disseminated rapidly.

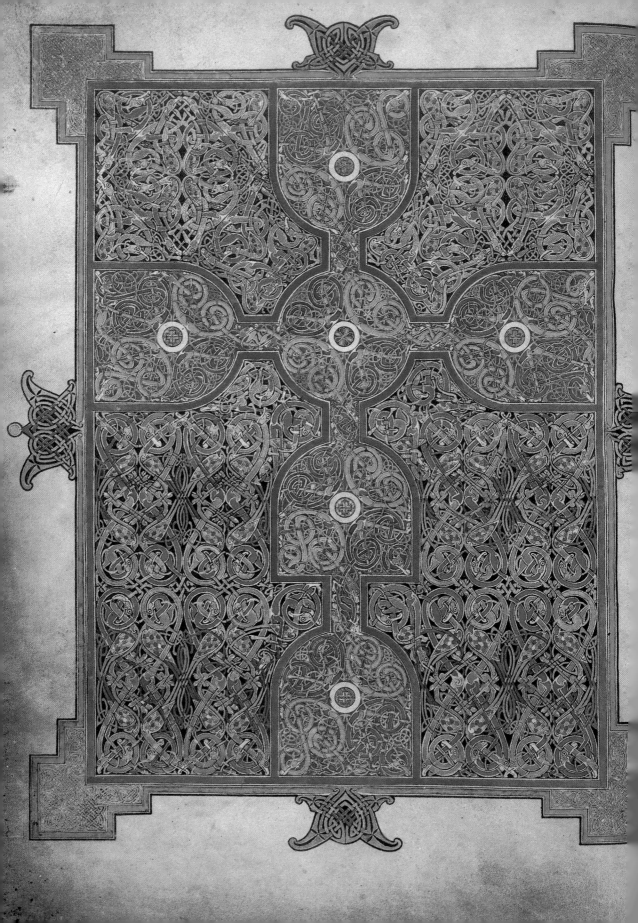

6 The European Middle Ages

Our current view of the European Middle Ages, and especially of their significance for craft, is confused. The term itself connotes not merely a vast geographical area, but a huge expanse of time. There is a tremendous difference between the Europe of Charlemagne and that of Charles VII of France and the rulers contemporary with him. During many centuries European society expanded, altered and developed, meeting with occasional setbacks, due to disease or natural disaster, as well as making continual advances. But to some extent modern enthusiasts for craft have been unwilling to accept this continual flux. In their minds, the accurate historical view — that of an extremely volatile and changeable society, often at odds with itself — is opposed by another. They still idealize the Middle Ages in a way which first became fashionable at the beginning of the nineteenth century.

This idealization arose in reaction to the horrors and evils of

Opposite page: 'Carpet' page from the Lindisfarne Gospels, Northumbria, 8th century A.D. London, British Library

Details of the embroidery on the stole of St Cuthbert, early 10th century. Durham Cathedral Museum

HIC·DVX·VVILGELM·CVM HAROLL

industrial society, and those responsible for it borrowed elements from very different medieval epochs, bringing together the Christian idealism of the earlier centuries and the fully developed urban guild system which came later, while to some extent misunderstanding both. Nineteenth-century enthusiasts for craft also tended to ignore the fact that the Middle Ages had witnessed an industrial and technological revolution of their own, which began in the thirteenth century.

Yet mixed in with these misconceptions there was a good deal of truth. There was, for example, a change in attitudes towards manual labour. In pagan society this had been almost universally despised, not least because it was often an activity of men who were unfree. Thanks to Christianity, handwork achieved a new dignity. Men did not forget that Christ had been brought up as a carpenter's son.

The Christian influence was reinforced by the fact that, during the early Middle Ages, and especially in the North, the monastic communities were the place where fine craftsmanship took refuge. In Anglo-Saxon England, for example, one finds that powerful churchmen were also famous as gifted craftsmen. Two saints, St Dunstan and St Ethelwold, won fame as metalsmiths. St Dunstan was also an illuminator, and made designs for embroideries. They were not isolated figures. Aelfsig, abbot of Ely from 981 to *c*.1019, was a worker in precious metal. Spearhavoci, monk of Bury and abbot of Abingdon in the mid-eleventh century, was a well-known goldsmith and was commissioned to make a crown for the Emperor Henry IV. Mannig, abbot of Evesham, made the shrine of St Eguin at his own monastery. The artist of the famous Lindisfarne Gospels, that masterpiece of early illumination, was probably

Detail from the Bayeux Tapestry; Harold of England accompanies Duke William of Normandy. 1080. Bayeux, Library

Eadfrith, bishop of Lindisfarne. Monkish craftsmen were also to be found at work in mainland Europe. Gozbert and Alcuin, who made a large bronze font for St Maxim's, Trier, in the twelfth century, were monks not laymen.

At the same period, noble ladies were also keen craftswomen, working particularly as embroideresses. In Germany Gisela, sister of the Emperor Henry II, was skilful with her needle, and organized an embroidery workshop near the imperial palace.

Anglo-Saxon queens were often celebrated for their mastery of this particular skill. The stole and maniple of St Cuthbert, now on display in the museum at Durham Cathedral, are sometimes said to be the work of Aelfled, queen of Edward the Elder (they were certainly commissioned by her, as an inscription tells us). Emma, successively the queen of Ethelred the Unready and Canute, was famous for her embroidery and so too was Edgitha, queen of Edward the Confessor, who was described by the historian William of Malmesbury as 'the perfect mistress of her needle'. She embroidered with her own hands a rich vestment in gold for the abbot of St Riquier in Picardy.

This particular tradition continued not only after the Norman Conquest (Matilda, queen of William the Conqueror, was closely associated with the making of the Bayeux Tapestry), but until the end of the Middle Ages and even beyond them. Queens were not ashamed both to weave and to sew. In the year 1290, for example, a messenger was sent to Burgh and to Aylesham to obtain weaving materials for the use of Queen Eleanor, wife of Edward I. Catherine

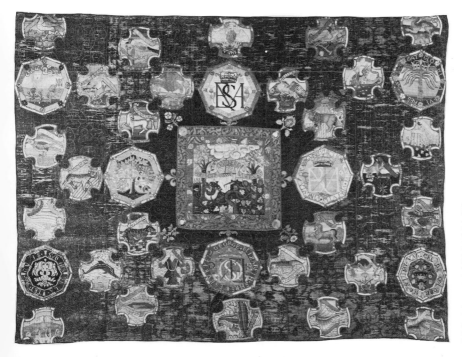

Oxburgh Hangings. Embroidered by Mary Queen of Scots and bearing her cipher, MSR, under a crown. 16th century. London, Victoria and Albert Museum

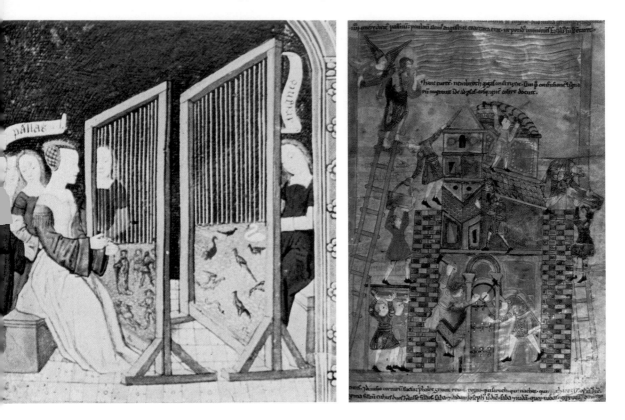

of Aragon, living in retirement at Ampthill in Bedfordshire after her rejection by her husband Henry VIII, consoled herself by doing embroidery and taught her skills to various friends and protegées. She also taught the craft of lace-making. Mary Queen of Scots did a great deal of needlework during her English captivity, some of it in collaboration with her hostess, Bess of Hardwick. The Oxburgh Hangings survive as evidence of their skill.

Noble women and nuns in fact continued to work at the crafts long after high-ranking churchmen had given up this kind of occupation. What kept them at it was another aspect of Christian doctrine as it developed in the writings of the Church fathers, who had a great suspicion of any form of female idleness. St Jerome, for instance, recommended a holy woman who had founded a convent to keep wool always in her own hands, to spin and weave and to see to it that her companions did the same. Manual labour, if demeaning for men, was not so for women.

In the world of the monasteries there soon grew up a distinction between 'learned religious', or true monks, and lay-brothers, who undertook all forms of manual labour. In Anglo-Norman times, the principal ecclesiastics were functionaries and administrators rather than artists and craftsmen. Craft had already begun to be left to specialists. Nevertheless the great monasteries remained, for some time to come, very important centres of craft production. They

Above Left: Women using a vertical loom. Detail of an illustration to Ovid's *Metamorphoses*. Flemish, *c*. 1497. Oxford, Bodleian Library

Above: Medieval builders at work, 11th-12th century. London, British Library

Jean Fouquet, *The Building of the Temple in Jerusalem*, *c*. 1470. Illumination from Josephus' *Antiquités Judaïques*. Paris, Bibliothèque Nationale

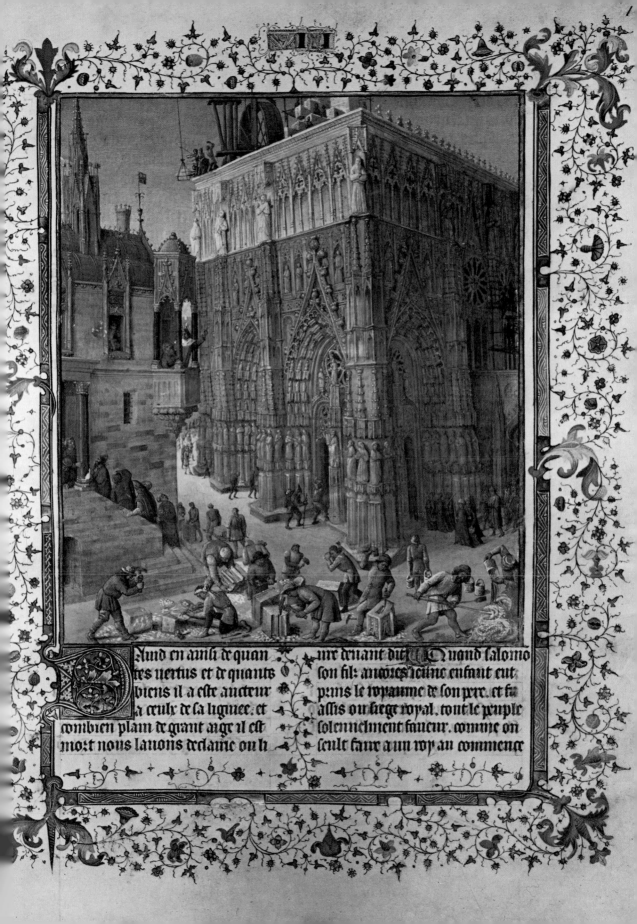

und en ainli de quan
tes uertus et de quants
biens il a este auckeur
a ceulx de sa lignee. et
combien plain de grant aige il est
mozt nous lauons declaire ou li

ure deuant dit. Quand salomo
son fil: ancores ieune enfant eut
pzins le royaume de son pere. et fa
assis ou siege royal. tout le peuple
solennelment faueur. comme on
seult faire a un roy au commence

resembled and were descended from the great villas of the Later Roman Empire, which took on a new role with the decline of urban centres. Like the villas, the monasteries had important workshops attached to them. For example, in the twelfth century the French abbey of Corbie had three large rooms which were used exclusively as workshops and housed a wide variety of trades — there were six blacksmiths, makers of edged tools and locksmiths, two goldsmiths, two shoemakers and a maker of parchment, among others. A big abbey would also act as a collecting-point for the goods made by its tenants. Rents were often paid, not in money but in kind — a smith had to bring six lance-heads: a farmer's wife had to produce stuff woven by her from wool provided by the abbey.

Secular estates operated in a similar way at the same period. Charlemagne, copying both the Late Roman and the monastic pattern, wanted to have numerous craftsmen attached to his farms, among them goldsmiths, shoemakers, armourers and carpenters. The workshops attached to great estates, whether the owners were lay people or clerics, employed women as well as men. The women

Early 15th-century builders at work. From *Livre des profits champêtres* by Pierre de Crescent. Paris, Bibliothèque de l'Arsenal

Detail of
Charlemagne's
tomb. Gilded and
enamelled bronze
set with stones,
9th century.
Aachen Cathedral

undertook such typically feminine tasks as weaving and spinning, and on secular estates they were generally supervised by the lord's wife, who perhaps worked beside them. The monasteries, however, employed professional overseers to look after their female work-force. In both cases there was often something approaching a factory organization — implements and materials were provided in the workshop.

It was not merely craft organization, but craft itself which was in certain respects highly developed at a very early date. Iron and steel tools, for instance, had mostly reached what we think of as their fully developed forms by the eighth century. Those used by early medieval wood-workers, ship-builders and stone-masons differed very little from their modern counterparts, though there was later to be a much greater degree of specialization, which led to tools being made in increasingly large and elaborate sets.

Yet in another sense the early medieval craftsman had a hard struggle to regain some of the skills lost in the social collapse which followed the Barbarian Invasions. In part of the northwest Roman Empire, for example, the making of good pottery on the wheel completely lapsed for a while. In Britain, outside Kent, the hiatus lasted from the fifth to the ninth century. Even where the wheel remained in use, as for example in the Rhineland, and where there was something approaching a continuous factory tradition, pottery

The Noah
window, 13th
century, Chartres
Cathedral, north
aisle of the nave

remained in other respects quite primitive. Stoneware developed in the Rhineland *c.* 800 A.D., apparently independent of Eastern influence. Lead silicate glazes, which had of course been known to the Romans, did not re-appear in northern Europe until the eleventh century. From the twelfth century onwards they were especially popular in Britain and in France. In the fourteenth century Rhenish stonewares were further developed by the addition of a salt glaze.

An immense amount of information about British medieval pottery in particular lies buried in archaeological reports, and this evidence presents an extremely curious and complicated picture, very different from the one put forward by late nineteenth and early twentieth-century enthusiasts for craft. There is no true continuity of development, only a fluctuating struggle with both natural and historical circumstances. In the first, or Saxo-Norman, phase, dating from about 850 to about 1150, one sees a rapid development of the potter's skill, stimulated rather than retarded by the Viking invasions and the Norman Conquest. Both of these encouraged overseas trade, and trade brought with it not only new markets but a knowledge of new types of pottery. The fast wheel once again came into use almost all over England, and standard forms appeared, for example a kind of glazed spouted pitcher with either one or three handles. These in turn indicate a high level of industrialization, almost on the Rhineland model. At this time most of the important potteries seem to have been located in towns — something which reflects the expansion of urban markets as well as the efforts made by the Saxon kings to limit trading to towns by means of legislation.

Yet the gains made were not consolidated. In the twelfth century this flourishing urban-based pottery industry started to decline. Potteries moved into the countryside and operated on a smaller scale, and there was even a tendency for developed techniques of throwing and kiln construction to be discarded. Only in a very few centres — the town of Stamford in Lincolnshire was one of them — do we find continuity of production on an industrial scale. The result was a huge proliferation of regional styles. Each district developed its own characteristic fabric and its own range of types. As the economy gradually improved, potting techniques became more sophisticated, though there was also less demand for certain items which had once been staple products. At this time, for instance, very large pottery cooking vessels were feeling the competition of more durable cooking pots made of bronze and iron. This, in turn, reflected the greater cheapness and availability of metals. In the fourteenth century, however, pottery-making collapsed, under the impact of a series of epidemics culminating in the Black Death of 1348. Fine wares almost ceased to be produced, and there was still a scarcity of them in the fifteenth century, even though coarse, utilitarian wares were being made in large quantities, under semi-industrial conditions, especially in potteries in the Midlands and around London. It was a symptom of the new climate that many such household wares, in addition to being made in standard shapes, were produced in a range of graded sizes.

The history of British pottery, in the seven centuries from the year 800 to the year 1500, suggests three things — first and most obviously the vulnerability of craft to an equally vulnerable economy, secondly the existence of a comparatively small and shallow reservoir of craft skills, and thirdly the absence of any independent craft aesthetic.

These conclusions, but particularly the last, can be reinforced by noting that, in the early Middle Ages at least, there was a conspicuous lack of any dividing line between crafts which later became sharply differentiated from one another. For instance, as can be seen from monastery and other records, the distinction between the craft of the bronze-founder and that of the goldsmith took a long time to establish itself. The craftsmen who chose to work under the protection of the monasteries were willing, in return for the shelter they received, to turn their hands to anything. It was much later that the situation altered, with the establishment of urban guilds.

The monasteries had another and different kind of importance as well. From the twelfth century onwards they were pioneers in the technological revolution which was eventually to change the face of medieval craftsmanship. The craft idealist sees the Middle Ages as a time when handwork was practised in praise of God, and also for its own sake, as a healthy spiritual and mental discipline. This is a fiction, but one which, like many fictions, does contain at least a small element of truth. The great cathedrals, for example, were indeed undertaken for the greater glory of God, and were adorned with infinite and devoted toil and care. Those who built and decorated them do not seem to have had any particular time-span in mind for their completion. A medieval church of any size always seems to have grown up in a completely natural and organic way, shedding some parts, perhaps, as others were added. Though we now speak of some churches as 'unfinished', with the assumption that other, comparable buildings were successfully brought to completion, there is a sense in which all such structures are incomplete and show a potential for further growth, which has only been halted by the social and other upheavals which brought the Middle Ages themselves to a conclusion.

There were also cases, though very few, where medieval men showed an actual prejudice in favour of the laboriously handmade. One example is supplied by guild-regulations in Florence, which, as late as the fifteenth century, laid it down that the warp, as opposed to the weft, threads in cloth must still be hand-spun. But then such threads were with some reason believed to be stronger.

On the whole, the instinct of the medieval craftsman was to find easier, less tedious and less backbreaking ways of doing things, even though both law and guild regulations seemed intent on putting a

English
medieval pitcher,
late 13th- early
14th century.
Museum of
London

brake on technological progress. There was no longer an enormous pool of slave labour of the kind supplied to Rome by her continuous conquests. Serfdom existed, but Christian doctrine was opposed to slavery itself. Indeed, there was often an actual labour shortage, and anything which enabled one man to do the work of several was therefore to be welcomed. The monasteries, with their large settled communities, were pioneers in this field as in so many others, the more so since early machines tended to be cumbersome and rooted to one spot. I have already listed in Chapter One some of the landmarks of this first industrial revolution — the introduction of tanning, fulling and iron mills. To obtain the necessary power was no problem. Medieval machine-builders made use of the energy of water above all. What was more difficult was the construction of the machinery itself. There was a lack of adequate materials. The early machine-builders were forced to use wood since metal was expensive and in short supply. Indeed, one can see how the pace very gradually accelerated as metal became more commonplace — machines were used to produce metal, and metal was made into more and better machines, supplying a greater and greater proportion of the vital parts. The earliest *moulin à fer* is recorded in

France in 1249, and by the end of the century the working of metal in power-driven mills was starting to be comparatively commonplace.

Both the development of a kind of industrialization and the unevenness of its growth had a decisive effect on attitudes towards craft activity in the second half of the medieval epoch. The unevenness manifests itself in some surprising ways. For example, the crank and connecting rod, which form the core of many modern machines, were not invented until comparatively late, at the very close of the period I am discussing. Other reasons for lack of industrial progress were less obvious. Although, as I have said, most of the tools we are familiar with today were known in already standardized forms by the eighth century, there remained certain surprising gaps, especially in the range of wood-working tools. The carpenter's plane, though known in antiquity, for some reason dropped almost completely out of use until it was revived in the twelfth century. It did not become common until nearly a hundred years later. Another implement which was slow to develop was the needle, which almost throughout the Middle Ages was made not with an eye but with a closed hook. The first modern needles with an eye were produced in the Netherlands in the fifteenth century.

The more efficient machines became, the greater the social

Charter of Henry II granting the weavers of London their guild, with the liberties already enjoyed under Henry I, 1155-8. London, Guildhall Library

Carpenters' workshop showing a plane in use. From *Les Quatre états de la vie de l'homme* by Jean Bourdichon, 15th century. Paris, Bibliothèque Nationale

difficulties they tended to cause. Highly developed silk-throwing machines already existed in Italy in the thirteenth century, and water-power was applied to them in the fourteenth. A water-powered mill of this kind required only two or three operatives to mind it, replacing the several hundred hand-throwsters who had been needed previously. A change of this sort, suddenly introduced, naturally brought with it a great degree of social dislocation, which the workers themselves would tend to resist by any means at their disposal.

The notion of craft protection brings us to the extremely complex subject of the medieval guilds. In Europe, the guild system seems to have had its beginnings in the eleventh century, though something very like a fully developed system of this type had existed in the ancient world and more especially in the cities of the ancient Near East. The purpose of the guild was to maintain standards of skill, and at the same time to protect the craftsman — not merely, or even primarily, against technological change, but against the burdensome demands of the feudal system. For this reason guilds were an urban phenomenon, for, as the medieval German proverb had it: 'Stadtluft macht frei' — 'The air of towns makes free'. But once installed in the towns, the medieval guilds soon began to go beyond the original aims of securing both protection of employment and actual freedom from serfdom for their members. They developed monopolistic tendencies, and soon began to try to limit rather than to expand the supply of skilled labour so that their members might demand as high a price for their work as possible.

By the thirteenth century the guild system was fully established. At Chartres, for instance, many of the celebrated stained-glass windows in the cathedral were gifts from the city guilds, and their activities are represented in the designs. 'The History of Noah', the first window to be put up, was made at the cost of the carpenters, cart-builders and barrel-makers — their interest is clearly the reason for the choice of subject. Soon the production of food, dress, ornament, domestic utensils and indeed almost every kind of manufacture was taken out of the sphere of the household, and at the same time became increasingly subdivided. The separation of the crafts, one from another, was in these circumstances carried to extreme lengths, and the divisions were frequently reinforced by government ordinance. By 1422 there were in London no fewer than one hundred and eleven recognized groups or guilds of merchants and craftsmen. Fourteen were concerned with leather alone — cofferers, cordwainers, curriers, girdlers, glovers, leather dyers, leather-sellers, lorimers, male-makers, pouchmakers, saddlers, skinners, tanners, and whitetawyers. In theory, none of these was allowed to undertake any activity which belonged in the sphere of one of the others. Fourteen years earlier, in 1408, there were no fewer than three different craft guilds concerned with making knives in London — the bladesmiths, who produced the blades, the cutlers, who made the handles, and the sheathers, who made the sheaths. It was the cutlers who had the right to sell the completed article.

At the same time, the regulations which laid down what might legitimately be done by a guild member within the boundaries of his own craft were continually and often burdensomely elaborated. At Rheims (1340) and Troyes (1360), the drapers' guilds determined in detail, for each particular species of cloth, not only the kind of wool which might be used, but also the number of threads to the inch, the selvedges, and the manner of dyeing.

This minute technical concern might seem to run counter to another factor in the development of the guilds, the fact that, in the late fourteenth and early fifteenth centuries, they started to turn into oligarchies, organizations run by 'master craftsmen', who no longer did much, or perhaps any, of the work themselves, but left it in the hands of journeymen, who were deliberately shut out of the mastership. In Germany, for example, prospective masters in the various armourers' guilds were usually required to provide their own suit of armour for inspection, since full membership of a guild in theory entailed the duty to fight in person for one's city. Newly appointed masters had therefore to purchase a suit of armour at their own expense within a certain number of months after passing

Suit of embossed armour, *c*. 1590, from the workshop of Lucio Piccinino London, Wallace Collection

the guild examination. The armour itself then officially became the property of the guild. The expense was such that membership was automatically confined to a small elite of wealthy craftsmen.

The differentiation of trades set in motion by the guilds continued well beyond the point at which the guild-system attained its greatest importance. In 1568 the German engraver Jost Amman illustrated ninety different trades in his collection of plates devoted to the subject. In the *Encyclopédie*, that bible of the eighteenth-century Enlightenment, Diderot described and illustrated more than 250. By 1826 Pigot and Company's commercial directory could record 846 trades in London alone. Yet there was, from the fifteenth century onwards, a distinct tendency for people of similar or related skills to amalgamate their efforts, even in the teeth of regulations to the contrary. Often this came about because of the continuing technological revolution which the established guilds, however strenuous their efforts, had been unable to bring to a halt. Armourers, as their craft gradually became obsolete after the invention of gunpowder, moved into making copper vessels, and thus became indistinguishable from the braziers, who were members of a very different craft mystery.

The art of war, with its emphasis on the practicalities of survival, was one of the great opponents of the traditional craft spirit. Armourers might bring their skill in handling metal to an astonishing pitch before the inevitable decline set in, but what was far more important in the long run was the invention of cast-iron, a material which depended, not on handicraft skill, but on the use of water-powered bellows — these alone made it possible to raise the temperature high enough to get the required result. But if cast-iron depended on the machine, it also depended on the stimulus of combat, the search for new and more effective weapons of aggression. The first cast-iron products were cannon-balls. The introduction of gunpowder and the cannon were themselves significant steps towards a technology which was no longer craft-based.

The development of the cloth industry, especially in England and Flanders, also challenged guild attitudes towards craft. The introduction of water-driven fulling machinery was a first step — this was in use in England as early as the thirteenth century. From that point onwards the medieval textile industries moved very rapidly towards a fully capitalist system. In Flanders, in the fifteenth century, making a piece of cloth required no less than twenty-six different processes, each of them carried out by a different operative. Guild-specialization was here pushed to a point where it became inimical to the kind of society which had stimulated the growth of associations based on craft.

The conflict between the guilds and the needs of the new capitalists eventually became acute, and a social revolution was the result. Following a pattern established by the potteries at an earlier epoch, the weaving-shops began to move out of the towns, and thus away from onerous guild-regulations. After about 1540 the great

Medieval building using a hoist and scaffolding. From the *Life of St Alban*, 12th century. Dublin, Trinity College

English and Flemish cloth manufactories transferred themselves to the suburbs, and sometimes even farther afield into the countryside itself. The workers followed, preferring to live at the gates of the factory and under the protection (or at the mercy) of their employers rather than of a craft-guild or city corporation. The nostalgic association between craft and the countryside stressed by nineteenth and twentieth-century critics of capitalism has some unexpected roots.

Not all medieval crafts developed towards capitalism in the same fashion or at the same pace. The building industry, which today is closely associated in people's minds with capitalist enterprise, followed patterns which illustrate the differences and not the similarities between medieval society and our own. It is true that medieval builder's craft has one or two surprisingly modern aspects. For example, builders already realized that it would be advantageous to standardize certain measurements, such as the size of blocks of building stone. In 1264 the city of Douai issued an ordinance specifying that *carreaux* must have six by eight inches of facing, and eight inches of bed. One good reason for thinking in

Opposite page:
'Building the
Tower of Babel';
medieval
stone-masons at
work. From *The
Bedford Hours*,
Paris, *c.* 1423.
London, British
Library

these terms was that transportation costs were high, and it was therefore customary to prepare building materials as far as possible before moving them to the chosen site.

The surviving accounts show that great cathedrals were built with the aid of simple scaffolding and hoists, and usually with only a small workforce at any one time. Illustrations showing builders at work in illuminated manuscripts — a favourite subject is the building of the Tower of Babel — confirm the impression which one gains from the documents.

Craft-specialization affected building just as it did many other forms of activity — in particular, the mason's and the carpenter's crafts were always distinct. Of the two, it was the mason's which predominated, and masonry eventually became identified with the notion of secret and independent doctrines, sometimes opposed to those officially professed by church and state. Trained masons, like other superior craftsmen, were not fixed to one spot, but sold their skills wherever work was to be found. This, too, accentuated their tendency towards independence and their separateness from the rest of the community. A mason identified his work by means of a personal mark, and associated with his fellow masons in the rough lodges which were built immediately adjacent to the building site.

Medieval architects, themselves usually master masons, occupied an anomalous position in medieval society. A secular architect (in the early Middle Ages many architects were monks) was classed as a kind of superior workman, and often himself worked with his hands. On the other hand, a successful architect frequently became possessed of considerable privileges, and his work was by no means anonymous — in fact, he often signed it. One also finds architects who supervised several projects at once. Methods were empirical rather than scientific, though master-builders did make use of rough plans, and also noted details which might be of use to them afterwards. The famous sketchbook of Villard de Honnecourt shows the kind of thing that interested them: details of existing buildings, which might serve again in the future. But it shows no signs of a general theory of architecture. Because of this empiricism, and also because of the restlessness and daring of the medieval imagination, the builder's craft of the period often over-reached its own resources, and some spectacular collapses were the result.

Section from
Villard de
Honnecourt's
sketchbook.
London, British
Library

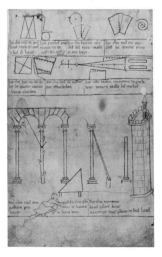

Another caste of craftsmen who enjoyed a special position in medieval society were the goldsmiths. Like master-masons, master-goldsmiths tended to be itinerant. They took their skills wherever there was a market for them. Because the materials used were costly, those who patronized the best goldsmiths came typically from the most powerful class, and the princes of Europe took great pride in their ability to command the skills of the most gifted artisans, and competed for their services. The objects the goldsmith produced were part of an intricate display of conspicuous wealth. The stepped buffet, an arrangement of shelves shown one above the

other like a set of steps, held a series of objects whose sole purpose was to impress the beholders. The number of shelves was supposed to be dependent on the rank of the person making the display — a king or queen might have five or even six stages, but a count or countess only three. Descriptions of the entertainments given by Philip the Good, Duke of Burgundy, give a good idea of the function of precious plate in terms of honour and its maintenance. At the Feast of the Pheasant, held at Lille in 1454, there was a six-staged buffet, which only the cupbearers were allowed to approach. At the Feast of the Knights of the Golden Fleece in 1456, there were no fewer than three buffets. One, solely for display, was loaded with golden objects set with precious stones. The other two, from which the tables were actually served, were filled with silver-gilt and plain silver plate respectively.

Yet there was always a hard-headed distinction in the medieval mind between the value of the workmanship and the value of actual materials, which the patron often produced from his own store. The difference was often specifically expressed in accounts and inventories. In the fourteenth century, the cost of manufacture was reckoned as approximately half that of the actual metal. When Edward the Black Prince returned to England from Gascony in 1371, the City of London presented him with six silver chargers 'weight £14.8s.9d., amounting with the making to £21.7s.2d.'

Medieval banquet scene, showing a three-staged stepped buffet. From *Epitre d'Othéa* by Christine de Pisan, 1461. Brussels, Bibliothèque Royale

Because they were primarily repositories for surplus wealth, master-pieces of goldsmiths' work were especially vulnerable to changes of political and economic fortune, and this is the reason why so little has come down to us. There are, however, a number of marvels that still survive — the royal gold cup of the Duke of Bedford in the British Museum, the reliquary showing Charles the Bold of Burgundy and his patron St George, presented by Charles the Bold himself to Liège, and the 'Little Gold Horse' at Altötting, com-missioned by Queen Isabeau of Bavaria for her husband Charles VI of France.

Reliquary of Charles the Bold, Duke of Burgundy, with his patron St George, by Gérard Loyet. Gold, partly painted and enamelled, with silver-gilt base, *c*. 1470-1. Liège, Cathedral and Chapter of St Paul

Like masonry, goldsmithing had a secretive, hermetic side. For obvious reasons, goldsmiths were particularly associated with the practice of alchemy— the search for a method of transforming base metals into gold. On occasion this might put them only one step away from the forbidden business of witchcraft. In addition, their financial operations and occasional service as bankers tempted them towards the equally forbidden practice of usury. The technical demands made by their craft gave medieval goldsmiths a working knowledge of almost all the problems which were later to interest the scientific metallurgist — change of melting point, the properties of alloying, the effects of cold-working and annealing, diffusion, surface tension, and the effects of oxidation and corrosion. Though most techniques were precisely the same as those employed at present — for example, the medieval goldsmith's solders were pretty much identical to those used by his present-day successor — the knowledge of the craft was apprehended in an empirical, not a scientific, way — the craftsman could not explain why he did certain things; he only knew that they worked. This, too, tended to turn goldsmithing into a thing of mysteries and secrets.

Because of their association with wealth, goldsmiths were relatively high in the social scale, and achieved recognition of their status fairly early. In London, for instance, the goldsmiths were the first of the city companies to receive a royal charter (1393).

One way in which goldsmithing differed from other European luxury trades was in being widely diffused. No urban community was conspicuously celebrated for its goldsmiths, even Paris, then the largest and wealthiest city in the Western world. Skilful workers in precious metals were to be found in every town which enjoyed a certain degree of prosperity. There is a contrast here with more specialized crafts such as enamelling and glass-making, both of which developed an association with specific centres — glass-making with Venice, where it is documented as early as 1090, and enamelling with Limoges and the valleys of the Rhine and Meuse. The development of glass-making in Venice shows how sharply a particular industry could move, given the right circumstances, against the general pattern of medieval craft practice. The Maggior Consiglio regulated the glass-manufacture by law, striving to keep its processes a secret. In 1291 all the glassworks were moved out of Venice itself to the island of Murano, and by 1450 the Murano factories were using recognizably industrial methods, with much teamwork and division of labour.

Enamelling was never so closely regulated, but its development illustrates one interesting point — the transition from monastic to lay workshops. The change was stimulated by demand — clients began to commission larger and more spectacular objects, and this led to a change from precious metals to less expensive ones. Gilded copper rather than gold became the preferred medium, and this in turn meant organization on a scale outside the scope of the monastic communities if they were to continue to fulfil their religious

The Eltenberg
Reliquary. Enamel
and copper-gilt,
with ivory figures,
Rhenish, *c*. 1150.
London, Victoria
and Albert
Museum

duties and other monastic functions.

Nor were glass-making and enamelling the only crafts to be
associated with particular cities or particular regions. The making
of fine swords was associated with Toledo in Spain, where, as we
have seen in Chapter Five, the craft was a legacy from the Moors,
and with Solingen in Germany, which was famous for swords as
early as the reign of the Emperor Frederick Barbarossa. The
Solingen smiths used registered marks which sometimes changed
hands for money, thus continuing in a more organized way the
tradition of their Viking predecessors.

In order to understand the complex structure of medieval craft
one must, however, look at some activity which was almost
universally practised. Embroidery, with its simple but demanding
techniques, is a case in point. The medieval instinct for decoration
ensured its continuing popularity. So did the medieval need for
precise visual identification by means of symbols. Embroidery was
the main vehicle for rendering the elaborate heraldic patterns which
ornamented garments of all kinds, ecclesiastical as well as lay. A

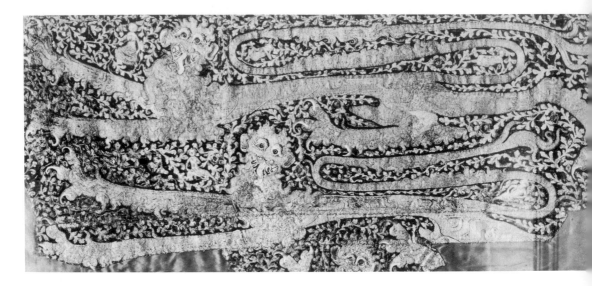

garment which was heraldically embroidered identified the wearer and showed both his allegiances and his position in the social hierarchy. Nevertheless, though fine embroidery spoke of wealth and position, it did not itself occupy the very highest position in its own particular scale of luxury. Woven silks were always valued more than embroideries because of the greater organization and greater complexity of the processes needed to produce them. Early medieval Europe showed its comparative lack of sophistication by using embroidery as the medium in which to copy the rare and sumptuous stuffs imported from Byzantium, and from workshops even further to the East.

Heraldic embroidery on velvet, with the Leopards of England in gold. English, 14th century. Paris, Musée Cluny

After starting its life in monasteries and in the hands of amateurs, embroidery eventually came to be a highly developed secular craft. There were embroiderers' guilds from the thirteenth century onwards, but they did not supersede either the monastic or the private workers. In fact, one finds fine embroidery being done in a very wide variety of circumstances — by noble ladies as a pastime, and by noble girls as a necessary part of their education as gentlewomen, by professional embroiders attached to large households — in fifteenth-century France every household with any pretensions retained the services of at least one professional embroiderer on an annual basis — and in organized workshops. The sumptuous embroideries created in England during the thirteenth and fourteenth centuries, and known throughout Europe as Opus Anglicanum, were professionally made. Commissions came from as far away as the papal court. Many of those employed on the work were men — the wardrobe accounts of the reign of Henry III give the names of several male embroiderers. Like nearly all medieval embroidery, whether professional or amateur, Opus Anglicanum was made on a frame — the circular or tambour frame which continues to be used today is of medieval origin.

Opus Anglicanum. Back of a chasuble embroidered in metal thread and silks on red velvet. English, early 14th century. New York, Metropolitan Museum of Art, Fletcher Fund, 1927

Medieval embroidery gives a good idea of the way in which craft at this period became specialized and professionalized without abandoning its domestic roots, and without a marked gap opening up between the processes used by the paid professional and the amateur working for private use and private satisfaction.

The two things which did most to change the nature of medieval society, and with it the character of medieval craft attitudes, were printing, revolutionized by the introduction of movable type, and the invention of the mechanical clock. Both printing and clockmaking are, in their early form, crafts which deviate from the expected pattern; and which, more importantly, accelerate change within society itself.

The revolutionary nature of printing is easy to perceive. The new craft faced in two directions, both of them implying radically new sets of attitudes. The printed sheet, whatever words or images it bore, was the first completely standardized product, standardized to the point of repeating the same mistakes of spelling or grammar, the same errors of drawing, over and over again if the type-setter or woodcut-maker happened to have made them.

In a broad sense, printing was important because it tended to standardize ideas — to provide a focus for the way in which reality was perceived as well as immensely speeding up the communication of those perceptions. In the craft field, the introduction of printed pattern-books, something which belongs to the sixteenth rather than the fifteenth century, had the effect of removing the craftsman's full independence, his freedom to invent his own forms and

Below: Printers' workshop. Woodcut by Jost Amman, 1568

Below right: 16th-century paper-making. Note the wire frame. Woodcut by Jost Amman, 1568. Paris, Bibliothèque Nationale

Above:
16th-century
printers' workshop
on a semi-
industrial scale.
Antwerp, Plantin
Museum

Above right:
Printed page with
hand-illuminated
border. From an
Italian manuscript,
1520. Oxford,
Bodleian Library

impose his own solutions on his chosen material. Medieval society was already ripe for printing, just as early Victorian society was ripe for the introduction of photography. Once introduced, it grew very rapidly. The first printing-office was set up in Mainz in 1447. Within ten years it was employing a hundred men.

The introduction of printing brought with it changes which affected other forms of production. Paper suddenly became of the first importance, as only paper provided a cheap enough receptive surface. A folio volume consisting of 200 pages of parchment needed the hides of no fewer than twenty-five sheep — the scribe's labour in producing a handwritten manuscript had always been the smaller part of its cost.

Although Europe was ready for the introduction of printing, the products of the new printing presses did meet with at least some opposition. This came from the aristocratic patrons who had traditionally commissioned and paid the scribes and illuminators. For them the printed book was an inferior product, and for some time to come they continued to prefer the old methods. Printers pandered to their tastes by making their products look as much like

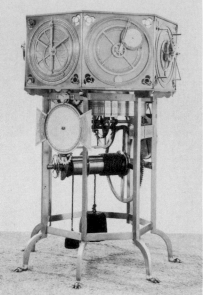

traditional manuscripts as possible, sometimes indeed leaving spaces for hand-illuminated initials. But the aristocratic resistance for some time remained immovable, supplying a first and clear instance of the prestige retained by an essentially inefficient craft process, even after a more efficient industrial method has been introduced to provide the same goods at lower cost.

The clock, like printing, first appeared in the Far East. The first clocks seem to have been made in China in the eleventh century. The invention arrived in Europe somewhere between 1277 and 1300, the way being perhaps prepared for it by the elaborate automata which had been created for the Byzantine emperors and the rulers of the Moslem Near East. In 1300, the first public clock was set up in Paris — it was made by one Pierre Pipelart. Other public clocks followed quite rapidly in various European cities, and also in large monasteries — an iron clock was installed in the church of S. Eustachio in Milan in 1309, and the cathedral at Beauvais had a clock with a bell before 1324. By 1340 the great monastery at Cluny had a clock, and a clock that struck the hours automatically was set up at Padua in 1344. Chartres cathedral had two clocks by 1359 and Wells Cathedral one, which still survives.

It is not surprising that early clocks were so often associated with churches, not only because of the need to mark the times of the various offices, but also because large churches were *par excellence* public gathering-places, within whose shelter all kinds of secular as well as religious activities took place. Lewis Mumford suggests in *Technics and Civilization* that it was in fact the transfer of the regular rhythm of monastic life to the secular sphere which led to the need for clocks and supplied the reason for their invention:

Above left:
Reconstruction of a Chinese astronomical clock-tower of A.D. 1090

Above:
Reconstruction of the elaborate astronomical clock designed by Giovanni Dondi, *c.* 1364. London, Science Museum

Striking mechanism of Wells Cathedral clock, *c.* 1360

the habit of order itself and the earnest regulation of time sequences had become almost second nature in the monastery. . . one is not straining the facts when one suggests that the monasteries — at one time there were 40,000 under the Benedictine rule — helped to give human enterprise the regular collective beat and rhythm of the machine; the clock is not merely a means of keeping track of the hours but of synchronising the actions of man.

Certainly with the introduction of public clocks men started to time activities they had never previously felt the need of timing. They became conscious of time, and the machine thus became the instrument of its own proliferation. All craft processes took on a different complexion as soon as they began to be costed according to the precise amount of time they consumed.

The invention of the European mechanical clock (in fact what one means by this is the invention of the verge escapement or foliot, in which a crown wheel engages with a vertical spindle whose movements are governed by a weighted cross-bar) coincided with a remarkable growth in the quality and number of metalworkers. These were also encouraged towards the development of new skills by the progress of another mechanism — the lock. Both clocks and locks put a premium on impersonal precision of workmanship. For the first time objects which combined precision and complexity began to be relatively commonplace. In one sense, this was a great step forward in the actual quality of craft — in the craftsman's sureness of hand and ability to repeat his effects. Yet progress was accompanied by a shift of attitude. It was not merely that the time of the craftsman was now precisely measured. Time was now also subjective. It could be changed, filled up or even expanded by the introduction of labour-saving instruments. The urge to introduce these was linked to a new consciousness of time and its value.

7 Renaissance Attitudes

Where attitudes towards craft are concerned, we instinctively feel that there is a great difference between the Middle Ages and the Renaissance. Indeed, this difference is one of the things which makes the Renaissance what it is. Yet the evidence itself often points another way. There is a strong continuity of attitudes, and an even stronger continuity of working conditions and technical methods, between Renaissance craft and what preceded it. The best way of recognizing this is to look at one craft in particular, and here the choice is obvious. There are a number of reasons for choosing goldsmithing as the craft which most fully displays the paradoxical nature of the Renaissance. The first reason is that the goldsmith's profession has been more minutely studied than any other craft occupation of the same epoch. This is especially true of the second half of the sixteenth century, covered by J.F. Hayward's recent monumental book, *Virtuoso Goldsmiths 1540–1620*. The second reason is the existence of a detailed craft autobiography, Benvenuto Cellini's celebrated story of his life.

Niklaus Manuel Deutsch, *St Eligius in his Workshop* (detail), 1515. The picture shows goldsmiths' implements, work in progress, and (on the shelves in the background) objects made for stock. Berne, Kunstmuseum

Two other reasons are less weighty, but are still important in their own fashion. One is the survival of a large number of designs for goldsmith's work, done by professional craftsmen and others, which enables us to study the relationship between the conception and the finished result. Finally there is the fact that Renaissance goldsmithing stood on a kind of frontier. Cellini's autobiography tells the story of his development from mere craftsman to independent fine artist. This would have been impossible from any other beginning. In the eyes of contemporaries, goldsmith's work was a stepping stone to an activity which was nevertheless very different in its fundamental character. But it was a stepping stone which was often used. If one reads Vasari's *Lives*, it is striking how many famous Renaissance artists are said to have at least started their careers in a goldsmith's shop. They include Ghiberti, Botticelli and Verrocchio. Brunelleschi, busy studying ancient art and architecture in Rome, worked as a jewel-setter for friends of his who were goldsmiths in order to make money. Of the artists mentioned, it was Verrocchio who seems to have maintained the longest and most intimate contact with the craft. Vasari describes him as being 'at once a goldsmith, a master of perspective, a sculptor, a woodcarver, a painter and a musician' — a list of accomplishments which gives a good picture of Renaissance universality.

Hayward, who relies more on German than on Italian documents, presents a somewhat different view of the goldsmith's situation. A German goldsmith could work either directly for some princely patron, which was Cellini's basic pattern, or for a much broader spectrum of clients — it might include princes, but also noblemen visiting the city where he lived, merchants and the City Council: in fact, any individual or organization with the money to buy his wares. German City Councils had particularly rich collections of plate. In 1610, for example, the city of Lübeck possessed more than two hundred and fifty vessels made of silver. The inflow of precious metal from the Spanish Indies greatly increased the production of such things during the sixteenth century. Goldsmiths who worked directly for a ruler and his court enjoyed one very important advantage in northern Europe, when compared to those who did not. They were usually exempted from guild regulations, which had by this time become extremely complicated and onerous.

Most important, it was the guild which had the power to determine its own membership, and to stop goods being sold by non-members. The apprenticeship period was long and strenuous and the tests set at the end of it were often elaborate. In Nuremberg, the aspirant had to prove his skills not only as a goldsmith, but also as a jeweller and seal-die engraver. He was required to make a cup, a gold ring set with a stone, and a seal-die. After 1572 the tests were refined still further. On three separate occasions each aspirant was shown a cup designed by the great goldsmith Wenzel Jamnitzer. He was then required to make, within three months and without help, his own version of the design.

Design and finished object: table centre in silver, with some details cast from life, by Wenzel Jamnitzer, *c*. 1549. Nuremberg, Germanisches Nationalmuseum and Amsterdam, Rijksmuseum

The goldsmiths' guilds kept a jealous eye open for any craftsman who attempted to infringe their regulations. They were particularly hard on those who had worked for ruling princes outside the established guild framework. A skilful man of journeyman status could easily be tempted to take up court employment before he had acquired the mastership. But he then ran the risk of being forever outcast from the guild, which might refuse him the right to have his work assayed, thus making it unsaleable. If such a goldsmith lost his court connection for any reason, for example through the death of his patron, then his troubles began in earnest. He either had to resign himself to being a humble employee in the workshop of another goldsmith or had to persuade a guild member to submit what he made for assaying and hall-marking as if these productions were his own. Yet the barrier was never rigid. We even hear of a commission being started in a guild workshop and finished in a court one.

Even when he had attained the mastership, the craftsman found himself hedged about with rules and regulations. For example, he was virtually tied to one spot, and had to get permission from the

City Council (not always easily granted) to go and work elsewhere. If he did obtain leave to go abroad, he was still supposed to report back in person at regular intervals, and to pay a fine according to the length of time he had been absent. Though the right to employ journeymen and apprentices to help with the work was one of the most important privileges of the mastership, their number was restricted. This meant that no one man, however fashionable or successful, could take on enough work to put his rivals out of business. Guild regulations extended to all aspects of the craftsman's life and work — even the most trivial. In some cities, he even had to obtain permission to put bars on the windows of his workshop. For it was felt that he might be concealing something irregular behind them.

Journeymen, however skilful, were increasingly an oppressed class, a tendency which had already begun to show itself in the Middle Ages. Their period of service was continually extended — it might be as long as ten years — and they were not allowed to marry before they had obtained the mastership. In fact, a social pattern established itself whereby the journeyman inherited his master's workshop by marrying the master's widow, only taking a young wife when this widow eventually died. However, the journeymen were freer than their masters in at least one important respect: they were allowed, and even encouraged, to travel, in order to gain as much experience as possible during their so-called 'wander years'. German journeymen often went to Italy, as well as moving restlessly throughout Germany.

Despite the stringency of guild regulations, and the length of the apprenticeship required in order to learn the goldsmith's trade, attitudes to craft were in many ways quite unlike modern ones. Hayward remarks that 'when considering the working methods of the sixteenth-century goldsmith it is necessary to set aside romantic conceptions of the nobility of handwork. The goldsmith had an eminently practical approach to his craft, and took as much interest in increasing efficiency and reducing costs of production as any modern factory manager.'

Methods of time-saving and cost-cutting took various forms. One, much favoured by German goldsmiths, was the casting of parts such as stems, finials and borders in series. Another was the use of repeating stamps. Wenzel Jamnitzer is said to have invented a revolving stamp to produce the friezes and repetitive borders which appear on pieces either from his own workshop or made under his influence. There was also considerable division of labour, as is proved by the fact that cups made by different German masters have identical figure finials, which were clearly purchased ready-made. Records show as many as twelve different craftsmen occupied with a single important piece. Small workshops set about things in a different way, by making use of specialist outside help. Among such specialists were the enamellers, who often worked for the trade as a whole, rather than for just one master; and the

Alessandro Fei,
16th-century
goldsmiths'
workshop.
Florence, Palazzo
Vecchio Studiolo

Benvenuto Cellini, drawing for a silver statue of Juno, commissioned by Francis I of France. Paris, Musée du Louvre, Cabinet des Dessins

pattern-carvers. The latter made original models carved in wood or honestone, from which casts could afterwards be taken. Many goldsmiths made a point of building up a good stock of such patterns, and once acquired they continued in use for many years, often regardless of the progress of fashion. Most goldsmiths had no scruples about using designs they had not created themselves. Vasari mentions that Verrocchio made a cup 'decorated with great numbers of animals and garlands and with other imaginative details, the mould of which still exists and is used by all the goldsmiths.' That is, Verrocchio's design continued to be popular during a span of at least eighty years.

The custom of making up a piece from pre-existing parts sometimes led to an undeclared struggle between craftsman and patron. A record exists of a negotiation between Duke Wilhelm of Saxe-Weimar and the Augsburg goldsmith Hans Schebel. In 1571 the Duke sent Schebel a drawing he had obtained (its author is unknown to us) showing an elaborate standing cup. The design is impressive — integrated and highly original for its time, but it does make some allowance for the use of pre-cast parts. Schebel was clearly not keen to make it up, nor were other Augsburg master-goldsmiths who were consulted. They explained that the design they had been shown would be very expensive to execute, as most of the ornament would have to be embossed, chased and finished by hand, while even the stem would have to be cast from a completely new model supplied by the pattern-carver. Schebel or somebody close to him supplied a drawing of a less expensive alternative — in the cheaper version the work would cost 12 thalers for every mark weight of silver used; in the more expensive, it would cost 20. In the alternative design the bowl could be cast in two or three segments, soldered together along the seams and carefully chased over. The cover and stem would also be cast, the wrought work thus being reduced to the lip of the bowl, the rim of the cover and the lowest part of the foot.

The Duke did not like this proposal, most likely because the

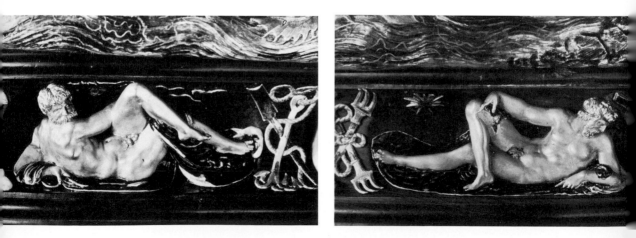

Benvenuto Cellini, The Vienna Salt, salt-cellar of chased gold and enamel on an ebony base. Made for Francis I of France in 1543. Vienna, Kunsthistorisches Museum

Benvenuto Cellini, details from the Vienna Salt, derived from Michelangelo's *Day* and *Night* on the Medici Tombs. Vienna, Kunsthistorisches Museum

alternative design was less well-integrated and also a good deal less novel than the one he had originally procured. Nevertheless a commission of some kind was given, which must have taken the craftsmen's protestations into account, as the Duke's agent mentioned that the finished cup could now be ready in only three or four weeks. At the same time he remarked that the very cheapest course of action would be simply to purchase a cup which could be obtained in Augsburg from stock.

The businesslike world of the Augsburg goldsmiths does not, at first glance, seem much like the one which Cellini describes in his autobiography, though some resemblances appear when one looks more closely. Cellini benefited from the freedom from guild restrictions enjoyed by Italian craftsmen. And in any case the whole point of his story is that he did not truly want to be regarded as a craftsman at all, though at the same time he liked his sheer skill to be acknowledged. His aim was always to establish himself as an independent fine artist, and this, by the end of his life, was what he had succeeded in doing.

Cellini learned his craft in Florence, but first made his reputation as a goldsmith in Rome, where he was employed on making large and showy pieces of plate for influential members of the papal

16th-century Isnik
tiles in the Harem,
Topkapi Palace,
Istanbul

Panel of Isnik
tiles, Ottoman
Turkish, 16th
century. Lisbon,
Gulbenkian
Foundation

court. It seems clear that his earliest important commissions were not made to his own designs but to those of his friend Giovanni Francesco Penni, an artist and a pupil of Raphael, who in fact introduced him to his first important patron, the Bishop of Salamanca. Cellini, however, soon began to assert his independence as a designer; and at the same time, by his own account, put himself on increasingly familiar terms with his illustrious patrons. He enjoyed a particularly stormy relationship with the most illustrious of them all, Pope Clement VII, who at one time, in his frustration at Cellini's refusal to finish an elaborate chalice, had him imprisoned.

Failure to finish important commissions was part of the story of Cellini's life, as it was that of more eminent Florentines, such as Leonardo and Michelangelo. When Cellini left Italy to work for Francis I of France, who furnished him with a considerable workshop, the parting of the ways came from Cellini's failure to complete a series of over-lifesize silver statues, meant for use as torchères, which the king had asked him to make. The king's rebuke to the errant craftsman has the ring of exasperated truth:

> I remember that I expressly ordered you to make me twelve silver statues; and I did not ask for anything else. You have undertaken to make a salt-cellar, and vases, and heads, and doors, and ever so many other things; so that I am quite overwhelmed, seeing all my particular wishes set aside, while you are bent on carrying out your own. So if you think you can go on like this, I'll soon let you see what I am wont to do, when I wish things done in my own way. Therefore I say to you: take care to obey the orders given to you; for if you are obstinate in pursuing your own fancies, you'll be running your head against a wall.

The salt-cellar mentioned by the king is extensively described elsewhere in Cellini's writings, and is also one of the most celebrated of all Renaissance craftworks. The design is governed by the elaborate symbolism typical of the period — the main figures represent Sea and Earth, the high reliefs on the ebony base are personifications of Night, Day, Twilight and Dawn, and they are accompanied by busts which personify the four chief winds. Symbolism of this type was often spelt out in words as well as in images. Surviving examples of Renaissance goldsmiths' work carry elaborate inscriptions, for example the cartouches with Latin verses which appear on Wenzel Jamnitzer's wildly ornate table-centre in the Rijksmuseum, Amsterdam. The style of the Cellini salt-cellar is closely related to that of Mannerist sculpture on a large scale — the female figure, in particular, with her elongated body, and small, neat, expressionless head, is a kind of Mannerist archetype. The high relief figures on the base are dependent on the similar but monumental personifications created by Michelangelo for the Medici chapel.

The story of the conception of the salt-cellar, originally commissioned by Cardinal Ippolito d'Este in 1539, but finally carried out

for Francis I, is instructive in itself. Two of the Cardinal's advisers, Luigi Alamanni and Gabriele Cesano, suggested differing programmes for the work. The Cardinal asked Cellini to choose between them. Cellini, according to his own account, then replied:

Above left: Hans Holbein, cup designed for Queen Jane Seymour, *c.* 1535. Oxford, Ashmolean Museum

> Reflect, my lord, of what great importance are the sons of kings and emperors, and what marvellous splendour and divinity appear in them! Nevertheless, if you ask a poor lowly shepherd what he loves and cherishes most, those kings' sons or his own, he will certainly tell you he loves his own children best. So I, too, cherish the children born of my own art. Therefore the first design I will show you, monsignor, my most reverend patron, shall be my own work, and of my own imagining; for many things are fine in words which, were they carried out, would produce but a poor effect.

Above right: Giulio Romano, design for a vase, 1st half of the 16th century. London, British Museum

Cellini's restlessness, when confronted with this kind of dictation, is something new — even the most eminent of medieval goldsmiths would not have questioned the patron's instructions in this fashion. Cellini is closer to us than to his predecessors, not so much because of Renaissance *amour propre*, but because of an easily bruised sense of his own individuality.

Other Renaissance craftsmen were less scrupulous about relying absolutely on their own powers, perhaps because, unlike Cellini, they had no aspirations to become fine artists. Those who were primarily painters and sculptors, on the other hand, frequently

Above: Venetian glasses from the Murano workshops, 15-16th century. Milan, Poldi-Pezzoli Museum

Far left: Blue glass and enamel wedding-bowl, made for the glass-making Barovier family, Venice, *c*. 1470-80. Venice, Museo Vetrario di Murano

Left: *Façon de Venise* goblet made in the Netherlands in the 18th century. London, Victoria and Albert Museum

Façon de Venise
wine-glass with
interwoven
colour-twist stem.
From the Low
Countries, late
17th century.
Bristol City Art
Gallery

supplied designs to be carried out in metalwork by others. Among them we find Albrecht Dürer, Albrecht Altdorfer, Hans Holbein the Younger and Giulio Romano. There are also a number of Fontainebleau School designs which are almost certainly by Rosso. The point about the designs by men not trained in the goldsmith's craft is that they were frequently impracticable, and had to be adapted to the needs of the material.

More subtly, there was also a tendency to impose a universal stylistic language. This took precedence over the means of expression arising directly from the particular tradition of the craft concerned. Indeed, one of the things one notices, in Renaissance texts about the fine arts, is a suspicion of traditionalist attitudes. The Renaissance, when it appealed to the example of the past, preferred to look back very far, to the world of antiquity.

If the men of the Renaissance looked back to the epoch which had immediately preceded their own, they felt themselves to be superior because nature itself was their authority, not an inherited tradition. Condivi puts the point well in his Life of the greatest artist of the period: 'Michelangelo has been from his youth a great worker; and to his natural gift has added knowledge, which he has been minded to acquire not from the labours and industry of

Italian majolica plate from Cafaggiolo, *c*. 1510-15. It shows a painter creating a commemorative wedding-plate for a young couple. London, Victoria and Albert Museum

others, but from nature herself; setting her before him as the true example.' Again, there is Michelangelo's own verdict on his one-time rival Raphael, as reported by the same biographer: 'Only have I heard him say, that Raffaello had not his art from nature, but from long study.' Vasari, like Condivi writing in Michelangelo's own lifetime, puts the same point in a slightly different way: 'All artists are under a great and permanent obligation to Michelangelo, seeing that he broke the bonds and chains that had previously confined them to the creation of traditional forms.'

It is not a mere rejection of tradition which is here being expressed, but a conviction that the fine arts, as the great artists of the Renaissance practised them, were something altogether different from mere craft. Craft-skills were an accumulated body of knowledge, which could be handed on from one generation to another. In art, one artist might liberate another by his example, just as one artist might teach another the basic techniques of painting and sculpture, but true success in art was the product of inborn genius. Michelangelo's fresco of *The Last Judgement* in the Sistine chapel, says Vasari: 'must be recognised as the great exemplar of the grand manner of painting, directly inspired by God and enabling mankind to see the fateful results when an artist of sublime intellect infused with divine grace and knowledge appears on earth.' Michelangelo himself wrote that his extraordinary design for the staircase in the Laurentian Library, which breaks all the Classical rules of architecture, came to his mind 'just like a dream.' Henceforth, it was painters and sculptors and perhaps architects who were to be licensed to dream. Their inferiors, the craftsmen, were stuck with quotidian rationality.

One of the easiest ways of tracing Renaissance attitudes towards craft is to look at the rise of Italian majolica. The prestige of decorative pottery, very low throughout the Middle Ages, first began to be raised by the wares, and most especially the lustre-wares, (decorated with iridescent metallic glazes), made in Spain in the fourteenth and fifteenth centuries by Moorish craftsmen working for Christian masters. Particularly fine pots and dishes were made at Manises, a suburb of Valencia, and these came to be widely exported. We hear of two potters from Manises supplying tiles for the Papal Palace at Avignon in 1362. In the first half of the fifteenth century the Hispano-Moresque potteries at Manises were supplying royal and noble families, and also important ecclesiastical patrons, almost throughout Europe. Much of their output was heraldic, and we can therefore identify the clients for whom their best wares were made. They were to be found in Aragon, Castile, Navarre, Savoy and Burgundy. But Hispano-Moresque pottery had a particular impact in Italy and Sicily. Its popularity was helped by other forms of Spanish penetration. For example, the Borgia family, who supplied the church with two popes at this period, came from the same region of Spain, and were patrons of the Manises kilns.

But Hispano-Moresque was not the only current of influence to affect Italian pottery in the fifteenth century — Italians also knew and admired the porcelains of the Far East, and the Turkish Isnik wares. During the sixteenth century sporadic attempts were made to discover the secret of porcelain, but that remained inaccessible to Europeans until the eighteenth, though a small factory under Medici patronage did succeed in producing the first soft-paste — the pseudo-porcelain which was to flourish at many European factories during the eighteenth century. Basically, however, Renaissance Italians were educated to think that fine ceramics were *ipso facto* decorated tin-glaze. Both the Hispano-Moresque and Isnik wares belonged to this essentially Islamic tradition.

During the second half of the fifteenth century Hispano-Moresque pottery began to suffer in Italian markets from the rapid improvement of the native product, which offered greater precision of drawing, plus a wider range of colours, than what was being made in Spain. In addition to this, being closer to the source of Renaissance decorative ideas, it responded in its own terms to the revolution which was overtaking the decorative arts in the Italian peninsula.

Italian potters began to explore the use of graded tones of colour, which created a sense of depth in the ornamental patterns they used. Majolica was now often enriched with lively but simple figurative line drawings. The custom grew up of making special items to celebrate certain occasions — betrothals, marriages and the birth of children. After a birth, for example, visitors would call on the mother carrying gifts and light refreshments on dishes specially painted to commemorate the occasion, often with the arms or badge of the family to whom the child had been born.

The eventual result was the birth of what was called the *stile istoriato* — pottery, more especially large dishes, with complex figurative scenes. From the very beginning most of the pottery decorated in this manner was intended for show, rather than for use, in this resembling the more impressive examples of Renaissance gold and silver plate. It has been suggested, indeed, that *istoriato* dishes originated from the elaborate commemorative plaques which it was customary to set into walls, and that they were looked upon as portable versions of such plaques.

The best painting of the type I have been describing was produced between 1510 and 1540, and thus is contemporary with the High Renaissance at the rise of Mannerism. Technically it is of extremely high quality, but its style and motifs are generally derivative, since the various scenes are borrowed from mural paintings, pattern-books, and most of all from engravings. Even where ornament predominates it tends to be in the so-called grotesque style borrowed from Roman wall-painting and used by the members of Raphael's studio for the decorations in the Vatican loggia. In its dependence on 'major' art *istoriato* majolica can be compared with the late phase of Athenian red-figure, which clearly derives from mural paintings by Polygnotus and others which are now lost to us. In both cases the conventions proper to large-scale mural work are somewhat recklessly adapted to a different and perhaps unsuitable purpose. In *istoriato* majolica of the most elaborate kind, however high its quality, one is often aware of a tension between the actual shape of the piece and what is represented on it. For instance, there is the evident difficulty of rendering perspective convincingly upon a concave surface.

Nevertheless, the Renaissance itself would have seen the whole process as part of a laudable attempt to ennoble an intrinsically humble medium. In terms of its own time, the attempt succeeded. As early as 1490 that great and sensitive patron of the arts Lorenzo de' Medici was speaking of the potters as possible rivals to the jewellers and silversmiths.

It is sometimes said that the Renaissance inherited from the Middle Ages a contempt of handwork in general. This is unsubtle. The Middle Ages, as we have seen, respected handwork for religious reasons. Yet medieval men also despised it for hierarchical ones. They had a clear vision of an ordered social structure, and the man who made things with his hands came somewhere near the bottom of it, not far above the agricultural labourer. The Renaissance was inclined to see the difference as being one between intellectual and purely physical endeavours — the life of the mind

Ottoman Isnik tankard, 16th century. Lisbon, Gulbenkian Foundation

Far left: Goblet with crizzled 'ice-glass' bowl. Venice, 16th century. London, Victoria and Albert Museum

Left: *Millefiori* glass ewer. Italian, 16th century. London, Victoria and Albert Museum

as opposed to the life of the body, intellectual activity always being superior to and governing the rest. Yet this paradoxically brings one face to face with what is now the most disconcerting aspect of Renaissance attitudes towards the crafts — the unbounded love of virtuosity. If Michelangelo was admired for his concepts, upon a lower rung the craftsman was admired for his power over materials, itself allied to Mannerist interest in the idea of transformation. Some Renaissance metalwork, like the table-centre by Wenzel Jamnitzer already referred to (p. 152), is so insanely elaborate that any vestigial trace of utility is submerged by the craftsman's pride in the refinements of his own skill.

To force the material to feats of imitation, to stress the utmost refinement and delicacy of handling, to surprise the viewer with unexpected forms — these were, especially in the second half of the sixteenth century, the chief aims of the craftsman seeking the respect of both patrons and peers.

Such qualities are pre-eminently displayed in the products of the Venetian glasshouses of the fifteenth and sixteenth centuries. Here luxuriousness of decoration is combined with all the capriciousness to which the material lends itself. Venetian glasses were often gilded and enamelled, but there were also other decorative techniques more intimately concerned with the actual making of the object. Opaque white threads might be embedded in clear glass to create *vetro a fili*, or the more elaborate *vetro a reticello* in which the threads cross over one another to form a net. There is crizzled 'ice-glass', there is glass in the Roman manner, made from fused slices of *millefiori* canes; there is glass made to resemble agate; there

Vetro a retorti goblet. Venice, late 16th century. London, British Museum

is glass with gold leaf sandwiched within its thickness; and there are the typical *façon de Venise* wineglasses, with fantastically elaborated stems.

Though we know the names of some leading Venetian glassmakers, for example Angelo Barovier, credited in the fifteenth century with raising the art of enamelling to a new artistic and technical level, the more elaborate products of the Venetian glasshouses must have been team efforts. No one man could handle the molten metal with sufficient dexterity to produce the effect required — each was the product of a kind of elaborate dance executed by the master glass-maker and his assistants. They are not the products of some solitary, independent craftsman, working out his own ideas.

The Venetian glass workshops are interesting for another reason as well. Though the Venetian state tried desperately to keep its glass-makers' methods a secret, in order to protect an important part of its export trade, gradually the techniques of *façon de Venise* glass became known across Europe, to the point where it is sometimes difficult to say whether a given piece was made within Venice or outside it. But later this particular fashion in glass was challenged by others, which involved different processes of manufacture. The English lead crystal glass, with its deep cutting, made at the end of the eighteenth century, represents a very different approach to the material, which has in any case been modified in response to a new aesthetic. But in Murano itself elaborate blown glass continued to be made, as indeed it still is at the present day. Venetian glass, from being the very latest fashion, became to some extent at least isolated and anachronistic, independent of the stylistic changes taking place elsewhere.

A somewhat different example of this sudden switch in the technical development of a particular craft is supplied by the furniture-making of northern Europe. Medieval furniture had been for the most part heavy and clumsy. In the sixteenth century a new method of construction was introduced. Instead of being made of large, solid pieces of riven oak, furniture was now 'joined', that is, it consisted of small panels set into frames and uprights, all pegged together with wooden dowels. This not only made it lighter and more easily movable, it was also better for damp climates, as it allowed the various parts to expand and contract without splitting.

The new craft of joinery was so successful that it led to a struggle within the guild system. New joiners' guilds were formed, to distinguish them from the turners and the carpenters — the latter, who had once made furniture, were now chiefly employed on housebuilding. Gradually, in the course of the sixteenth century, joinery established itself as the standard method of making furniture — this was recognized in England at the time of the accession of Elizabeth I. But instead of ossifying, furniture-making techniques continued to develop throughout the next forty years, and at the end of Elizabeth's reign joinery was already beginning to be

Flask in glass imitating agate. Italian, *c*. 1500. London, Victoria and Albert Museum

challenged in metropolitan workshops by something new and different. Dovetails were now used to fix the boards together to make a solid piece as wide as the craftsman wanted, and these boards, in turn, were given a skin of veneer or elaborate marquetry. The new technique — cabinet-making as opposed to joinery — called for workmen with more sophisticated skills, as well as for larger workshops. But joined furniture survived, having retreated from the creative centre. Joinery became the typical and recognizable idiom of the country craftsman, who made furniture for use rather than for show. For the first time there grew up a distinction between town craft and country craft. Different clienteles expected different things of the craftsman. This was nearly as important as the new theoretical division between the intellectual, who worked with his head, and the artisan, who worked only with his hands.

Joined chest in oak, pegged construction. English, 16th century. London, Victoria and Albert Museum

8   Craft against Art

The seventeenth and eighteenth centuries, far more so than the Middle Ages and the Renaissance, established a pattern for the crafts as we know them today. That is, what we see growing up during this period is a fully developed range of craft skills, which now provide a basis for the techniques used by the modern hand-craftsman. But we also see at this period — or seem to see — the evolution of social attitudes which the contemporary craft movement is still struggling to overthrow. The separation of the fine artist from the craftsman, which appears as an essential part of Renaissance art-theory, is now translated into practical everyday terms. The fine artist began to accumulate the outward honours and signs of respect which confirmed his rise in the social hierarchy. Sir Peter Paul Rubens was given a knighthood by Charles I, and served the Habsburg Regents of the Netherlands as their ambassador on more than one occasion. Rubens himself aspired to be a kind of universal man. Contemporary accounts of his way of life at his house in Antwerp describe him as painting, conversing with visitors, and dictating a letter, all at the same time. His correspondence deals not only with artistic and diplomatic concerns, but with matters of scholarship and with his activity as an art collector.

The pattern Rubens set in the seventeenth century was followed in the eighteenth by artists such as Sir Joshua Reynolds. The Royal Academy, which Reynolds presided over, was a body which quite deliberately set out to give artists 'professional' status — to make it clear that they were something more than mere tradesmen.

If one looks at the career of Reynolds, then at that of Thomas Chippendale, the most famous English furniture-maker of the same period, one can immediately appreciate the difference. Chippendale never aspired to be more than a successful businessman, running a workshop which undertook more and more extensive commissions — sometimes, indeed, the entire furnishing of a house, including wallpapers, curtains and blinds. However successful he became, he did not expect to be received by his clients as a social equal. Reynolds, on the contrary, saw success in terms of recognition, as well as of money. Money counted for something, of course. Reynolds raised his charges progressively, as he came to portray more aristocratic and important sitters. But he did not (unlike, for example, Rubens) turn himself into the head of a kind of factory. The farthest he could go in this direction, if he was to remain true to his image of himself, was to use the occasional services of a professional drapery-painter.

We can even see the difference in the books which were

The saloon at Saltram House, Devon, 1768. An example of Robert Adam's interior design, including the carpet, picture-frames and much of the furniture

published by the two men. In his *Discourses*, originally delivered as public lectures, Reynolds tried to provide his epoch with a unified theory of art which would, among other things, justify his own practice as a painter. Chippendale, in *The Director*, was concerned only to popularize a style and to provide practical guidance for fellow-craftsmen. He knew that his was only one possible style among many. Indeed, there is a discrepancy between Chippendale's book and some of the finest pieces to come from his own workshop. These abandon the modified Rococo which *The Director* set out to popularize, and adopt instead the very different design principles of Neoclassicism. The reason is that they were designed, not by Chippendale himself, but by the architect Robert Adam, who made Chippendale his collaborator on many of his most important commissions.

Adam is significant for more reasons than one. We see in him not merely a gifted architect but one of those 'dictators of taste' who sprang up with some frequency during the eighteenth century. Usually, like Adam and his predecessor William Kent, they were professional architects. Sometimes they were gentlemen with a more or less thorough architectural training, like Kent's patron Lord Burlington. And sometimes, like Mme de Pompadour's brother, the Marquis de Marigny, or like Thomas Hope at the beginning of the following century, they were simply men whose official positions or private fortunes enabled them to influence the whole process of stylistic change. The actual craftsman thus

Above: Designs for chair backs in modified Rococo style made by Thomas Chippendale for the 3rd edition of his *Director*, 1762. London, Victoria and Albert Museum

Above left: Henri Staben, *The Archduke Albert and the Archduchess Isabella visiting Rubens' Studio*. Brussels, Musées Royaux des Beaux-Arts

Desk designed by Robert Adam and made by Thomas Chippendale for Harewood House. Leeds Art Gallery

became only a pair of hands. Above him was the head of the workshop, such as Chippendale; and above the head of the workshop was the man who actually determined the form of a given object, and whose interest lay in attaining a particular stylistic objective.

Craftsmen who worked in these circumstances were only part of an extremely complex physical and economic structure. The governing fact, the circumstance which controlled the whole orbit of craft, was that, until the tentative beginnings of the Industrial Revolution in the mid-eighteenth century, all processes of manufacture, however stultifying and tedious, remained pure handwork. Luckily, the rational and enquiring spirit of the period saw to it that many detailed descriptions were written of the way in which ordinary articles were made.

One of the most famous of these is the description of a pin factory written by Adam Smith, author of *The Wealth of Nations*:

> One man draws out the wire; another straightens it; a third cuts it; a fourth points it; a fifth grinds it at the top for receiving the head; to make the head requires two or three distinct operations; to put it on is a peculiar business; to whiten the pin is another; it

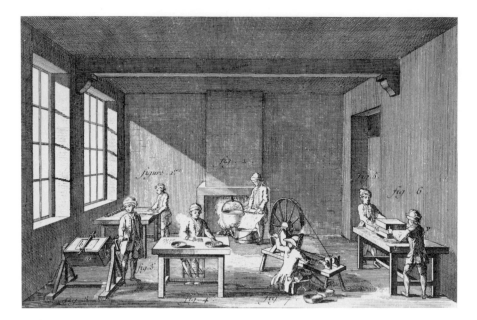

is even a trade by itself to put them in the paper; and the important business of making a pin is in this manner divided into about eighteen distinct operations.

This makes a very important point — that though all objects of daily use were still made by hand, the principle of the division of labour was firmly established. In many trades it went back to the Middle Ages. Now, however, it was to be found in almost every sphere of manufacture. Even the making of Brussels lace was split up into at least seven different operations, each one carried out by a different person. The design itself was handed out in sections by the master of the workshop.

Part of the reason why the division of labour entrenched itself so firmly in the manufacturing process was the drive, from the seventeenth century onwards, towards the standardization of products. Men wanted to overcome not only the uncertainty of organic variations, springing from the nature of the material used, but also any differences which might spring from the worker's insistence on pursuing his or her own methods.

In addition, there was the fact that the great progress made in the physical sciences during the seventeenth and eighteenth centuries brought with it an increasingly mechanistic view of the universe. Even though industrialism itself had not arrived, attention was fixed upon mechanical systems of all kinds, and men themselves were sometimes regarded, not as entities in themselves, but as mere parts in something larger. Workshop organization therefore followed a universal intellectual tendency.

A clear view of an immense variety of manufacturing processes, as they were practised in France in the decades which immediately preceded the Revolution of 1789, can be obtained from two

Needle-makers' shop, which is very close in organization to Adam Smith's description of a pin factory, with its division of labour. From Diderot's *Encyclopédie*, 1751-80

sources. One is the relevant sections of Diderot's great *Encyclopédie*; the other, somewhat more technical, is the long series of *Descriptions of the Arts and Crafts* published by the French Académie Royale des Sciences. Both are illustrated with engravings showing typical workshops and their personnel. The illustrations confirm what the texts already suggest — that most manufacturing operations remained relatively small in scale, with only a handful of employees in each shop. In some cases, for example the making of saddlery, craft methods have remained stable to the present day. What the texts and their accompanying illustrations never suggest, however, is that the writer is himself a craftsman. He describes what he himself has observed from outside. In this respect, eighteenth-century writings about craft are very different from what was penned later.

There is another respect in which these descriptions are surprising — they concentrate almost entirely on craft as it was practised in towns. If one looks at the same period now, the craftwork of the time can be divided into three categories. In the first place, there were the sophisticated urban craftsmen, in close touch with fashions in design, which changed with ever-increasing capriciousness and rapidity. Secondly, there were provincial craftsmen, influenced intermittently by urban fashions, but basically content to repeat utilitarian designs. In small agricultural communities, in particular, there grew up an almost independent tradition, in which form was moulded, not by aesthetic preference, but by a pragmatic preference for what seemed to work best. Once a good and efficient design was found, through a process of trial and error, neither the rural craftsman nor his customers saw any reason to change it. This applied to the making of things such as carts, ploughs and harrows,

Above: Tapestry showing Louis XIV (left) inspecting the Manufacture Royale at the Gobelins. Note the different kinds of objects on view – tapestry, furniture, silver plate. Cartoon by St André after Le Brun, 1729-34. Musée National du Château de Versailles

A contemporary saddle-maker using traditional handicraft techniques

as well as to certain kinds of furniture. Finally, there were the crafts which were practised at home — people, mostly women, making objects without thought of resale. At the lower economic levels, these activities were undertaken out of necessity; higher up the scale, they served as a pastime.

The fashionable crafts, city-based, evolved in step with the progress of urban society. For example, they gradually freed themselves from court influence, and became available to anyone with the money to afford such luxuries. France is once again the best place to trace this evolution, as it took place during the reigns of Louis XIV, Louis XV and Louis XVI. Louis XIV, with his strong sense of what was due to the monarchy, and his equally strong centralizing instinct, attempted to organize matters so that the court would be supplied from a number of royal manufactories. The most important was the furniture manufactory at the Gobelins, set up to supply the royal palaces, which was in 1667 officially designated as the 'Manufacture Royale des Meubles de la Couronne'. There were other establishments at Savonnerie and Beauvais, and there was even an attempt at one time to establish a royal monopoly over the production of lace.

Yet the Gobelins could not supply everything the court wanted, and furniture was therefore ordered for royal use from leading

ébénistes and *menuisiers*, members of the two furniture-makers'
guilds, one concerned with cabinet-making; the other with chair-
frames and anything carved. Their efforts were co-ordinated,
where royal commissions were concerned, by the Superintendent of
the royal Garde-Meuble. But these craftsmen did not work for the
king alone. They worked for other members of the royal family, for
the aristocrats, and eventually for a whole newly rich class —
bankers, and the *fermiers-généraux* who bought the right to collect
taxes from the government. The only difference was that, when he
worked on a non-royal commission, the craftsman (who was also a
guild-member) was forced to affix his guild mark or *poinçon*. Where
royal commissions were concerned, this was not, strictly speaking,
necessary.

The leading furniture-makers, and especially the *ébénistes*, were
by no means independent of other and subsidiary craftsmen. The
chassis, the actual carcase to which the *ébéniste* affixed his elaborate
marquetry, was often supplied by an outside workshop; and the
gilt-bronze handles and other ornaments which provided the
finishing touches were also bought in. As the materials of
which very luxurious furniture was made became increasingly

Secretaire by
Adam Weisweiler,
decorated with
Sèvres porcelain
plaques. French,
c. 1780. London,
Wallace Collection

heterogeneous, a new figure made his appearance. This was the *marchand mercier*. The mercers were an important and old-established Paris guild — one which enjoyed a special status. Savary's *Dictionary of Commerce*, published in 1750, says that their corporation was considered the most noble and most excellent of all those which existed in Paris, since those who belonged to it did no manual work except to embellish articles already made. In the case of furniture, their activities soon went a long way beyond embellishment.

The *marchands merciers* had long traded in exotic material of all kinds. For example, they had imported lacquer cabinets from the Far East. They, or one of their clients, now got the notion that it would be amusing to incorporate lacquer panels in furniture of European form. It thus became natural for the *marchand mercier* to commission furniture himself, paying the craftsman and holding it for resale. The *merciers* had also made a speciality of having porcelain figures, first Oriental ones then pieces from Meissen and Sèvres as well, mounted in ormolu (the finest cast and chased gilt bronze, gilded by the mercury gilding process). From this it was a short step to having porcelain plaques mounted on furniture. Many plaques were commissioned in special shapes and sizes. Soon the *merciers* were well on the way to becoming dictators of taste, and

Bureau Mazarin in the style of André Charles Boulle. Veneered with brass, ebony, ivory, tortoiseshell, lapis-lazuli and mother of pearl. French, late 17th century. London, Victoria and Albert Museum

towards the end of the Ancien Régime certain leading *ébénistes*, such as Martin Carlin and Adam Weisweiler, worked for these intermediaries almost exclusively.

The collaborative nature of work in the luxury trades, and the firm separation between the conception of the piece and the actual making of it, is equally well illustrated by the mode of organization in the great eighteenth-century porcelain factories. Porcelain, whether it was true hard-paste, like the wares produced at Meissen, where the secret of the Chinese use of kaolin had at last been discovered, or the soft-paste imitation produced at Vincennes and later at Sèvres, enjoyed a very special status at this period,

Hard-paste European porcelain. Meissen tankard, *c*. 1735. Basel, Historisches Museum, Kirschgarten, Collection Pauls - Eisenbeiss

equivalent and more than equivalent to the status enjoyed by majolica in Italy in the first half of the sixteenth century. Louis XV was a shareholder in the Vincennes factory from the beginning; and in 1753, three years after the move to Sèvres, the king bought out the other shareholders and became sole proprietor, though in theory at least the factory remained a commercial enterprise and was supposed to pay its own way.

The man responsible for its financial health was the director appointed by the king, and he was also responsible for the aesthetic quality of the product. Designs could be supplied from outside the

Wedgwood plate from a dinner service for Catherine the Great for her country palace 'La Grenouillère' (hence the frogs), 1778. London, Victoria and Albert Museum

factory — this was the case with statuettes, for example, which were often the work of celebrated sculptors such as Falconet. Or else, equally often, they could be copied from some existing source, not created for this medium at all. Or they could be radically adapted or designed completely afresh within the organization itself. Under the director, and ready to realize whatever design was chosen, were various technical specialists. A single dinner-plate in the elaborate service commissioned by Catherine the Great of Russia in 1775-7 went through no less than eight different pairs of hands before it was completed — those of the moulder, the *répareur*, the glaze painter, the ground artist, the painter of flowers, the painter of cameos, the gilder and the burnisher.

Many different forces influenced the final appearance of the product. Sèvres was created for a public which was conscious to the

Sèvres plate from a dinner service designed for Catherine the Great, 1775. London, Victoria and Albert Museum

last degree of the nuances of fashion and luxury. Naturally, its development followed the general development of French decorative styles during the eighteenth and early nineteenth centuries, moving from the Rococo to the Neoclassical, and then to such fancies as the Egyptian style popularized by Napoleon's raid across the Mediterranean. On the other hand, this stylistic progress was neither steady nor inexorable. The Rococo style typical of the mid-eighteenth century established itself as one particularly suitable for luxurious porcelain, and continued in use throughout the next half-century. In the English royal collection, for example, there is a sumptuous green-ground dinner-and-dessert service, made at Sèvres in 1795–7. Many of the pieces, instead of carrying the familiar crossed L's — the standard Sèvres mark since the foundation of the factory — are marked RF, for *République Française*. But both the style of decoration and the shapes are indistinguishable from those in use much earlier. The tureens and covers follow the model created by J.-C. Duplessis during the reign of Louis XV.

The reasons for this occasional stylistic conservatism are in some respects different from and in some respects the same as those which affected the country crafts of the same period. There was no need, for instance, to look for the most economical, or even the simplest way of producing a particular category of object. On the other hand, the workmen at Sèvres, though they laboured for a

Pieces from a Sèvres green-ground dinner-and-dessert service, marked R.F. (République Française), 1795-7. Royal Collection. Reproduced by gracious permission of Her Majesty the Queen

fickle and fashionable public, were themselves artisans, blessed with the artisan's instinctive conservatism. The decorators' marks on the apple-green Sèvres service already described show that some of them — J.-F. Micaud and E.-F. Bouillat, for instance — were the very same men who had painted exactly similar bouquets of flowers on Vincennes and early Sèvres porcelain some forty years previously. But, most of all, the luxury crafts were affected by the

Porcelain painter at work in the Sèvres workshop, 18th century. Archives de la Manufacture Nationale de Sèvres

buying public's idea of decorum and suitability. Sèvres services were used on state occasions, just as the English royal family uses them today for State Banquets to welcome visiting heads of state, and the Rococo idiom had established itself as being particularly in keeping with this kind of festive occasion.

Today we instinctively think about and define the more luxurious artefacts produced during the eighteenth century, not so much in terms of those who made them, as in terms of those who used and possessed them. This approach is surely correct. The artisan at Sèvres was wholly separated from his product, which had nothing to do with his own way of life. Yet these magnificent porcelains are in no sense of the term industrial objects. They show us all the finesse, dexterity and refinement of which the craftsman's hand is capable.

The country craftsman of the same period found himself in a different situation. Not only was he closer to his consumers than the urban artisan, living the same kind of life as they did and producing goods which fitted into his own life-style just as they did into theirs, but he usually worked in a far more modest and less elaborately organized workshop, perhaps with one or two assistants to help him, often blood-relations and the eventual heirs to the business. In his situation an elaborate division of labour was impossible. He therefore needed to master a wider spectrum of skills within his chosen trade. He also had much less financial

leeway, and his profit margin was probably much smaller.

While it is a mistake to think that the country crafts were not affected by stylistic fashions, the effects of this influence were both varied and unpredictable. Country-made furniture, for example, did involve the repetition of archetypes, some of which had no precise equivalent in town — the quasi-independent evolution of the Windsor stick-back chair is a case in point; and here, too, one sees the influence exerted by a kind of technical logic — the country craftsman had to find the way of doing things which best suited the material at hand, as he had neither time nor inclination to force it to go against its own nature. Other, very simple furniture continued to be made, as I have already noted, following joiners' patterns established as early as the late sixteenth century.

Yet much country furniture was only a simplification of what fashionable cabinet-makers had been producing in town a few years previously. Occasionally, but not invariably, this process of assimilation involved a complete stylistic sea-change. French provincial furniture, ranging in date from the mid-eighteenth century to the late nineteenth, is often made in a transitional Baroque-Rococo style which recognizably derives from what was being produced in

Carpenters' workshop producing furniture in the French provincial style. From Diderot's *Encyclopédie*, 1751-80

Early form of
Windsor
stick-back chair,
c. 1750. London,
Victoria and
Albert Museum

Paris in the earliest years of Louis XV. But this furniture has evolved its own range of types, most of them modifications of ideas inherited from the late Middle Ages — the *armoire*, or large cupboard; the *buffet-bas*, or sideboard. It is made of native woods — oak and walnut — and the cabinet-furniture, instead of being veneered, is constructed of carved wooden panels. The techniques of the urban *ébéniste* are rejected, but the glamour of urban ornamentation continues to exercise its spell.

Louis XV
provincial oak
armoire. French,
18th century

Those who idealize the eighteenth-century country craftsman often seem to think of country life as a mode of existence where everything was of a piece, where all domestic articles had the same modest sobriety and fitness for use. In fact this view is mistaken. Country people made use of local products, such as baskets, where these provided the obvious solution to a particular problem, and it was therefore unnecessary to look elsewhere. But they also valued,

Hippolyte Bellangé, a pedlar selling ornaments in plaster to Norman peasants, 1883. An example of the way such traders carried 'town taste' to the countryside until well into the 19th century. Paris, Musée des Arts et Traditions Populaires

perhaps in some cases over-valued, products which came to them from long distances, often via itinerant pedlars if there were no convenient shops. From the sixteenth century onwards ordinary households began to accumulate more and more personal possessions. Certain industries — among them the making of pewter, pottery and glass — were considerably enlarged to meet demand and there was a decisive shift to an economy based on money rather than barter.

Changes in the glass industry help to make the point. New techniques of glass-making depended upon two things. One was the introduction of the glass-maker's 'chair', somewhere between 1575 and 1662. This device enabled the craftsman to work with less trained assistance, and therefore more efficiently and rapidly, as well as more cheaply. More significant, however, was the substitution of coal for wood in glass-maker's furnaces. In England, coal imports to London increased between twenty and twenty-five fold in the years between 1580 and 1660. It was natural that the glass-makers should wish to avail themselves of the new fuel, but from their point of view it had significant disadvantages, since it was 'dirty' and polluted the metal. This led to the introduction of closed crucibles. The substitution of coal for wood and the economic and technical complications it brought with it led to a concentration of capital and labour within the glass industry just as it did elsewhere. The emphasis was no longer on the luxurious fantasies of the Venetian glass-makers, but on increasing the output of cheap and useful commodities, available as far down the social scale as possible.

The birth of a kind of proto-industrialism did not, however, lead to the total collapse of domestic skills. Handicrafts continued to be very widely practised in the home environment. In fact, as will appear in a moment, there was sometimes a kind of unholy alliance between mass production on the one hand, and domestic craft on the other.

The handicraft of 'amateurs' covered an enormous spectrum, and arose from a wide variety of motivations. I have already said something about the activity of royal embroideresses and weavers in Chapter Six. This tradition continued throughout the seventeenth and eighteenth centuries. Mary II of England, great-great-granddaughter of Mary Queen of Scots, was as enthusiastic a needlewoman as her ancestress, and Celia Fiennes records in her *Journeys* that the Queen and her Maids of Honour did much work for Hampton Court. While the emphasis, in domestic embroidery, had switched away from clothes, as patterned stuffs were more easily available and less expensive, there was still a good deal of enthusiasm for upholstery. In particular, sets of embroidered chair-covers were often the work of amateurs — a group of friends and relatives would labour upon such a project as a team. Mrs Delany, one of the most famous amateur craftswomen of the eighteenth century, greatly admired by George III and his family, describes in her letters how she helped the Duchess of Portland with just such a set of chair-seats.

Mrs Delany's 'fancy work' covered an immense range. In addition to embroidery, she did shell-work, feather-work and cut paper-work. She made paper figures, paper mosaics and paper and lambswool flowers. She imitated medals, making them out of cardboard covered with gold leaf; she did chenille work and made pillow-lace. Her friends and rivals practised these occupations and others as well. The Duchess of Portland worked in jet, amber, tortoiseshell and ivory. Mrs Delany says in one of her letters: 'The Duchess has just finished a bunch of barberries in amber that are beautiful, and she is finishing an ear of barley turned in amber, the stalk ivory, the beards tortoiseshell.'

Paper mosaic of flowers by Mrs Delany, 18th century. London, British Museum

It was not only gentlewomen, but sometimes also gentlemen who practised the crafts, though such conduct was often considered eccentric. Two kings of France were enthusiastic metalsmiths. In the sixteenth century the decadent Valois, Charles IX, astonished the Spanish ambassador when he promised the King of Spain a gun of his own making. In the eighteenth, Marie Antoinette had reason to complain that her husband neglected her for the delights of his workshop, where he investigated the mysteries of clocks and locks.

In these two cases we seem to catch a glimpse of individuals who were tragically unsuited for the great roles into which fate had thrust them, and who found a consolation and a retreat in manual work.

The situation of women was different from that of men. Most of them were denied the intellectual satisfactions open to men, though the female 'bluestocking' was of course a familiar phenomenon in

Mrs Delany's day. Even more firmly were they denied the right to engage in politics or business. 'Fancy work' provided an outlet for energies which could not be employed elsewhere. On the other hand, except when it came to traditionally and firmly female occupations such as needlework, sanctioned over the centuries as being a fit occupation for women of gentle, noble or even royal birth, there was always the danger of doing things with too much expertise, and thus losing caste by becoming in some sense a professional. What strikes one now about many of Mrs Delany's crafts is their essential triviality — they are displays of dexterity for dexterity's sake. Things must be 'pretty' rather than beautiful, and fanciful rather than useful. The woman who had time for such matters was guaranteed to be a woman of leisure.

One of the strangest of eighteenth-century crazes was that for what was called *parfilage*. *Parfilage* or 'drizzling' was a process, not of making, but of unmaking. Gold and silver thread were unravelled from pieces of old lace or embroidery — in theory, in order to sell the metal thus recovered. In fact, the process became an end in itself. Women took drizzling-bags with them to social gatherings, and special sets of unravelling instruments were made in luxurious materials such as ivory. They sometimes form part of the equipment of old work-boxes. Lady Mary Coke, visiting the Austrian Court in Vienna, noted that: 'All the ladies who don't play cards pick gold.'

These upper-class rituals must be seen against the background of women's crafts lower down the social scale. Here, if the man brought money into the household by going out to work, then it was the woman's place to make it go as far as possible by making as many household necessities as she could. But women, working at home, also provided the backbone of certain important industries which were still technically in the 'craft' stage of their development. In late seventeenth-century England, for example, nearly one million people were employed in the woollen trade — an enormous proportion of the population as a whole. Only one in eight was a male; the rest were women and children. Spinning, in particular, was regarded as women's work — an occupation which could be carried out in almost any circumstances, even in poor light or when the spinster's mind was elsewhere. The crisis in employment which occurred in the woollen industry at the close of the eighteenth century — to be precise after 1792 — was due, not to the introduction of the power-loom, which came later, but to the fact that home-spun yarn was being driven out of the market by yarn spun mechanically. Many women put aside their spinning-wheels and learned to work the looms, which had in the professional sense come to be regarded as a male occupation. But women brought with them into the labour-market traditionally low financial expectations. Spinning had always been poorly paid, not least because it could be done part-time as well as with only part of one's attention. Now the effect of women's competition with men was to force down the level of wages generally.

The history of the woollen industry teaches one to see women's craft not as the enemy but as the ally of capitalism. The textile industry pioneered the way towards the factory system, which significantly was always being resisted by the authorities. In 1603, to take just one example among many, the Wiltshire Quarter Sessions published a regulation that 'no clothman shall keep above one loom in his house, neither shall any weaver that hath a ploughland keep more than one loom in his house. No person or persons shall keep any loom or looms going in any other houses beside their own.' But there was nothing to prevent the budding capitalist from organizing his supplies of yarn from a great body of female out-workers, eager to supplement the family income. A good supply of yarn was even more crucial than the ability to bring a number of looms together in one place and to control their output, since, until the appearance of the mechanical mule, it took a number of spinsters to keep one loom supplied with the amount of material it needed to work to capacity.

Women's craft, or, rather, the fact of women being traditionally tied to certain types of craft, was paradoxically one of the reasons for the overthrow of the craft-system as a whole. Capitalism relied, on the one hand, on the steady progression triggered off by the rise to the British coal industry. Coal led to an improvement in metallurgy. Iron and steel became cheaper and more plentiful. In the sixteenth and seventeenth centuries wood, with all its innate disadvantages, was still used for making most machines, and metals were employed only for special strength and durability. Gradually, however, it became possible to make large machines completely of metal, with a great improvement in strength and in precision of working. But the machine-economy still required a pool of docile labour. In the textile industry, where industrialism and capitalism first came together, this essential element was largely supplied by women. Unlike the male craftsman in a still craft-orientated society, the woman who made things by hand was already fully habituated to repetitive and stultifying work.

9 The Industrial Revolution

The Industrial Revolution is often represented as a matter of direct and open conflict between industry and craft. On the one hand the desire for quantity and uniformity; on the other that for quality and individuality. This is an over-simplification. The Industrial Revolution was a combination of many factors, the majority of them economic but some aesthetic. It did not happen all at once. One can detect traces of its coming from the Middle Ages onward — substitution of machines for hand-tools, the organization of a primitive factory system, increasing division of labour. The sixteenth and seventeenth centuries, for example, saw great progress in the use of gears and screws and in substituting positive mechanical action for movements produced by the weight of the apparatus itself, or the muscles of the operative. This affected all processes where strength as well as skill was required. Skill itself was

J. Hunton, man using a stocking machine, with one woman spinning and another winding yarn. From *The Universal Magazine*, London, 1750

discounted by the progress of invention — the seventeenth century saw the introduction of the stocking machine, which now competed successfully with the domestic hand-knitter. As we have already seen, there were continual efforts, often resisted both by governments and by local authorities, to bring certain crafts within the scope of what we should now call factory organization. To choose a French rather than an English example, as early as the reign of Henry IV a textile factory of 350 looms had been set up at Saint-Sever, near Rouen.

Division of labour can be observed not only in the pin manufactory described by Adam Smith, but also in the development of the clock and watch industry. Thomas Tompion (1639–1713), the greatest English clockmaker of the late seventeenth century, produced about 6,000 watches in the course of his working life, at the rate of three or four a week, and about 550 clocks. His methods were described by his contemporary Sir William Petty, the political economist: 'In the making of a Watch, if one man shall make the *Wheels*, another the *Spring,* another shall engrave the *Dial-plate*, and another shall make the *Cases*, then the *Watch* will be better and cheaper, than if the whole work be put upon one Man.' Tompion introduced 'engines' for cutting wheel teeth, to replace hand-cutting — his products were themselves mechanical, and clearly he had no objection in principle to mechanical devices. Later, at the end of the eighteenth century, the celebrated French watchmaker Bréguet kept up to one hundred workers occupied in making the watches that bore his name. Many of these workers lived outside Paris, some even as far away as Switzerland. Bréguet's annual turnover exceeded 400,000 francs a year.

If these innovations were already changing the face of craft in Europe, it is also necessary to think of the Industrial Revolution in a broader context. Industrialism was preceded and stimulated by a growth of trade, by the establishment of European colonies in Asia, Africa and the Americas, and by the creation of the mercantilist system.

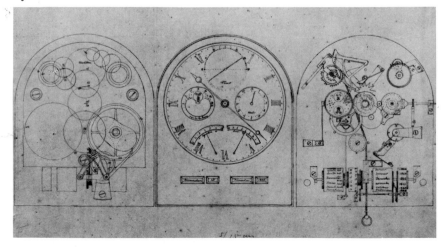

Bréguet, design for a complex carriage clock, *c*. 1815. It gives the phases of the moon, the day of the week, the date, the month and the year. Private Collection

Detail of a long-case clock by Thomas Tompion, once owned by Josiah Wedgwood. It marks the seconds and gives the day of the week.
Private Collection

Essentially, Europeans saw colonies as a captive market for their own goods. The mother-country manufactured; the colony took finished goods and sent raw materials in return. Tariff barriers were used to control and regulate the flow of trade. But matters did not work out as simply as this may suggest. From the earliest times, as we have already seen, Europe had been an eager market for goods imported from India and the Far East. To begin with, these goods were high-priced luxuries, things Europe could neither grow nor make, such as pepper and porcelain. Gradually, however, the nature of European trade with the Indies began to change. The establishment of reliable sea-routes, from the time of Vasco da Gama onwards meant that by the seventeenth century it was possible to transport Indian and Far Eastern products in bulk to European markets. This commerce, conducted through the English East India Company and its rivals on the Continent, was a hugely profitable one.

The reason for this profitability was not merely that East Indian goods were superior in certain spheres, nor even their novelty, but sheer cheapness. Sir Dudley North wrote, in *Considerations upon the East India Trade*:

> The cheapest things are bought in India; as much labour or manufacture can be had there for two pence as in England for a shilling. The carriage there is dear, the customs are high, the merchant has great gains, and so has the retailer; yet still with all

this charge, the Indians are a great deal cheaper than equal English manufacture.

One part of the European responses was to look for ways of reducing the amount of labour required in order to produce a given article. The low cost of Indian and Chinese labour was to be answered with European logic and technical ingenuity. To some extent, the situation which the North recognized and described at the end of the seventeenth century still exists today. The cheapness of labour in India means that imported Indian craft products compete in the same market with European goods mass-produced by machinery.

The European decorative styles of the seventeenth and eighteenth centuries were heavily influenced by this massive inflow of exotic goods. In England, for example, *chinoiserie* (a playful imitation of what was genuinely Chinese, with a touch of irony thrown in) had a long life from its first appearance in the mid-seventeenth century. For an essentially rational and puritanical nation it was a way of reconciling the fantasy of the Baroque and the Rococo with English self-consciousness and unwillingness to overstep the bounds of decorum. The early phase of the Gothic revival was an example of the same thing, only here the decorative imagination travelled in time rather than space.

One thing which amateurs of the Gothic such as Horace Walpole could not do was to travel back through the centuries and commis-

Above left: *Chinoiserie*. 'Old Dragon Japan Pattern' vase in Worcester porcelain, *c*. 1770. London, Victoria and Albert Museum

Above: Copy of Japanese kakiemon plate. Meissen, *c*. 1723. Basel, Historisches Museum, Kirschgarten, Collection Pauls - Eisenbeiss

Chinoiserie.
China-cabinet with
pagoda roof and
Chinese fret.
Attributed to
Chippendale,
c. 1755. Port
Sunlight, Lady
Lever Art Gallery

18th-century
Chinese coffee-pot
made for the
European market.
The shape is
entirely European,
and the decoration
is copied from
European
engravings.
London, Victoria
and Albert
Museum

Chinese plate for
export, late 17th
century. The
decoration, which
shows the Baptism
of Christ, is copied
from a European
print. London,
Victoria and
Albert Museum

sion the craftsmen of the Middle Ages to make things which fitted the society of the eighteenth century. With the East India trade this was perfectly possible. Porcelain, perhaps the most typical craft of the period, supplies examples of two very different kinds of imitation. On the one hand, European factories copied Chinese and Japanese patterns with astonishing fidelity. On the other, European merchants increasingly tended to impose their own ideas on the workshops which supplied them. The Chinese and Japanese kilns had long been accustomed to accommodating the whims of foreign clients, and certain shapes, such as the spouted so-called *narghili* bottles, were made specifically for the Near East. The Chinese and Japanese therefore had no objection to making any shape the European customer required — barbers' bowls and tankards in particular. They were also quite amenable on the question of decoration, to the point where, in the eighteenth century, it became customary to send out patterns, often armorial designs, to be copied on porcelain by Chinese artisans. There was also a trade in porcelains decorated with copies of European religious prints.

Yet there was one drawback. These goods, produced by potters and painters who had never experienced the European way of life at first hand, suffered from a certain clumsiness. Though the Europe

Christian Precht, designs for porcelain to be manufactured in China. Swedish, *c*. 1738. Gothenburg, Röhsska Konstslöjdmuseet

of the eighteenth century never overcame its dependence on cheap East Indian goods, there was a subconscious longing for something different — in particular, for something more in step with a key concept of the time — the idea of rationality.

'Neoclassicism', which was the name the nineteenth century later gave to the new style which arose to combat the capriciousness of the Baroque and the Rococo, was not, as this label implies, merely a matter of copying the achievements of Greece and Rome. It was true, of course, that the ancient world enjoyed enormous intellectual prestige — the education received by all those who were educated at all was firmly based on surviving Greek and Latin texts. But there was much more to it than that. Neoclassicism was the product of a powerful intellectual and even moral impulse. The licentiousness — in every sense — of what had gone before was now found to be offensive. The new art was to pursue truth, purity, nobility and honesty. A study of antiquity was merely the shortest route to these virtues — the real end was, in the fine arts, the true imitation of nature. But the word 'nature' was not defined as we should define it today. Hugh Honour, in his preface to the catalogue of the exhibition in 1972, quotes from a Royal Academy lecture of the late eighteenth century, in which nature was defined 'as the general and permanent principles of visible objects, not disfigured by accident nor distempered by disease, not modified by fashion or local habits. Nature is a collective idea and, though its essence exists in each individual of the species, can never in its perfection inhabit a single object.'

Where the decorative arts were concerned, this doctrine led to a search for very simple, authoritative forms, usually with a minimum of extraneous decoration. The search was not conducted by the craftsman out of inner compulsion, which is a myth constructed by the nineteenth century about the craft activity of the Middle Ages, but by the craftsman at the behest of the intellectual. The social barrier between those who worked with their minds and those who worked with their hands remained strong, even after the upheaval of the French Revolution. At first sight, this may look like the kind of scholarly dictatorship which already existed in the Renaissance — the kind of thing Cellini objected to. But in fact matters had been taken farther. The educated man now wished to rationalize the whole process of making, to provide the craftsman with a set of rules and standards which would guide him upon any occasion, and which would enable him to resolve any problem of decoration or form.

One consequence of the rise of Neoclassicism was a loss of feeling for the actual nature of materials. A rational design would succeed no matter what substance it was made of — wood or stone, glass or ceramic. Josiah Wedgwood, for instance, felt no qualms about copying the Portland Vase, a masterpiece of Imperial Roman cameo glass, in his newly invented ceramic jasper-ware.

Wedgwood is, in fact, a key figure in the story of what happened

Above: Wedgwood
jasper-ware
reproduction of
the Portland Vase.
An example from
the first issue sold
to Thomas Hope
in 1793.
Staffordshire,
Wedgwood
Museum. (See also
p. 54)

Above right: Pair
of Wedgwood
black basalt ewers
(modern replicas
from the original
plasters), designed
by John
Flaxman in 1775.
Staffordshire,
Wedgwood
Museum

to craft, and to attitudes towards craft, in the late eighteenth
century. Manufacturing enterprise, not merely design, was becoming increasingly logical. Wedgwood's interest combined art,
science, and the profitable conduct of business in a way entirely
characteristic of the time.

He first set himself up as a master potter in 1759, after having
been first an indentured apprentice to his elder brother and then a
partner in two other potteries. In 1769 he opened a new manufactory which he called 'Etruria' (the name signified his Neoclassical
allegiances). This was at first used for the production of ornamental
wares only, but later the whole business was removed there. Etruria
comprised not only a factory but also a model village for Wedgwood's workmen.

As an independent potter, Wedgwood made both 'useful' and
'ornamental' wares, and each of these has its own significance in the
retreat from established craft attitudes. The difference between the
two was something which was quite clear in Wedgwood's own
mind, and this had significance for the future. His best-known
ornamental wares were made of the famous black basalt and jasper
ceramic bodies which he invented. The first was a dense black
stoneware of extreme hardness, which would withstand high-
temperature firing and which could be polished on a lapidary
wheel. Like the plain black gloss pottery of the Greeks and
Etruscans and the red Arretine of the Romans, it had a strong

affinity to metalwork, and, apart from some sculpture, most of the forms are visibly derived from metal. Jasper was a white biscuit, which could be coloured throughout with metallic oxides or (later) dipped in a coloured slip of the same material so as to give a matt ground of absolutely even hue, in shades of blue, and in green, lilac, yellow, brown and black. The grounds were used to set off relief decoration moulded in white. Jasper therefore had a strong affinity to hardstone cameos, and on a small scale was frequently used to imitate these. The characteristic of both black basalt and jasper was that they were essentially immaculate. They showed no trace of the maker's touch — far less so than the elaborate wares produced at Sèvres.

Josiah Wedgwood's first pattern-book, showing borders for Queen's Ware Service, 1773–1814. Staffordshire, Wedgwood Museum

Wedgwood jasper-wares became, in their particular field, one of the most important expressions of Neoclassical taste. Wedgwood not only made copies of Classical antiquities, such as the copy of the Portland Vase already mentioned, but employed some of the most celebrated artists of the time to make designs for him. They included the animal-painter George Stubbs, John Flaxman and Lady Diana Beauclerk. However successful their designs, and some are indeed beautiful, it is clear that these artists knew nothing and cared little about the exact nature of the material in which they were to be carried out.

Like black basalt and jasper, Wedgwood's useful wares were the result of a long period of study and experiment. This culminated in the appearance of Queen's Ware — a fine cream-coloured earthenware body with an even, clear glaze which Wedgwood had perfected by 1763. He succeeded in attracting the attention of the English royal family with this (hence the name), and in 1772 crowned his success by getting an order for a vast table service from the Empress Catherine II of Russia. It consisted of 952 pieces, ornamented with 1,244 different views of English country houses and scenery. This meant that Wedgwood was for a moment competing in precisely the same market as Sèvres and the other great European porcelain factories. Yet the real significance of Queen's Ware was different. Through it, Wedgwood made fine table-ware of absolutely even and reliable quality available to a much larger range of customers than formerly. Catherine's dinner service was hand-painted, but only in sepia monochrome, as full colour proved to be too expensive. But much ordinary Queen's Ware had on-glaze printed decoration: the technique had been invented over a decade previously, in 1762. Where painted decoration was used it tended to be deliberately simple, just like the shapes themselves. In fact, simplicity and uniformity were the most important watchwords of Wedgwood's business enterprises.

Within the Etruria factory, production methods were organized and rationalized to the uttermost, though Wedgwood remained sufficiently a man — and a tradesman — of his own age to supply numerous table services embellished with individual crests or initials. Yet perhaps the most important thing about him was not so much his capacity as an organizer of his own workforce but the fact that his activity as a businessman was not confined to manufacture alone. He understood that, in order to make Etruria flourish, he had both to find new markets and make old ones easier to reach. He was the leading spokesman for his fellow-potters in advocating the extension of the system of turnpike roads, and he was also — and perhaps this was even more significant — a leader in promoting the Duke of Bridgewater's plan to build a new Trent and Mersey Canal. It was Wedgwood himself who cut the first sod at Brownhills, near Burselm, Stoke-on-Trent, on 26 July 1766. Linking two major rivers across the whole breadth of the Midlands, the canal passed through Wedgwood's estate at Etruria and alongside the factory, making it infinitely easier and cheaper both to bring in raw materials and ship out finished products. For England, the growth of the canal system, perhaps even more than the later growth of the

The Wedgwood factory at Etruria, with the Trent and Mersey canal in the foreground

Sèvres copy of
Wedgwood
jasper-ware, made
in blue-and-white
biscuit porcelain,
c. 1785. London,
Victoria and
Albert Museum

railways, had something of the significance which the discovery of
the sea-route to India had had for the European economy in
general.

When we look at Wedgwood's products in general — both
Queen's Ware and the more elaborate and expensive jasper-ware —
they impress us not with manual dexterity, but with the evidence
they offer of a single controlling intelligence. In this case, it was
more accurately a pair of intelligences, perfectly attuned to one
another — that of Wedgwood himself and of his partner Thomas
Bentley. It was Bentley in particular who sensed the power of the
new Neoclassical current of design, and it was Wedgwood who
responded. With what excitement we may judge from a letter he
wrote to Bentley in September 1769. It reads in part:

If you continue to write such letters as your last there is no saying
where our improvements will stop. I read it over, & over again,

and still profit by every repetition of your agreeable lessons.

And do you really think we may make a *complete conquest* of France? Conquer France in Burslem? My blood moves quicker, I feel my strength increase for the contest. Assist me my friend, & the victory is our own. We will make them (now I must say *Potts*, and how vulgar it sounds), I won't though, I say we will fashion our Porcelain after their own hearts, & captivate them with the Elegance and simplicity of the Ancients . . .

Wedgwood proved as true a prophet as he could have hoped. Sèvres itself was soon copying the cameo-effects to be found in Wedgwood jasper.

Though not all items made in the Neoclassical style are as divorced as Wedgwood's own products from traditional ideas about the nature of craftsmanship, Neoclassical emphasis on simplicity and regularity of form combined with rigorous intellectual control did have an impact on the craft tradition which was sometimes wholly practical in its consequences. For example, in furniture carved work went out of favour, though there continued to be a demand for skilful veneering and inlay. The results can be traced in the history of the English furniture industry. There was a great loss of wood-carving skills simply because the carvers could no longer find work. In the early nineteenth century there were only eleven master-carvers and about sixty journeymen carvers still at work in the whole of London. When the vogue for carved furniture returned, other methods of producing it had to be found. This led to a reliance on wood-carving machines. The new furniture, thus adorned, was produced for a new class, one which had been formed by the now firmly established Industrial Revolution and one whose disposable income, very often, was directly or indirectly taken from the profits made by the new factories. Yet it would still be incorrect to see the growth of industry alone as leading directly to a collapse in standards of handworkmanship, a collapse which it took the great effort of the Arts and Crafts Movement to stem, if not wholly to reverse.

An example of the reaction against carved decoration: Sheraton mahogany tambour bureau bookcase, *c.* 1780. Private Collection

10 The Decline of Craft

It was during the second phase of the Industrial Revolution, from 1820 to about 1850, that standards of design in England and almost throughout Europe got themselves into a muddle. This muddle attracted the wrath of some of the leading thinkers of the time — for example Sir Henry Cole, founder of Summerly's Art Manufactures and publisher of the *Journal of Design and Manufacture*, and still more so the impassioned Gothic Revivalist A.W.N. Pugin. Eventually it provoked a response from Ruskin and led to the foundation of the Arts and Crafts Movement.

By this time the impact of industry and its growth on standards of craftsmanship and design in everyday objects had become very complex. Neoclassicism eased the transition from one set of attitudes to craft to quite another — design was no longer a matter of interaction between the prevailing taste of the time, the particular patron and the maker, but rather something imposed unilaterally from above. It had now come to seem unacceptably austere. The class which the revolution enriched associated wealth and its enjoyment with all the luxuries laboriously hand-made for their predecessors. There was a vogue for the complex richness of the Elizabethan style, popularized by the historical novels of Sir Walter Scott. There was also, from about 1830 onwards, a renewed taste for the Rococo. But the so-called Grecian style was also liked, and carried on Neoclassical ideas in somewhat attenuated form. The chief characteristic of the period was therefore its eclecticism and lack of stylistic coherence. The effects of this were compounded by the fact that the growth of population and of wealth reduced the direct influence of the small group of educated arbiters of taste, who had succeeded in imposing their ideas almost throughout the eighteenth century. As had already happened in Wedgwood's case, the real responsibility for design passed to the manufacturer, and the manufacturers of the period, unlike their great predecessor, were in many respects ill prepared to bear the responsibility.

Yet this was not the whole of the story. Victorian inventiveness led to a continual expansion in the range of manufacturing techniques. Many inventions were ways of reproducing things more cheaply and more quickly. The eighteenth century had already had a taste for substitute techniques of ornament — *Vernis Martin* and other japanning techniques had been invented as a way of imitating the costly Oriental lacquer beloved by furniture-makers and others. Now there was a great rush to find new methods. These were protected by patents, and the emphasis on patents was a sign of the times, as it stressed the importance of the man who invented

American Palm Leaf quilt, 19th century. Bath, American Museum in Britain

techniques, as opposed to that of the man who actually employed them, and at the same time separated the idea of invention from that of day-to-day use. Between 1837 and 1846 thirty-five patents were taken out at the British Patent Office for processes which involved coating one substance or material so that it looked like another and (usually) more expensive one. Sheffield plate was already established as a way of making silver-ware less costly — copper sheet was rolled between and thus fused with two thinner sheets of silver. But now this comparatively simple mechanical process was replaced by a more scientific one. In 1840 G.R. Elkington took out a patent for electroplating. By means of electrolysis, a thin layer of silver could now be deposited on an article of base metal. The method was not only easier and cheaper, it released the manufacturer from many of the disciplines imposed by his material, since the base-metal base could be of any shape, however convoluted. Electroplate marked a decisive step away from the direct handling of metal.

Even more significant was the related process of electrotyping. This enabled the whole article to be created in the plating vat. It was at first regarded simply as a way of making exceptionally faithful copies. The original might be a piece of contemporary metalwork, a piece of early silver, or even a natural object such as a leaf or a shell — the latter possibility led Victorian designers in directions which had already been explored by Mannerist gold-smiths such as Wenzel Jamnitzer. Soon, however, designers and craftsmen began to think of electrotyping as a technique in its own right and created objects specifically for multiple reproduction. Yet because the technique itself was so impersonal, and so far removed from the making processes of the past, they remained uncertain

Below: Sheffield plate cake-basket, 1760–70. London, Victoria and Albert Museum

Below right: The original Jacquard loom, *c.* 1805. Paris, Musée des Techniques

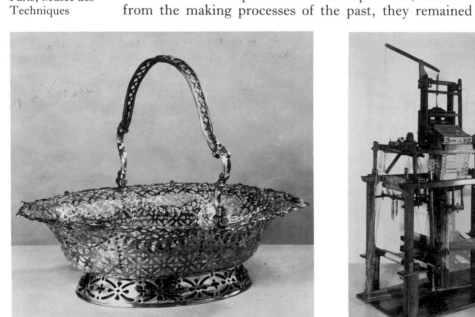

about the best and most authoritative way in which to use it.

An even more striking case of this stylistic uncertainty can be found in Early Victorian carpet design. The cause was the introduction of the mechanized Jacquard loom. A hand loom capable of weaving very complicated patterns and needing only one man to operate it had been invented in about 1805 by the Frenchman Joseph-Marie Jacquard (1752–1834). His loom was the culmination of about seventy-five years of progress, which began with the systems devised by his fellow-countrymen Bouchier (1725) and Falcon (1728). Now machine-powered Jacquard looms came into widespread use for the manufacture of elaborately patterned carpets. These could be made, not only in any design, but in almost any breadth. Woven stuffs thus entirely escaped not merely from the limits imposed by human strength and skill, but also from any direct connection with the human scale.

Yet many books on the nature of domestic design during the nineteenth century have made the mistake of concentrating too exclusively on English examples. It is true that England was, and remained for a long while, the heartland of industrialism. Nevertheless another very active centre of innovation in the decorative arts, especially during the first half of the century, was Austria. Here the post-Napoleonic period saw the creation of the characteristic style we now call Biedermeier. The word implies the notion of bourgeois comfort, and it was in Austria that a number of innovations were made which are usually and wrongly credited to the English. For example, it was an Austrian, the Viennese upholsterer Georg Junigl, who in 1822 took out the first patent for coiled spring upholstery. The first English patent was not taken out until six years later. Austria was also the place where Michael Thonet made his radical experiments with bentwood furniture, starting in about the year 1830, and taking out a series of patents in 1841 which covered France, England and Belgium as well as his

Thonet oval-top
bentwood table,
late 1850s.
Courtesy of the
Art Institute of
Chicago

own country. Thonet's bentwood furniture was one of the first and
most successful examples of the application of genuinely industrial
thinking to furniture production, and by the early 1850s, thanks to
standardization and mass production, his furniture was making
serious inroads into both the British and American markets. His
designs are still in production today. He is an even more historic
figure than he is usually held to be, since his success marks the
triumph of the designer, who is responsible for the appearance of
objects he may never touch, as opposed to the craftsman, who
handles the materials himself.

Thonet bentwood is also important because it marks the start of
an alternative tradition — that of objects designed for, and in a
certain sense by, the machine. Thonet chairs are the direct
ancestors of the tubular steel furniture which emerged from the
Bauhaus in the 1920s, and of the laminated bentwood furniture
designed by the Finnish architect Alvar Aalto in the early 1930s.
Thonet implicitly rejected the idea of craft long before the modern
tradition of design came into being, but he did not reject it in favour
of a plethora of mechanically created ornament.

It is also worth looking at the position of craft in early nineteenth-
century America. Looked at from one angle, it can seem as if
America had, at this period, become the refuge of the craft spirit. It
was only in the second part of the century that major industrialization began, though when it did its progress was very rapid. Craft,
the need to make things for oneself rather than relying on outside
suppliers, played a large role in American pioneer communities for
obvious reasons. The country was still underpopulated and un-
developed; there were few specialists; people therefore made what
they needed from the resources they found on the spot. Often the
actual process of making was an expression of community spirit.
The magnificent patchwork quilts in a wide variety of patterns,

many with symbolic meaning attached to them, were often the product of quilting bees — family and neighbourhood gatherings where menfolk cut the plywood patterns used to make the basic patterns and needlewomen contributed their share of the labour. Yet it is also worth noting that these quilts are not completely independent of industrial society, since the actual stuffs of which they are made were industrially produced, and are here transformed by a process of re-cycling.

American craft could also be a direct reflection of the stubborn individualistic beliefs which led people to take their chance on the other side of the Atlantic. The characteristic Shaker furniture, produced by the religious sect of that name from about 1815 onwards, has a spareness which echoes not only the religious fundamentalism of the people who created it but also their practical country background. From existing rural tradition they evolved a limited series of standard designs — ladder-back side-chairs and rocking-chairs and small tripod tables with circular tops.

The virtues of Shaker design were so obvious, even to those who did not belong to the cult, that this furniture very soon found a steady market among outsiders. The Shakers therefore

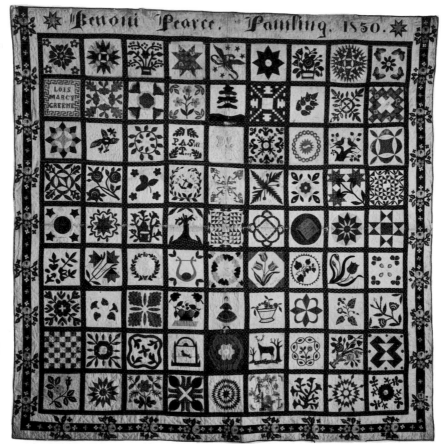

American Album quilt, 1850, with each square made by a different friend or relative of Benoni Pearce, New York. Washington, Smithsonian Institution

began to make it commercially, establishing what amounted to communal factories in order to finance their way of life. Long before the end of the nineteenth century furniture closely based on Shaker patterns was being turned out by ordinary commercial manufacturers.

There is a paradox about the history of craft in nineteenth-century America. It was encouraged by the factors I have mentioned — sparse population and the need to do the most one could for oneself. But these were precisely the factors which, only a little later, encouraged the exceedingly rapid growth of American industry. The pioneers who settled the prairies of the Midwest were initially thrown back on their own resources, true enough, but they were not content to remain in such a primitive condition. Perhaps naturally, tools evolved ahead of ordinary domestic artefacts. While the primitive prairie plough, the bull-tongue plough, continued to be used in southern Illinois until as late as 1850, many other tools were already altering their form. One was the axe. By 1848, the year in which it was eulogistically described in a German *Handbook for Settlers in the United States*, the American 'Kentucky' axe was both different from and distinctly superior to the hand-axes which intending settlers might know in Europe: 'Its curved cutting edge, its heavier head, counterbalanced by the handle, gives the axe greater power in its swing, facilitates its penetration, reduces the expenditure of human energy, speeds up the work . . .'

Psychologically, it was a short step from improved tools to new kinds of agricultural machinery, and in the long run these machines had a decisive effect on the whole of the American economy and the position of craft within it. The mechanical reaper, an idea first formulated in England as early as 1783, was perfected in America by Cyrus McCormick, who took out a patent for his invention in 1834. In 1846 a factory ventured to build a series of a hundred of McCormick's machines. They were instantly successful on the level land of the prairie, and between 1846 and 1854 over 8,000 of them

McCormick's patent mechanical reaper of 1834 (modern replica). Collections of Greenfield Village and the Henry Ford Museum, Dearborn, Michigan

Two Shaker interiors. The simple designs and materials reflect Shaker ideals of plain, simple living

were sold and used. Innovations such as this brought a complete and rapid revolution to American agriculture. The revolution did not stop at agriculture alone — abundant corn very soon produced a surplus of hogs and this in turn led to the mechanization of abattoirs and pork-packing plants.

The mid-nineteenth century Cincinnati packing houses, the first to be organized in such a rational way and on such a large scale (the scale, indeed, was something that rationalization alone made possible) are generally considered to be the real ancestors of the modern assembly line. Hog-carcasses, heavy and awkward lumps with a complex structure of tendons and bones within them, were not things which could be handled directly by machine. The solution was to hang them from an endlessly moving chain, which moved each carcass in turn past a row of workers, each of whom was responsible for a single operation — opening, disembowelling, semi-decapitating, splitting or stamping. This overhead railway system in the Cincinnati slaughterhouses led eventually to the fully developed conveyor system, which belongs to our own century. It was the root of the assembly-line concept which made real mass-production possible.

Long before this, however, industrialism had brought with it a further and decisive expansion in the market for goods. It was not merely the newly rich manufacturers who could afford to buy. Most people, even the poorly paid workers in the factories, had more possessions than ever before. More important still, their attitude towards these possessions had altered. The hand-made objects of pre-industrial society were in this sense unique — that each, however often the craftsman had performed a particular task, was a little different from the others. This quality of uniqueness was subconsciously present in people's minds. They bought for use, and they did not expect to use and discard. Now that expectation was in the process of being changed.

Cincinnati meat-packing plant, 1873. Collections of Greenfield Village and the Henry Ford Museum, Dearborn, Michigan

11 The British Arts and Crafts Movement

The precursor of the attitudes which characterized the Arts and Crafts Movement in the second half of the nineteenth century was A.W.N. Pugin. Born in 1812, Pugin was precociously gifted as a designer — before he was fifteen he was designing furniture for the flamboyant restoration of Windsor Castle undertaken by George IV. Later, he was Charles Barry's collaborator in the building, decorating and furnishing of the new Houses of Parliament. All his life (he died relatively young, in 1852) he was the apostle of the Gothic style, and his attachment to it was particularly vehement after his conversion to Roman Catholicism in 1835. Unlike eighteenth-century enthusiasts for Gothic, Pugin saw it as a moral force, and a means of reforming the 'confused jumble of styles and symbols borrowed from all ages and periods' which he saw surrounding him in the England of his day. In fact, though the prescription he recommended was totally different, his attitude towards the decorative arts was not at all unlike that professed by the original promoters of Neoclassicism. They, too, had found in objects a moral force, a means of changing the condition of society. Indeed, there was another important resemblance as well. Pugin stressed, as the Neoclassical theorists had once done, the supremacy of nature — but his 'nature' was that which supplied the models for the decorators of the great medieval buildings. It was therefore in a sense deeply ironic that, of all the opposing styles he saw about him, the Neoclassical should have been the one Pugin most deeply detested. This was because of his religious convictions; he saw it as the emblem of pagan rather than Christian culture.

There was, however, one sense in which Pugin went much farther than the Neoclassicists. He insisted not only on integrity of design, but also on integrity of construction. Where architecture was concerned, he wrote that 'the two great rules for design are these: 1st, that there should be no features about a building which are not necessary for convenience, construction, or "propriety"; 2nd, that all ornament should consist of enrichment of the essential construction of the building.' He extended these rules from architecture to the design of furniture, disliking 'staircase turrets for inkstands, monumental crosses for light-shades, gable-ends hung on handles for door-porters, and four doorways and a cluster of pillars to support a French lamp.' The furniture Pugin himself designed, especially the later pieces, shows a deliberate simplicity and sturdiness. But the craftsmen who made it came from the

Couch designed for Windsor Castle, 1820–30, attributed to A.W.N. Pugin, and now in the Queen's Robing Room, Palace of Westminster

ordinary furniture-trade and no doubt made up very different designs by other hands. The firm of J.G. Crace, who usually worked for Pugin, had been employed by George IV on the extravagant decorations of the Brighton Pavilion.

Pugin stood at the parting of the ways. One road led towards contemporary industrial design, and the other towards the craft movement as we know it today. The true prophet of that movement was not however Pugin, but John Ruskin. Ruskin's fervent idealization of craft handwork, in his books *The Seven Lamps of Architecture* and *The Stones of Venice*, gave the idea of craft an impetus which it was never afterwards to lose.

One of Ruskin's great hatreds was for what he called 'architectural deceit', the well-established practice of using one material to imitate another. But deceit lay not in imitation alone, but in the species of labour:

> He who would form the creations of his own mind by any other
> instrument than his own hand, would also, if he might, give
> grinding organs to Heaven's angels, to make their music easier.

This sentence forms part of the conclusion of 'The Lamp of Life' in *The Seven Lamps of Architecture*.

The real impetus towards the foundation of the Arts and Crafts Movement was given not by this, but by *The Stones of Venice*. The first book was published in 1851, significantly the year of the Great Exhibition, many of whose displays horrified both Ruskin and Morris; the second and third in 1853, and it continued to be reprinted throughout the century. The chapter 'On the Nature of Gothic', which appears in the second book, was taken up as a kind of manifesto, and was printed as a separate pamphlet in 1854. Ruskin's thesis was that artefacts must reflect man's own essential humanity, and could never, therefore, attain the absolute perfection of finish demanded by the Neoclassical theoreticians: 'Men

were not intended to work with the accuracy of tools, to be precise and perfect in all their actions. If you would have that precision out of them, and make their fingers measure degrees like cogwheels, and their arms strike curves like compasses, you must unhumanise them.'

The rules for craft which Ruskin laid down have often been quoted, but are nevertheless worth quoting again. There were three of them:

1. Never encourage the manufacture of any article not absolutely necessary, in the production of which *Invention* has no share.
2. Never demand an exact finish for its own sake, but only for some practical or noble end.
3. Never encourage imitation or copying of any kind, except for the sake of preserving records of great works.

The ideas enunciated in *The Stones of Venice* had an enormous appeal for a new generation of young men. Among them were a group of Oxford undergraduates. Two, William Morris and Edward Burne-Jones, both at Exeter College, were dissatisfied with the intellectual climate at the university, which they found 'languid and indifferent'. In addition to being energized by Ruskin, they were attracted towards the Pre-Raphaelite Brotherhood of painters, to which Ruskin had lent powerful support.

A.W.N. Pugin, The Prime Minister's Room, *c.* 1852. Palace of Westminster

Morris was then, as his friend and first biographer Mackail records, 'an aristocrat and a High Churchman'. He was also the fortunate possessor of a private income. After he left Oxford, he studied architecture, and then, under the influence of Dante Gabriel Rossetti, he tried without much success to become a painter. He was by this time living in London, in the studio in Red Lion Square which had once been Rossetti's. Morris and Burne-Jones, who shared it with him, decorated their living quarters to suit their own medieval tastes. One conspicuous item was a huge settle with three cupboards above it. Rossetti painted scenes from Malory and Dante on the doors. But Morris's fascination with the domestic interior increased greatly after his marriage in 1859. In 1860 he moved into a new house, the Red House at Bexleyheath, which his close friend the architect Philip Webb had built for him, and set about creating interiors to suit his own taste. From this beginning grew the Firm, afterwards to be more formally called Morris & Co.

The Firm made its first great impact on the public at the International Exhibition held at South Kensington in 1862, showing stained glass, embroideries, furniture, tiles, table-glass and candlesticks, and was awarded two gold medals. Stained glass, and ecclesiastical work in general, provided Morris with much business in the earlier years. But his main importance is not as a church furnisher. Though he was not gifted as a painter, he turned out to be a pattern-maker of genius. A number of his designs for wallpapers and textiles are still in production. And he went farther than this — he evolved a theory of design which has remained influential to the present day. 'A designer', he wrote, '... should always thoroughly understand the process of the special manufacture he is dealing with, or the result will be a mere *tour de force*. On the other hand, it is the pleasure of understanding the capabilities of the special material, and using them for suggesting (not imitating) natural beauty and incident, that gives the *raison d'être* for decorative art.'

Though brought up as a gentleman, Morris plunged with a will into the actual business of craftsmanship. The Icelander Eríkir Magnússon, who helped Morris to translate the Icelandic sagas, left this vivid description of his friend at work:

> In the cellars of his old house in Bloomsbury Square ... on heavy sabots of French make, aproned from the armpits, with tucked-up shirt-sleeves, his fore-arms dyed up to the elbow, the great man lectured most brilliantly on the high art of dyeing, illustrating his lecture with experiments in the various dyes he wanted for his silks and wools.

It was Morris who actually put into practice Ruskin's dictum that 'It would be well if all of us were good handicraftsmen of some kind, and the dishonour of manual labour done away with altogether .... In each several profession, no master should be too proud to do the hardest work.'

Morris gave the example to a number of other leading craftsmen in England, though the Arts and Crafts Movement did not truly gather impetus, despite the success of Morris's own firm, until the

1880s, after the Aesthetic Movement, which had quite different sources, had created its own impact. Arthur Heygate Mackmurdo established the Century Guild in 1882; the Art-Workers' Guild was founded in 1884, and in 1888 Charles Robert Ashbee set up the Guild and School of Handicraft. This was also the year in which the Arts and Crafts Exhibition Society was founded. The influence of the second wave of pioneers lingered well into our own century — one reason for this being the fact that many of them were long-lived. Mackmurdo and Ashbee both lived until 1942. It was therefore the generation of the 1880s, even more than Morris himself, who created the pattern for the artist craftsman as we know him today. Mackmurdo, for example, founded the Century Guild in order to 'restore building, decoration, glass painting, pottery, wood-carving and metal to their rightful place beside painting and sculpture', and thus initiated the rivalry with the fine arts which was to be one of the distinguishing marks of the new movement. The Arts and Crafts Exhibition Society provided a place where the movement's achievements and ambitions could be publicly demonstrated.

Perhaps the most interesting figure in the Arts and Crafts Movement of the 1880s was Charles Robert Ashbee. He was of upper middle-class origin, educated at Wellington and at King's College, Cambridge. His first idea, when he emerged from university, was to train as an architect, and he articled himself to G.F. Bodley, the most important early patron of Morris & Co. He went to live at Toynbee Hall, the pioneer university settlement in the East End of London, and started a class in drawing and decoration there. It was the members of this class who were the early members of the Guild of Handicraft, which in 1890, two years after its

Above left: The Flower Pot, panel designed by William Morris and embroidered by May Morris. Walthamstow, William Morris Gallery

Above: William Morris, the original design for his *Chrysanthemum* wallpaper, 1874. Walthamstow, William Morris Gallery

foundation, moved into Essex House, a Georgian Mansion stranded in Mile End. It had retail premises in fashionable Brook Street.

At the end of his life, in 1892, when the Guild of Handicraft was already flourishing, Morris expressed regret that the craftsmen who worked for him at Morris & Co. had been offered so little creative initiative:

> Except with a small part of the more artistic side of the work I could not do anything (or at least but a little) to give this pleasure to the workmen, because I should have had to change their method of work so utterly that I should have disqualified them from earning their living elsewhere.

Ashbee was more sanguine. He considered both art school and trade workshop experience a 'positive disadvantage' to the people who came to work with him, and preferred to teach them himself:

> Each pupil is taught first to conceive the design, and then to apply it through the help of the other classes to the different materials, the wood, the metal, the clay, the gesso, the flat surface for painting. The effort here, therefore, is not to emulate the ordinary Technical School but to follow in the lines laid down by leading artists who have the encouragement of the handicrafts at heart, in the belief that the modern cry for the education of the hand and eye can only be fully achieved in the education of the individuality of the workman.

Ashbee's venture was in its early years a success, and he himself built up a considerable reputation as a working silversmith. By the

C.R. Ashbee, desk made by the Guild of Handicraft for the Duchess of Leeds, *c.* 1900. The silverware is also by Ashbee. London, Victoria and Albert Museum. Photograph by Alan Crawford

late 1890s his reputation, and that of the Guild he had founded, was widespread both within England and abroad. One particularly prestigious commission was for decorations in the Grand-Ducal Palace at Darmstadt. In 1902, however, Ashbee decided to transfer the Guild to the country, to Chipping Campden in Gloucestershire.

One of the great discoveries made by the craft movement was that country workshops were a reservoir of skills which often seemed to have been forgotten in town. Certain types of furniture, for example, seemed to reach back to the tradition of joinery, which fashionable urban cabinet-makers had progressively abandoned since the seventeenth century. Morris, in his efforts to reform Victorian taste, had turned to these designs for inspiration, and his simple Sussex chair, with its rush seat and turned legs and stretchers became one of the firm's best-sellers. From a personal point of view, Morris preferred furniture of this type to the elaborately decorated pieces which Morris & Co. also produced, saying to Edward Carpenter at the end of his life:

> I have spent, I know, a vast amount of time designing furniture and wallpapers, carpets and curtains; but after all I am inclined to think that sort of thing is mostly rubbish, and I would prefer for my part to live with the simplest white-washed walls and wooden chairs and tables.

There was something more to it than that. As many of his published writings show, Morris was very far from condemning the machine — it was the misuse of the machine he objected to, as did his disciple Ashbee. Yet there was undoubtedly within the Arts and Crafts Movement a nostalgia for the past, a backward-looking idealism which the country seemed better able to satisfy than the modern city. Ashbee wanted to set up a new and healthier community, which the countryside would protect. Unfortunately, the move meant the decline and eventual extinction of his enterprise.

The Guild of Handicraft had cut itself from its market, which was essentially an urban and luxury one. Ashbee blamed other factors as well — for example, the passion for antiques, which had been rising steadily since the 1840s, and which made new designs of any quality difficult to sell; and the competition of a throng of amateur craftsmen and particularly craftswomen (his contemptuous collective name for them was 'dear Emily') who now hung about the fringes of the true Arts and Crafts Movement — but he had to admit that the Guild had failed to stand the test. By 1908, when the organization was dissolved and reconstructed on a far more modest scale as a trust, he had concluded that it was useless to rebel against the industrial system, but more than ever necessary to try and reconstruct it from within. The 'intellectual Ludditism' of Ruskin and Morris, as Ashbee now called it, was something which would no longer do.

It is perhaps symbolic that one of the things which most closely linked Morris to Ashbee, at least in a practical sense, was an interest

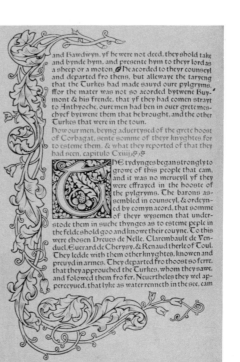

in luxury book-production. Morris's last venture into the crafts was the Kelmscott Press, founded in 1890. In the space of six years it issued more than fifty titles, including a reprint of Ruskin's seminal chapter 'On the Nature of Gothic'. Morris intended the Kelmscott Press to oppose everything he detested about ordinary nineteenth-century commercial book-production. He designed the type-faces himself, and the borders and initials, commissioned woodcuts from Burne-Jones and Walter Crane, and printed the books on paper hand-made to his own specifications, with specially imported ink. Ashbee's Essex House Press, named after the Guild of Handicraft's original London headquarters in Mile End, was only one of a number of private presses that followed Kelmscott's lead. There were St John Hornby's Ashendene Press, founded in 1894; the Vale Press and the Eragny Press, both founded by artists — Charles Ricketts and Lucien Pissarro; and there was T.J. Cobden-Sanderson's Doves Press. Between them they did a huge amount to raise standards of book-production, and indeed to change people's whole notion of its potentialities. Nevertheless what they published could only be available to the few. There is an irony in the fact that printing, which was at the time of its introduction an assault on craft, became one of the chief preoccupations of a flourishing craft revival.

I have said less about Arts and Crafts style than about Arts and Crafts ideals and organization because stylistically the movement is hard to pinpoint. Morris favoured the medieval tradition, and borrowed from the English rustic crafts; but by the 1880s what craftsmen produced had accommodated itself to the so-called Aesthetic Movement, which intervened between Ruskin's trumpet

Above left:
Sussex armchair by Morris & Co., in ebonized wood with rush seat, 1870s

Above:
Page from *The History of Godfrey of Boulogne,* printed by the Kelmscott Press, 1893. Walthamstow, William Morris Gallery

blast and the craft activity of these last two decades of the century.

To understand what the Aesthetic Movement was about, it is necessary to look briefly at Late Victorian design in general, and to notice the fact that the Arts and Crafts enjoyed no special monopoly of handicraft. Ruskin and Morris did not put an end to the confusion of styles they denounced. They only made people momentarily uneasy. In the 1860s and 1870s, for example, old established firms like Gillow & Co. and Holland & Sons were producing furniture even grander than Morris's most stately productions. It was not medieval, but was loosely based on Louis XVI originals. The actual workmanship of this furniture was in many respects superior to that of the eighteenth century — the very acme of traditional craftsmanship. Holland & Sons produced intricate veneers in ivory and precious woods almost as a matter of course, for exhibition purposes or the pleasure of rich clients. The repoussé silver, often combined with steel and gold, which the Frenchman Léonard Morel-Ladeuil made for the firm of Elkington & Co. at the same period is equally impressive as a revival of traditional handicraft techniques. Morel-Ladeuil's creations included the Milton Shield, shown at the Paris Exhibition of 1867, and the Helicon Vase, exhibited at the South Kensington International Exhibition of 1872. Both were in a kind of Neo-Renaissance style, and from the point of view of workmanship were fully worthy of Cellini or of Wenzel Jamnitzer.

The future did not, however, lie with Neo-Renaissance or with

Inlaid cabinet by Holland & Sons, *c*. 1870. London, Victoria and Albert Museum adaptations of Louis XVI. The 1860s saw the beginning of a powerful new fashion, stimulated by a renewal of interest in Japanese art — Japan itself having been opened to commerce by Commodore Perry's expedition of 1854. All the leading English commercial manufacturers took to Japonisme — makers of ceramics such as Worcester, Minton and Copeland; commercial silversmiths such as Elkington and the Sheffield manufacturer James Dixon & Sons. By the 1870s imitative Japonisme had evolved further into a new style, perhaps the first wholly original one thrown up by the Victoria era. This was the so-called 'Art' style, which was the expression of the Aesthetic Movement. This allied ideas borrowed directly from Japan with the remnants of early Victorian Naturalism, and added a kind of spindly black-and-gold dandyism which was entirely its own.

Sideboard in Anglo-Japanese style, designed by E.W. Godwin and made by William Watt, *c.* 1867. London, Victoria and Albert Museum

The importance of the Aesthetic Movement lay, not in the means whereby the objects associated with it were made, but in the manner in which people were encouraged to look at them: in isolation from their surroundings and presumed function. The fashion for collecting antiques, denounced by Ashbee, may have had something to do with this. Quite certainly such an attitude would in time create uncertainties within the craft movement itself. And meanwhile, with the crafts for the moment dormant, it led to the idea that works of art (with all the density of emotional reference this phrase implies) could be replicated by straightforwardly commercial means. By the 1870s art-furniture manufacturer's were being listed in the London Trade Directory as a separate category, as if to make it plain that they were different from other cabinet-makers and furnishers. Yet when one looks at things more closely, it seems that the London furniture trade was well able to accommodate the new vogue with no alteration in its own structure or workshop methods, which remained as they had been since 1830. The architect E.W. Godwin, perhaps the most distinguished designer of Aesthetic Movement art-furniture, worked in association with the firm of William Watt of Grafton Street, just as Pugin had once worked with Crace. Watt issued a catalogue of *Art Furniture* in 1877, which features a number of Godwin's designs. Gillow & Co., in addition to making the Louis XVI-influenced furniture already mentioned, made Aesthetic designs by E.J. Talbert.

As far as design was concerned, the new handicraft workshops followed the lead which had been set them in the commercial sphere. Their products in fact sometimes competed for attention

Below:
Christopher Dresser, twin-necked vessel showing Pre-Columbian influence, designed for the Linthorpe Pottery. Private Collection

Below right:
Christopher Dresser, jug with sweeping handle, designed for the Linthorpe Pottery. Private Collection

with those which owed their existence to a new species — the professional industrial designer. The greatest design-innovator of the period, far greater than anyone directly associated with the Arts and Crafts Movement, was Christopher Dresser.

Born in 1834, Dresser studied at the Government School of Design from 1847 to 1856. He was a fully qualified scientist in addition to being a designer, specializing in botany. Plant forms inspired much of his decorative work although, like Pugin before him, he thought too great a degree of naturalism was inappropriate. But what really inspires both his writings about design and his practice as a designer is a rational and scientific spirit. In one sense, he is the first ancestor of the twentieth-century Functionalists: 'An object', he wrote, 'should not only be so far fitted for the work for which it is intended that it is possible to use it for the purpose of its production, but should be perfectly adapted to meet all the requirements of the work for which it is designed, and that in the easiest and simplest manner.'

If one looks at Dresser's designs for metalwork, this seems a

Christopher Dresser, electroplated soup tureen and ladle with ivory handles, 1880, designed for Hukin & Heath. Private Collection

simple and self-evident statement of his practice. Produced chiefly for two firms — the ubiquitous Elkington & Co., and J.W. Hukin and T. Heath — they were used both for silver and for electroplate, and often one finds the same article made in both materials. The forms Dresser invented seem at first sight extremely surprising for their period, not only simple, but almost aggressively industrial — severely geometric, smoothly impersonal in finish, and often with rivets and other constructional details sharply revealed. Dresser is always concerned to use the metal not only starkly but sparingly. In his toast-racks, for example, the simple uprights serve as legs, and also as partitions to separate the slices. His oval sugar basins with swing handles have the long sides curved inward to stiffen the metal without the need to add a rim.

Dresser's porcelain and glass are a different matter. Sometimes, it is true, he lost control of what was done to his designs. At Mintons, his patterns were put on shapes for which they were never intended, and unsuitable decoration was applied to shapes of his invention which he had meant to be ornamented differently. This was not the case with the wares turned out by the Linthorpe Art Pottery in Middlesbrough, where he seems to have enjoyed almost total control. The forms, unlike those for metalwork, are organic. They show traces of historical influence — there is a clear current from Pre-Columbian pottery, with its squat forms and stirrup handles, while a number of the splashed glazes are unmistakably Chinese in inspiration. There is a strong emphasis on three-dimensionality, on the abstract interplay of solid and void, and on forms which seem ready to turn on their own axis. Yet it is chiefly important that these are ornamental rather than useful objects, quasi-sculptures, produced by openly industrial means. Linthorpe ware is marked with Dresser's facsimile signature, and thus in one sense stakes its claim to be both 'original' and 'artistic'. But it was mould-made, and was turned out in large quantity by means of standard factory production methods. The mould-numbers are often found impressed beside the signature itself.

Far more than the historicist commercial artefacts which had originally provoked Ruskin to denunciation, Linthorpe wares offered a challenge to the Ruskinian theory of craft. In some ways, it is a challenge which has not as yet been satisfactorily answered.

12   The Arts and Crafts Movement in America

The Arts and Crafts Movement, which had sprung up in England, was influential both in the United States and in Europe. The United States was more easily able to understand and absorb the Ruskinian notion of the decorative arts as a moral force, but perhaps the practical consequences of the movement were more profound and longer lasting elsewhere.

Pottery was always one of the preferred media of the artist-craftsman, and it was through ceramics that the new gospel launched by Ruskin and Morris made its first practical impact across the Atlantic. The year was 1871, and the place, suitably enough, was the meat-packing city of Cincinnati, the place where the assembly line was even then in its birth-throes. It was important, and also characteristic of the American situation, that the movement was launched by amateurs — socially prominent young women. Their first enthusiasm was overglaze china painting, and a class to teach this skill was set up at the Cincinnati School of Art. Among the pupils was Mary Louise McLaughlin, the daughter of

the city's leading architect. She and her colleagues became so skilful that they were able to send a display of their products to the Centennial Exposition held at Philadelphia in 1876.

Naturally, they visited the Exposition, and there they saw foreign ceramics on display which further excited their imaginations. They were particularly impressed with a group of French wares, decorated in 'barbotine' technique with coloured slips under the glaze. Miss McLaughlin experimented on her own account, and was soon able to produce something like it. In 1879 she organized a Women's Pottery Club. In doing so, she managed to offend Maria Longworth Nichols, another wealthy young woman who had been among the early Cincinnati enthusiasts for china painting.

Mrs Nichols' response was to found a pottery of her own. She called it Rookwood, after her family estate, and also, as she said, because the name 'reminded one of Wedgwood'. Mrs Nichols was endowed with a sound commercial instinct, and her aim was always to put Rookwood on a paying basis. First she reconciled herself sufficiently to the Women's Pottery Club to agree to supply them with greenware, and to fire it after it was decorated. This arrangement lasted until 1883, but then Rookwood withdrew, further assuring its own dominance. A number of rival enterprises had by this time sprung up, but they were never able to challenge Mrs Nichols successfully. By 1881 she had already started the transition from independent studio work by amateurs to a fully professional attitude — it was in this year that she hired her first full-time professional decorator. In 1883, the style of decoration was changed. An atomizer was now used to produce smoother, less 'hand-crafted', colour transitions. The new ware became known, significantly, as 'Rookwood Standard', a name which implied continuity of production.

In 1889, Rookwood won a gold medal at the World's Fair in

Above left:
Rookwood
monumental vase,
1887

Above:
William F.
McDonald, plate
with turtle and
leafy branch,
1885, made at the
Rookwood Pottery.
Washington,
Smithsonian
Institution, Gift of
Mrs Page Kirk

Paris. It was at this point that Mrs Nichols, now Mrs Bellamy Storer, decided to sell her interest to her partner William Taylor. Rookwood had thus traced a typically American pattern in the Arts and Crafts: what was started for private satisfaction became a fully commercial enterprise. Mrs Bellamy Storer did however retain a studio of her own at the pottery and now produced a much more Oriental type of ware, with a deep, lustrous copper-red glaze. Her work as a potter was at this time limited by the successful political career of her new husband, who served as American ambassador, from 1897 onwards, in Belgium, in Spain, and at the Austro-Hungarian court in Vienna. Her trajectory from amateur status to being a professional, and then to amateur status again, illustrates many of the ambiguities which have continued to haunt the American crafts and especially, perhaps, American craftswomen.

Rookwood was only one of a number of studio potteries, not only in Cincinnati or near it but in other parts of America, which operated in the 1870s, 1880s and 1890s with varying degrees of artistic and commercial success. Both in temperament and in aim they differed widely. Hugh C. Robertson conducted years of impassioned research into the secrets of Oriental monochrome and crackle glazes at Chelsea, near Boston. The one-time painter, Theophilus A. Brouwer Jr, set up a studio in East Hampton, Long Island, around 1893, and without much care for chemistry or the technical niceties of his medium, succeeded in making some remarkably free and beautiful pottery until, in 1910, he abandoned the medium in order to make sculpture in concrete. Even more original in his way of thinking was George Ohr, dubbed the 'mad genius of Biloxi', who threw pots with incredibly thin walls, squeezed, twisted and folded into bizarre shapes. At Newcomb College, New Orleans, a different attitude prevailed. Here the aim was to train young women and provide them with a skill which would permit them to go out into the world and earn a living. The pottery also gave employment to girls who wanted to stay on after their graduation. Significantly, however, the actual throwing of the pots was always done by male professionals, and only the decoration was the work of women. The motifs used were usually plants and animals indigenous to the American South — one finds magnolia, live-oak, palm-trees and wisteria.

Though there was not continuity of style, pottery provides a glimpse of the wide spectrum of American attitudes towards the crafts — the involvement of amateurs, and particularly of women (a heritage perhaps from the pioneer communities of much earlier in the century), the willingness to take decorative and technical ideas from any source, an interest in experiment for its own sake, a thrust towards individual self-expression without worrying too much about utility, a strong commercial acumen which contrasts with this, and an interest in craft not for its own sake but as a medium of education.

Though the potters made an early start, the American craft

George Ohr, vase made at Biloxi Art Pottery, *c.* 1900

movement did not really get going until the 1890s. Before that, in 1882–3, Oscar Wilde, then still essentially a young hanger-on of the founders of the Aesthetic Movement such as Whistler, had made his lecture tour in the United States, and had reaped enormous publicity for ideas which were not originally his own. These were added to the stock that Americans had inherited from Ruskin and Morris. They did not find prophets of their own until the appearance of Frank Lloyd Wright.

It is customary for students of American craft to divide the country into three schools — the East, Chicago and the Midwest, and California. The craft movement of the eastern states was the most eclectic of the three. The city of New York itself was chiefly important for Louis Comfort Tiffany and his studio, but this is such a special case that it is better dealt with on its own. Tiffany was preceded, in certain of his enterprises, by Christian Herter, whose firm, known as Herter Brothers, made an extremely refined variant of the art furniture designed in England by men such as Godwin and E.J. Talbert. But since Herter, though of German origin, had trained in France, his furniture of the late 1870s and early 1880s sometimes seems to foreshadow the French Art Deco of the 1920s. It is a luxury product, made especially to appeal to rich people.

Boston and Rhode Island had flourishing crafts associations — the Boston Arts and Crafts Society was founded in 1897. *Handicraft* magazine began to be published from Boston in 1902, ceasing publication in 1904 and being revived in 1910. There were good craft silversmiths in and around Boston. One of the best known was Elizabeth E. Copeland. Providence, Rhode Island, had an Art Workers' Guild by the mid-1880s, named after the famous English enterprise. This was followed by the foundation of a Handicraft Club. Providence was also the base of the Gorham Manufacturing Company, a highly successful firm of commercial silversmiths, who are said to have been the first silver manufacturers in America to use mass-production methods. They were so impressed by the success of the craft movement after the turn of the century that they started using imitation handicraft techniques. One line, related both to French Art Nouveau and to Liberty Cymric silver, was christened Martelé, because of its hammered finish.

Not unexpectedly, since Californian society was itself so new, the leading craft personalities in California mostly came from elsewhere. Perhaps the most important were two brothers who worked as architects, Charles Sumner Greene and Henry Mather Greene. They were born near Cincinnati, raised in St Louis, and trained at the Massachusetts Institute of Technology and with various architectural firms in Boston. They then went to Pasadena to set up their practice. Their mature work mixes Japanese influence with elements taken from the traditional American shingle style. The hightide of their joint career was very brief — from 1907 to 1909 — but during this period they designed and also fitted out some

notable houses. The furniture they supplied is as deliberately luxurious as that made by the Herter Brothers earlier — the basic material is walnut, and there are inlays of ebony, ivory and semi-precious stones, inspired by Japanese originals but not copying them. Similarly luxurious furniture was sometimes supplied, through their Furniture Shop in San Francisco by Lucia and Arthur F. Mathews, professional painters who were also interior decorators. The scale of the enterprise — there was much work to be done in the city after the 1906 fire and earthquake — is suggested by the fact that it at one time gave employment to about fifty workmen. Here as with the Greenes, and with Herter Brothers in New York, craft provided a basis for conspicuous consumption.

It was, however, the Midwest where the American craft movement seems to have flourished most vigorously, in part through its association with the Prairie School of Architecture. Connections between Chicago and the English Arts and Crafts Movement were both direct and numerous. Walter Crane, closely associated with Morris, lectured at the Art Institute, which became a focus for the whole craft movement, with annual craft exhibitions from 1902 to 1921. Ashbee came to Chicago twice, in 1896 and 1901. Morris fabrics, wallpaper and furniture were imported by the famous department store Marshall Field, and there was even a William Morris Society, founded in 1903. There were numerous craft workshops and salerooms, a number of them grouped together in the Fine Arts Building on South Michigan Avenue.

Above left:
Charles and Henry Greene, detail of panelling, Gamble House, Pasadena, California, 1908

Above:
Herter Brothers, ebonized wardrobe in maple, cherry and cedar, 1880. New York, Metropolitan Museum of Art

Frank Lloyd Wright, print table in stained white oak. New York, Metropolitan Museum of Art, Emily C. Chadbourne Bequest, 1903

In Chicago, as in Cincinnati, fashionable women were eager to involve themselves with craft. One such was the silversmith Frances M. Glessner, who turned the conservatory at her house on Prairie Avenue into her private workshop. She studied, as did a number of other such women, at Hull House, Chicago.

The greatest of the Prairie School of architects associated with Chicago and the surrounding region was Frank Lloyd Wright. The houses he built in his first period, up to his departure for Europe in 1909, combine Arts and Crafts influences with Japanese ones. Often these pointed in the same direction. 'Bring out the nature of your materials,' Wright wrote, 'let this nature intimately into your scheme. Strip the wood of varnish and let it alone. Stain it.'

Wright built in much of the furniture in his houses, but he also designed free-standing pieces — chairs and tables, usually in oak — and decorative objects such as copper lamps, urns and vases. All of these were in a version of what was by now standard Arts and Crafts idiom, and the metalwork in particular seemed to lay stress on the whole process of handmaking (inevitable, in fact, since each piece was designed specifically for a given interior). The furniture has been described as being 'architectural sculpture rather than merely utilitarian objects — part of a larger sculptural whole. As such, the furniture can take on symbolic significance that a decorative object does not usually convey.'

Yet Wright, though he admired Morris, regarded him as wrong-headed, and said so in a famous lecture delivered at Hull House in 1901 — 'The Art and Craft of the Machine'. In this he took a sorrowful farewell of Morris's doctrines: 'That he miscalculated the machine does not matter. He did sublime work for it when he pleaded so well for the process of elimination its abuse had made necessary; when he fought the innate vulgarity of theocratic impulse in art as opposed to democratic, and when he preached the gospel of simplicity.' 'The machine is here to stay', Wright declared upon the same occasion. 'It is the forerunner of the democracy that is our dearest hope.' The craft movement was here being served notice that it must modify some of its most cherished tenets or be discarded by the new architecture with which it had seemed to make such a fruitful alliance.

What are perhaps the most interesting aspects of the American Arts and Crafts movement in its heyday have not yet been touched on in this brief survey. They lie at opposite ends of the social and economic spectrum. They are the work of Louis C. Tiffany on the one hand, and of Gustav Stickley and the Roycrofters on the other. Tiffany never pretended to be anything other than a maker of luxury items. Like other craftsmen of the period, he began his career as a fine artist, studying painting under George Inness, and exhibiting at the Philadelphia Centennial Exhibition of 1876. But it was also in 1876 that he made his first stained-glass window, thus

Below left:
Louis Comfort Tiffany, silver-mounted 'Magnolia' vase. New York, Metropolitan Museum of Art

Below:
Louis Comfort Tiffany, Jack-in-the-pulpit vase, *c.* 1906–12. St Louis Art Museum, Gift of Miss G. Spalding

straying into an area closely associated with William Morris and with the Arts and Crafts Movement in general. Though some of Tiffany's glass was ecclesiastical, the vast majority of his designs were purely secular. Before 1890 many were abstract or near-abstract. Tiffany was also anxious to keep to the essential nature of his medium:

> By the aid of studies in chemistry and through years of experiments, I have found means to avoid the use of paints, etching or burning, or otherwise treating the surface of the glass so that now it is possible to produce figures in glass of which even the flesh tones are not superficially treated — built up of what I call 'genuine glass' because there are no tricks of the glassmaker needed to express flesh.

Tiffany soon became a well-known decorator, redoing some of the rooms at the White House in Washington, and creating much admired interiors for the H.O. Havemeyers, New York's most famous collectors of Impressionist paintings. By 1902, when, after several previous changes of name, his firm became known as Tiffany Studios, he was the head of a large and prosperous commercial enterprise, employing many workmen and turning out a large range of decorative objects. Glass, however, remained his first love, and Tiffany made not only stained-glass windows, but lampshades and lamps in stained-glass technique and a vast array of decorative glass vases. In 1880 he filed a patent for making the decorative iridescent glass which was to be especially associated with his name. He later gave it the name *Favrile*, from the obsolete English word fabrile meaning 'made by hand'.

The vases Tiffany made — or which, to speak more accurately, were made under his supervision and control by the immensely skilful artisans he discovered — were, like his stained-glass windows, based on the very nature of the material itself. The ornamental motifs were an integral part of each piece, not applied to the surface. Though Tiffany looked everywhere for inspiration — to ancient Greek and Roman glass, to Venice and Nailsea and even to early nineteenth-century Bohemia — what struck contemporary critics was an essential simplicity and naturalness. A critic of our own day, Mario Amaya, in his book on Tiffany glass remarks, apropos of this air of spontaneity, that 'it may not be too farfetched to see in Tiffany's *Favrile* glass the seeds of American abstract-expressionist painting which was to become so fashionable half a century later, about the same time that Tiffany glass underwent a revival of interest.'

To my mind there is more to it than this. With Tiffany glass craftwork broke free of any ties with utilitarian purpose, and staked a claim to be looked at and thought about in the same way as a painting or a piece of sculpture. Stained glass, that halfway house between the fine arts and the crafts, provided a logical stepping stone from one to another. The second important thing about Tiffany's products was the stress which was put on the importance

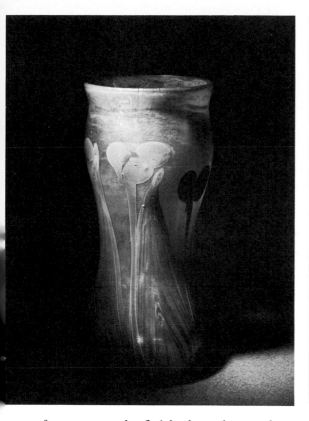

of process — the finished result was always, as much as anything, a statement about technique.

Gustav Stickley and the Roycrofters are important in a different way — not so much for the achievements, as for the attitudes they expressed. It was natural that the community spirit which showed itself so naturally in some of the early nineteenth-century folk crafts should be revived when the Arts and Crafts Movement began to exert its influence. Some of the new craft workers banded together in settlements, such as the Rose Valley community founded in 1901 by the architect William L. Price, in a group of abandoned mill buildings, fourteen miles southwest of Philadelphia. This group was not unlike Ashbee's Guild of Handicraft in its Chipping Campden phase, and it suffered the same fate at more or less the same moment, going bankrupt in 1909. Before that there had been pottery and furniture workshops, as well as a private press.

The Roycroft community at East Aurora, New York, was more successful and much longer-lived — from the mid-1890s to 1938. Its founder and presiding genius was Elbert Hubbard, who drowned in the *Lusitania* in 1915. He began his career as a soap salesman. In 1894, having just sold his partnership in the Larkin Soap Company, he visited England, went to see the Kelmscott Press, and fell under William Morris's spell. He set up his own press in East Aurora on his return, and this led to the creation of a bindery, and this in turn to a shop where other kinds of handcrafted leather were made — table mats, purses and wallets. In 1901 the

Above left:
Louis Comfort Tiffany, *Favrile* glass vase, *c.* 1896. London, Victoria and Albert Museum

Above:
Louis Comfort Tiffany, iridescent *Favrile* glass vase with peacock's feather design, *c.* 1895. New York, Metropolitan Museum of Art, Gift of H.O. Havemeyer 1896

Roycroft Shops began to offer simple, Morris-inspired furniture to their customers. An apprentice system was set up; there were lectures, concerts and organized sports.

The furniture made in the workshops of the Roycroft Community has a close resemblance in its rather clumsy heaviness and plainness to that produced under the auspices of Gustav Stickley. Stickley was brought up in the furniture trade, unlike Hubbard; but he resembled Hubbard in suffering a change of heart after visiting England and meeting leaders of the Arts and Crafts Movement there. At first he remained within the framework of commercial American furniture manufacturing, showing a line of simple massive furniture with some Art Nouveau influence at the 1900 furniture show in Grand Rapids. The style caught on, and Stickley began to emphasize the trade name he had chosen, which was Craftsman, and to develop the actual organization of his business in a new way. In his workshops at Syracuse, New York, he introduced a semi-cooperative scheme, but it proved to be unsuccessful and was dropped after only three years. A little later he tried again, buying land near Morris Plains, New Jersey, where he planned to build up a model farm and small family community. But this too did not prosper. On the other hand, the Stickley business empire continued to flourish. Craftsman furniture became popular throughout the United States, and there were franchises as far apart as Boston and Los Angeles. It was not until 1915, when the tide was beginning to set strongly against the aesthetic Stickley promoted, that he overstretched his resources completely and collapsed into bankruptcy.

Gustav Stickley, couch in oak and leather, *c.* 1909. Courtesy of the Art Institute of Chicago

Stickley's chief instrument of propaganda, both for his own products and for the crafts ethos in general, was a magazine called *The Craftsman* which he founded. The first issue appeared in October 1901, and was devoted to William Morris. But *The Craftsman* rapidly widened its scope — it covered everything and

Gustav Stickley,
oak furniture,
1902–13.
The copper
candlesticks are by
the Roycrofters

The Craftsman
workshop
illustrated in *The
Craftsman*
magazine

anything — art, architecture, poetry, drama, politics, economics, history, gardening, city planning and education. It printed stories by Tolstoy and Gorky; poems by Robert Frost and Carl Sandburg, and offered practical instruction in weaving, coppersmithing, furniture construction and leatherwork. It tackled the subject of women's liberation — one article was entitled 'Is There Sex Distinction in Art? The Attitude of the Critic Towards Women's Exhibits'. It also promoted an interest in the crafts produced by ethnic minorities within America, especially those of the American Indian. Though its circulation never rose very much above 20,000, *The Craftsman* tackled nearly all the issues which a craft-oriented public today might consider interesting and important.

Stickley made many contributions to his own magazine. One of them, entitled 'The Use and Abuse of Machinery, and its Relation to the Arts and Crafts', is a trumpet call for the birth of a national art in the United States. 'But like all art', Stickley warns:

it must spring in the first place from the common needs of the common people ... Merely to make things by hand implies no advance in the development of an art that shall make its own place in world-history as a true record of the thought and life of this age, any more than the making of them after 'original designs' implies that these designs are the outgrowth of thought based upon that need which is the root of inspiration to the true craftsman, as well as upon his personal desire for self-expression. Fine words indeed, but somehow the popular wing of the

American craft movement, to which both Gustav Stickley and Elbert Hubbard belonged, failed to live up to them.

Tiffany was the unrepentant aristocrat of the American crafts, and his attitudes are reflected today in the work of numerous American craftsmen who work chiefly for a collectors' market. The only important difference is that there are now no workshops on the scale of Tiffany Studios, and if such workshops existed they would for various reasons be considered suspect — a topic I shall look at later.

Stickley and Hubbard claimed to be the servants of a far more inclusive philosophy. To do them justice, they indeed saw themselves in this role — they played it without irony, and took their considerable applause without uneasiness. But it was playacting all the same. The craft movement, despite its rapid and widespread popularity, never succeeded in altering or deflecting the mechanisms which governed the economic and social development of America. Even its work for women lay dormant until it was revived in the 1970s. At the very instant when the Arts and Crafts were nearest to winning mass acclaim — that is, during the first decade of the present century — the modern industrial assembly line was about to come into being. The example of the Cincinnati meat-packers had been taken up by the motor manufacturer Henry Ford, who had a fully developed assembly line in operation in his Highland Park plant in 1915.

Craft, as Stickley and the Roycrofters purveyed it, did not finally affect the way people lived, but only the way in which they wanted to see themselves. And soon enough they wanted to see themselves quite differently, and craft fell out of fashion. Ironically enough, one of the chief enemies of the sort of design Stickley and his immediate rivals purveyed was the motor-car which Henry Ford turned from an exotic luxury to something which was within almost everybody's reach. The heavy, rooted solidity of Stickley's artefacts, particularly his furniture, came to seem impossibly clumsy and out of tune with the needs of the society which mechanization had produced.

Yet Stickley did, nevertheless, leave an enduring legacy behind him. Though his furniture reflected a philosophy which was eventually abandoned, he never entirely sundered himself from the Grand Rapids way of thinking. His furniture was factory furniture, designed to be manufactured on a large scale. His methods of handling wood with industrial simplicity lived on, survived the war years, and re-emerged in the basic wood furniture — parsons tables and butcher-block tables — being retailed successfully at the present day.

13 Art Nouveau and Jugendstil

Though rooted in Britain, the Arts and Crafts Movement and the Aesthetic Movement (themselves simultaneously allies and rivals) had an effect in Europe as well as in America. The precise nature of that effect is, however, difficult to define; and the matter becomes still more difficult when one considers the question, not merely of style, but of the actual circumstances in which household objects were produced.

One direct link between the English Arts and Crafts has already been noted — the invitation to the Guild of Handicraft to provide furnishings for the Grand Duke of Hesse's new palace in Darmstadt. There was another link as well — between the architect Charles Rennie Mackintosh and his associates and the Vienna Secession. But its precise nature is admittedly obscure.

Mackintosh is now universally recognized as the most original British architect of his time, and also as the only important British exponent of Art Nouveau. He had three close associates — his wife Margaret Macdonald, her sister Frances, and Herbert McNair, who became Frances's husband. They made their first impact

Charles Rennie Mackintosh, reception and music-room, from the house designed for the *Zeitschrift für Innendekoration*, 1901, Glasgow School of Art

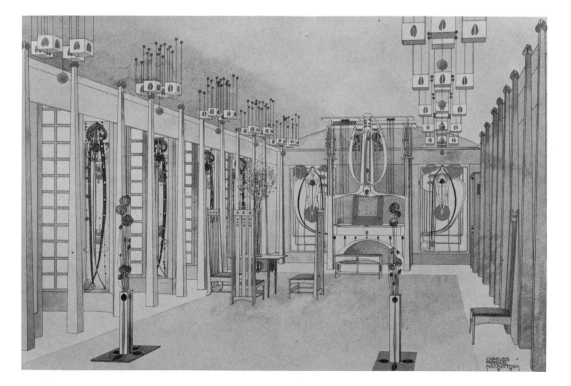

outside London when they showed at the Arts and Crafts Exhibition Society's Exhibition, held in London in 1896. There what they produced must in many ways have seemed typical of the products of the more 'literary' wing of the movement. For example, Mackintosh himself showed a panel in beaten brass with the legend 'Art and Literature seeking Inspiration at the Tree of Knowledge and Beauty'. But on the whole the Scottish contribution to the show was not well received, and this did much to isolate Mackintosh and his colleagues from what was going on in England.

In the years immediately following, Mackintosh carried out a series of important decorative commissions in Glasgow, the majority for the tea-rooms owned by his chief patron Miss Cranston. He also took second prize, in a competition sponsored by Alexander Koch, an art-promoter in Darmstadt, for a design for a house for an imaginary art-patron. This design was duly published in the *Zeitschrift für Innendekoration*, and made Mackintosh's name and personal style known to the people interested in such matters in Germany. Just previous to this publication he and his group had exhibited with the Vienna Secession. They also showed in Venice, Turin, Budapest and Dresden, always very successfully.

The furniture Mackintosh exhibited on these occasions was very

Charles Rennie Mackintosh, furniture for the 'Rose Boudoir', 1902, with typical high-backed chairs. University of Glasgow, Hunterian Art Gallery

much the sort of thing he had devised for the tea-room interiors, and also for the various domestic commissions he was working on at the same time. The metalwork and other decorative accessories were in the personal variant of Arts and Crafts style devised by him and carried out by other members of the group. Jessie Newbery, an associate but not actually one of the so-called 'Glasgow Four', summed up their aims when she said: 'I believe in everything being beautiful, pleasant, and if need be, useful. To descend to particulars, I like the opposition of straight lines to curved, of horizontal to vertical; of purple to green, of green to blue. I delight in correspondence and the inevitable relationship of part to part.' Mackintosh's furniture usually has a marked verticality. His most typical chairs have exaggeratedly high backs. Unusual features were the use of stained-glass inserts for ornament, and the contrast of very dark or very light colours — pieces stained black or enamelled white.

Though extremely, even wilfully original in design, these Mackintosh pieces are not examples of fine craftsmanship, for example, it has proved possible for an Italian manufacturer of the present time to copy some of them, and re-issue them in series. Nor, despite

Charles Rennie Mackintosh, The Willow Tea Rooms, Glasgow

their severe forms, are these pieces recognizably 'functional'. The chairs, indeed, are notoriously uncomfortable to sit in. Their real purpose was to articulate the spaces Mackintosh designed, and make them eloquent, and in this sense they are typical architect's furniture, close in spirit to the at first sight very different designs produced in the eighteenth century by William Kent.

The Viennese Secessionists were sufficiently impressed by the English Arts and Crafts Movement as a whole to set up the Wiener Werkstätte in 1903, under the leadership of two of their number, Josef Hoffmann and Koloman Moser. Hoffmann, a leading architect, had also, by the time the workshops were founded, had a

Above left:
Koloman Moser, silver vase set with lapis-lazuli and silver sugar bowl. Vienna, Österreichisches Museum für Angewandte Kunst

Above:
Josef Hoffmann, tea set. Vienna, Österreichisches Museum für Angewandte Kunst

Josef Hoffmann, bentwood armchair. Courtesy of the Art Institute of Chicago

good deal of experience as a book-illustrator, especially for the periodical *Ver Sacrum*, which was the organ of the Secession Movement in Vienna. The squares and straight lines he experimented with look back to the Austrian Neoclassical tradition on the one hand, and forward to the Functionalism of the twenties on the other. The interiors designed by the Viennese architect Adolf Loos were similarly prophetic of twenties' taste with their cubic forms and smooth, undecorated surfaces. Essentially, however, the Viennese designers, most of them architects, who were associated with the Secession catered to a thoroughly aristocratic appetite for luxury, though this was expressed in more restrained form than elsewhere. Nothing, for example, could be more essentially luxurious than the furniture and decorations devised by Hoffmann for the Palais Stoclet in Brussels. Joseph Maria Olbrich's furniture for the new music room in the Palace in Darmstadt combines maplewood, brass and various inlays in a way that seems a distant echo of the French Empire style and certainly springs from the same cabinet-making tradition.

The link between Mackintosh and his Continental admirers was therefore not so much a question of stylistic similarities as one of similarity of attitude — certain Arts and Crafts ideas applied within the broad discipline of a new approach to architecture. Perhaps

Adolf Loos, Café Museum, Vienna, 1899. Note the use of Thonet bentwood chairs

inevitably, the thing which did not have much impact on the Continent was the vague and somewhat sentimental idealism of many of Ruskin's most vocal English followers. Instead, new approaches to design often owed a good deal to the irritable nationalism of the period following the Franco-Prussian War of 1870. In France, Art Nouveau was a re-assertion of long-standing French supremacy in matters of novelty and luxury — it was no accident that Nancy, close to the German frontier, was one of the places where the style flourished most luxuriantly. German Jugendstil, developing increasingly close links with industry in the decade before the First World War, was, amongst other things, an instrument of commercial superiority. Like the naval arms race with Britain, it asserted Germany's determination to overtake the older-established industrial nations, and to beat them at their own game by producing better and more efficient products in greater quantity. Without the machine, the Kaiser's new empire could never triumph. The difference between French Art Nouveau and Jugendstil was not one of stylistic nuance, but of fundamental attitude, and both movements involved radical modification of the theories put forward by the rival camps in Britain — moralists on the one hand and supporters of art-for-art's sake on the other.

French and Belgian Art Nouveau certainly did owe something important to the English Aesthetic Movement. But it also had debts elsewhere. One was to the great Symbolist Movement which revivified both European literature and the European visual arts from about 1885 onwards. The other was to the strong taste for Naturalism — direct dependence on forms discovered in nature — which crops up throughout the history of nineteenth-century design. The inscriptions Mackintosh and his colleagues put on

Josef Hoffmann, design for the kitchen, Palais Stoclet, Brussels

decorative objects, with the aim of creating a specific mood, had
plenty of precedent in Britain, from the time of the great 1851
Exhibition onwards. The habit soon spread to France and Germany, and the pioneering Art Nouveau designers did not disdain it.
In 1889, Emile Gallé, the pioneer designer of the School of Nancy,
exhibited a glass vase with floral decoration and bearing a line from
Verlaine: 'Je récolte en secret les fleurs mystérieuses'. (In secret, I
glean mysterious flowers.) But an object did not have to be
inscribed to be symbolic. One of the claims made by Art Nouveau
designers was that the decorative arts were on a par with the fine
arts, in the sense that they had just as much power over the
spectator's ideas and feelings. They constantly claimed a place for
the applied arts side by side with fine art in the official Salons of the
time.

Where French Art Nouveau was concerned, the urge towards
luxury and novelty was always predominant, and this was one
reason why the claim was taken seriously — people were impressed
that so much thought and work and feeling had gone to produce
objects which were obviously unique of their kind. Yet it can also
be argued that the best Art Nouveau furniture, and other Art
Nouveau objects as well, have strong links to a tradition of luxury

craftsmanship which had existed continuously in France since the mid-seventeenth century, and which indeed was to survive until the Second World War or even longer. They were the product of small specialist workshops akin to the sewing and cutting rooms of the *haute couture*.

Like *haute couture*, Art Nouveau furniture was often an extraordinary mixture of both daringly novel and absolutely traditional elements. Looked at from one angle, it was an attempt to revive the Rococo of the Louis XV period in a new dress. For different types of furniture, it also referred to relevant historical precedents — for desks to Louis XV, but for chairs to Louis XVI and for large cupboards to the Renaissance. Forms were daringly remoulded, but seldom invented entirely afresh. Where the Art Nouveau designers moved away from traditional procedures they also moved away from the emphasis on structure, which now seems the most 'modern' thing about the Arts and Crafts. Louis Majorelle, perhaps the most original of the Nancy School furniture-makers, modelled some of his most important furniture in clay, thus forcing a comparison with sculpture. Yet some leading designers mistrusted this restless plasticity and lack of obvious construction, even when they surrendered to it. In 1906, quite late in the development of Art Nouveau, the Paris designer Eugène Gaillard said that furniture ought to obey five main rules:

1. A piece of furniture shall as far as possible express its function.
2. Respect for the nature of the material.
3. No unnecessary constructive elements.
4. In wood an arch is only to be regarded as a decorative element.
5. The ornament should be abstract.

The uneasy Arts and Crafts conscience can here be found re-exerting itself.

The true dilemma of the Art Nouveau craftsman can be more easily understood by looking at Gallé's career, not as a furniture-maker, which in fact he was, but as a designer of glass. It follows a strange, but not very reassuring trajectory.

Gallé was born in 1846, the only son of a producer of luxury goods. In 1865 he started designing crystal-ware for his father's factory, and in 1867 he established a workshop for decorating glass. In 1874 he went into partnership with his father, making glass on a regular basis, and at the Paris Exhibition of 1878 he scored a big success with his products. There were further successes at the Exhibitions of 1884 and 1889, when the Musée des Arts Décoratifs bought a large group of work. During this period, Gallé shows two characteristics — a systematic search through all periods of glass-making history for ideas which might be useful to himself, and an ever-increasing technical sophistication. By 1889, his search had led him to the newly-fashionable Japanese style. Nature was his source (he was also a skilled gardener); and his products were subtle individual masterpieces. His aim, he said at this time, was that his glass should 'adoucir les hommes'.

Gallé's tremendous success at the 1889 Exhibition came just at the right time to make him one of the leaders of the Art Nouveau style. He was a good businessman, and had already started to expand. By 1884 he was taking pupils; in 1889 he set up a decorators' studio. Moulds were now made for the use of the glassblowers he employed; designs for decoration were worked out beforehand in watercolour, not worked directly in the glass itself. Gallé became the head of a large organization. He still showed remarkable inventive powers — inventing new colours, trying new technical tricks, such as adding semi-precious stones or sea-shells to the basic glass. But a gap opened between the few, increasingly elaborate masterpieces, with which he concerned himself directly, and the standard Gallé product. Exact repetition is very rare in Gallé vases. Designs and shapes are combined and recombined to

Far left:
Emile Gallé, glass vase with silver mounts by Bonvallet, inscribed 'We shall win, God is leading us'. Exhibited at the Paris Exhibition, 1900. Paris, Musée des Arts Décoratifs

Left:
Maurice Marinot, vase in acid-engraved glass, c. 1920. Paris, Musée des Arts Décoratifs

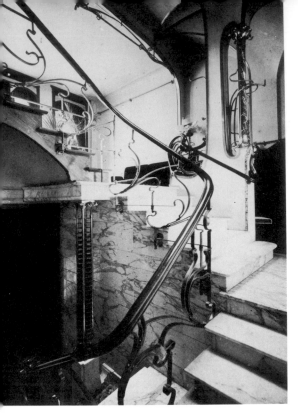

produce something which can be called 'unique'. The effect —
decoration of one colour on a white ground — is nevertheless
repetitive. Gallé paid the price of expansion by losing artistic
quality, and became a durable financial success as a result.

It was perhaps in part a determination not to fall into the same
trap which shaped the career of Maurice Marinot, the greatest
French maker of art-glass of the next generation. Marinot began as
a painter — he was one of the Fauves and, between 1905 and 1914,
exhibited regularly as a fine artist at the Salon d'Automne and the
Salon des Indépendants. His interest in glass did not start till 1911,
and he then painfully acquired the basic elements of the craft. 'Tout
ce que j'ai fait, j'ai fait difficilement', he was to say afterwards. The
style he developed was quite different from Gallé's. From designing
and directing the work of other glass-makers with greater technical
knowledge than himself, Marinot moved towards direct handling of
the material, making massive sculptural pieces, working either
alone or with one assistant to help with the heaviest work. 'C'est
chaque fois une belle bataille, un plaisir profond dans l'effort
physique.'

Each of Marinot's products therefore bears his own completely
personal stamp — the idea it incorporates is never separable from
its actual execution. Each is purely and simply an object for
contemplation, as much as a painting or a sculpture. But his
restricted production was allied to restricted influence. Marinot was
immensely admired, but, unlike Gallé, seldom copied. The price,
in terms of dedication, was too high.

Belgian Art Nouveau, far more than French, was under the

influence of architects, chief among them Victor Horta. The artistic climate in Belgium in the late nineteenth century was restless and daring. The exhibition society called *Les XX* provided a focus for avant-garde art, usually Symbolist in tendency, from all over Europe. At the same time the wealth pouring in from King Leopold II's private fief, the great colony in the Congo, was creating a new and adventurous plutocracy, while Belgium itself had risen to prominence as an industrial power. It seemed almost as if the great days of the late medieval Valois Dukes of Burgundy had returned in a different guise to the territories they had once ruled.

Horta's town houses, a number of which still survive in Brussels, including the pair at 22–23 rue Américaine which he constructed for himself, show very clearly the nature of his genius. His manipulation of interior space is extremely free and daring, and he constructs with industrial materials, that is to say, he uses iron and glass even when the setting is frankly domestic, as well as using them freely in public buildings. Like the other leading architects of his time, he created furniture and fittings for the houses he designed, and these, spare but dynamic, are fully in tune with the setting he provided. They are not, however, industrial objects.

A more important figure from the point of view of the relationship between craft and industry was Henry van de Velde. His influence was exercised less decisively in Belgium than in Germany. Born in 1863, he first of all studied painting, first at Antwerp, then in Paris, before returning to Belgium and participating in the activities of *Les XX*. From 1893, under the influence of William Morris, he began to devote himself to the decorative arts. This led him eventually to architecture.

Richard Riemerschmid, oak chair, 1900. London, Victoria and Albert Museum

Van de Velde's first significant venture was the house he designed for himself at Uccle near Brussels. This and its contents were conceived as a whole, and exemplified the theories Van de Velde had now formulated and put into print. Domestic objects, he thought, should be made in such a way that the process of fabrication remained 'proudly and frankly' visible in the finished result. Ornament must be original, not historical, and the materials must be logically used. He had as yet not reached the point, as he later admitted, where he could consider the possibility of 'form without ornament'. Nevertheless both his theories and what he designed were sufficiently new to attract attention in both France and Germany. He furnished four rooms for the Maison de l'Art Nouveau, the revolutionary shop which Samuel Bing was opening in Paris (it was of course this shop which gave its name to the whole Art Nouveau movement). He showed work at the exhibition of applied arts held in Dresden in 1897. Most important of all, he attracted the attention of Julius Meier-Graefe, an entrepreneur, editor and art-historian who was influential both in Paris and in Berlin. In 1900–1 Van de Velde went on a lecture tour in Germany. He became an advisor to the Grand-Duke of Saxe-Weimar, and in 1906 directed the foundation and construction of the Weimar

Kunstgewerbeschule. Here he pioneered a new teaching method, which did not rely on the imitation of former styles. The new forms which resulted were eagerly seized upon by German industry. Though Van de Velde did not always get his own way in Weimar, and had many difficulties to contend with, his experiments there represented a significant change in the relationship between the creative designer and industry.

Long before this, his ideas rather than his actual practice had been a stimulus to German designers. In 1897 two important craft workshops were founded, one in Munich and one in Dresden. Both took as their platform the search for a national art — Germany had after all only been united after the war of 1870 — but one which rejected stylistic imitation and depended on a close collaboration between artist and artisan. Though a kind of Art Nouveau flourished briefly in Germany under the name Jugendstil (taken from the periodical *Jugend*, founded in 1896), it was very restrained compared to the French version of the style. After the turn of the century the decorative arts developed very rapidly, in the hands of men such as Richard Riemerschmid, Bernhard Pankock and Peter Behrens, towards a kind of proto-modernism. A chair designed by Riemerschmid, even one created as early as 1900, might easily be taken for the work of one of the leading Scandinavian designers of the 1930s.

Peter Behrens, electric kettles designed for AEG

In 1907, a decisive step was taken towards bringing the new designers and German industry together. This was the foundation of the Werkbund. The man who sponsored the organization was Hermann Muthesius, the German architect who was the admirer and apostle of 'matter-of-factness' in industrial architecture. Among the members were Behrens, Riemerschmid, Olbrich and Hoffmann. In the same year Behrens was appointed design consultant by one of the most important industrial concerns in Germany, AEG (the German General Electrical Company). His brief was not only to design items of electrical equipment (cookers, radiators, lamps), but also to design packaging, posters, catalogues and leaflets, and even the shops in which the goods were sold and the factories in which they were made. The conjunction of events is significant because the Werkbund, while still inspired by the more positive aspects of William Morris's doctrines, was resolved to come to terms with the machine. For the members of the Werkbund the machine was not something apart, but an extension of the hand tool. It was necessary to use it in such a way that goods could be produced in large quantities, but also so that there was no loss of quality. It was felt that only in this way could the new Germany hope to catch up with her longer-established competitors.

The organization did not reach this position without prolonged internal struggles. At the annual meeting of the Werkbund held in 1914, Muthesius came out as an advocate of standardization not only in the interests of quality but also of perfection of form. He was opposed by Henry van de Velde, who believed that a rigid

Peter Behrens,
set of drinking
glasses. Cologne,
Kunstgewerbe-
museum

discipline of this type would kill the individuality of the artist. In fact, travelling by the route of practicality, the advocates of the new industrial design had arrived, by 1914, at a position which was close to that taken up by leading Neoclassicists at the very start of the Industrial Revolution. Once more, it seemed logical and necessary to evolve the authoritative type-object. The development is perhaps less surprising if one considers where it took place — in Central Europe, where Biedermeier taste had never quite died out. In fact, if one takes a second and more thoughtful look at some of the more radical designs evolved by Riemerschmid and even Behrens, one sees in them not merely a foreshadowing of the Scandinavian products of the thirties, but a far from distant echo of what Austrian and German craftsmen had been producing, in the name of good sense, practicality and comfort, in the second quarter of the nineteenth century.

Peter Behrens,
electric fans
designed for AEG

14 Art Deco versus the Bauhaus

The contrast between French Art Deco and the new Functionalism sponsored by the Bauhaus in Germany, during the fifteen years or so that followed the Armistice of 1918, is at first sight very similar to that between Art Nouveau and the products of the designers associated with the Deutscher Werkbund. Indeed, the coincidence of dates is more precise, since French Art Nouveau was already past its peak by 1907, when the Werkbund was founded; and the difference is more clear-cut and startling.

The relationship between Art Nouveau and Art Deco is very much that between the Rococo of Louis XV and the classicism of Louis XVI in the France of the eighteenth century. Art Deco was, even more than its predecessor, a luxury style, addressing itself to a small elite. Its chief patrons were people very much involved with the idea of fashionability — fashionable actresses, the leading Parisian *couturiers* and *couturières*. Later, in the 1930s, it became an 'official' style — the one favoured for important public commissions, such as the interiors of the new liner *Normandie*, launched in 1935, and meant to be representative of the very best in French craftsmanship.

In the Art Deco domestic interior the emphasis was on exotic materials, handled with great suavity. Cabinet-makers such as Emile-Jacques Ruhlmann, Maurice Dufrêne and Süe et Mare favoured exotic woods — amboyna, amaranth, thuya, palissander, ebony and lemonwood. Ivory and shagreen were used for trimming. The workshops which produced such furniture were organized along exactly the same lines as those directed by Riesener and

Opposite page:
Carl Malmsten,
drawing-room
designed for the
Swedish royal
residence of
Ulriksdal, 1923

Süe et Mare,
ebony commode
with marquetry
doors, *c.* 1925.
Private Collection

Jean Dunand,
copper vase inlaid
with bronzed and
patinated iron,
c. 1914. Paris,
Musée des Arts
Décoratifs

Weisweiler at the end of the eighteenth century, save that the
distinction between chairmakers and cabinet-makers had long since
broken down.

It is of course also true that some of the great Paris department
stores launched a more popular version of Deco. Paul Follot, with
Laurent Mauclès, became director of the special department called
'Pomone' at Bon Marché in 1923; and Maurice Dufrêne presided
over 'La Maîtrise' at Galeries Lafayette. These departments were
backed by workshops which made furniture in small series, rather
than directly to commission. The workshops were manned by
artisans equipped with a broad range of traditional cabinet-maker's
skills. There was no question of factory production.

A number of independent artist-craftsmen were associated with
the Art Deco ethos, but they were surprisingly few in number. One
was the glass-maker, Maurice Marinot, already mentioned.
Another was the potter Emile Decoeur, heavily influenced by the
newly fashionable Chinese monochrome wares, and as fastidious as
Marinot about what left his workshop. Most of the big specialist
names were, however, the heads of busy workshops, or even of
actual factories, rather than men who worked on their own. Jean
Dunand produced metal vases, and later a range of objects in
lacquer, often working in collaboration with the leading Art Deco
cabinet-makers, and employing up to a hundred workers, including
specially trained artisans imported from French Indo-China, in
order to fulfil the commissions he was offered. René Lalique, once
the most spectacular and original of Art Nouveau jewellers, turned
to glass, and in 1918 acquired a factory at Wingen-sur-Moder near
the German border, where he turned out moulded glass bowls and
other objects which now seem the very essence of Art Deco taste.
Most of his products came from the power-press. Only a very few
especially ambitious and elaborate items were made singly, cast,
like bronzes, by the *cire-perdue* process.

Edgar Brandt,
L'Oasis, iron-work
screen, 1925.
Private Collection

Emile-Jacques
Ruhlmann, group
of furniture

Below:
René Lalique,
moulded glass
vase, 1925.
Copenhagen,
Kunstindustri
Museum

Below right:
René Lalique,
L'Oiseau de Feu,
glass and bronze
lamp, 1920s

Art Deco, innovating within an essentially conservative system of workmanship, had room for old-established concerns such as the great National Manufacture at Sèvres, where a special studio for producing 'artistic' porcelain and faience was set up under Maurice Gensoli, while the standard factory product also began to show strong Deco influences. The most startlingly innovative Art Deco table-silver was created by Jean Puiforçat, designing for his family firm.

Very few French designers stood out against Art Deco's luxurious elitism. The most effective and impassioned opponent of the style was the architect Le Corbusier. His first major book, *Vers une architecture*, published in 1923, stressed the importance of the new 'machine aesthetic'. For him, far more than for the pre-war members of the Deutscher Werkbund, the standardization imposed by the machine was a good, not an evil, because it suggested the possibility of a logical architectural vocabulary. In 1925, Le

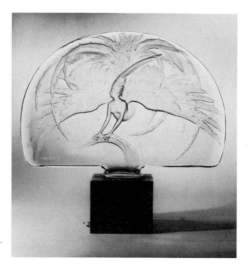

Corbusier put his ideas into practical form, with his Pavillon de l'Esprit Nouveau, which formed part of the Exposition des Arts Décoratifs held in Paris. It was this very exhibition which gave its name to the Art Deco style, and the contrast between the two philosophies, that of the young architect and that which animated the leading Deco designers, was starkly exposed. As he said at the time, Le Corbusier's intention was to show 'how, by virtue of ... standardization ... industry creates pure forms, and to stress the intrinsic value of the pure form of art that is the result.'

Le Corbusier was ready to fit some already existing furniture into his schemes — designs from the long-established Thonet range, which appealed to him not only because of their purity of outline but also because they were the result of typically industrial rather

Jean Puiforçat, silver tea service, 1925. Paris, Musée des Arts Décoratifs

Below left: Room with typical furniture by Bauhaus designers Walter Gropius and Marcel Breuer

than handicraft processes. His own designs for furniture were based on the use of steel tubes. These had already been used as materials for furniture by designers connected with the German Bauhaus. In one case, he used these tubes to make what he called a 'British officer's chair'. It was a version of nineteenth-century travelling furniture, simple, elegant and light. While Le Corbusier's version looked industrial, because of what it was made of, it was in fact quite complicated to manufacture. What one encounters here, in fact, is an example of handwork imitating the machine.

This was by no means an uncommon phenomenon, as the so-called 'machine aesthetic' began to take hold. Makers of expensive glass, for example, were tempted to imitate forms which had originally been evolved for use in the laboratory.

The place where the new relationship between art, craft and industry was being hammered out was not France, but Germany, where the Bauhaus had been set up in 1919. Significantly, its first home was at Weimar, where Henry van de Velde had taught. The aim of the Bauhaus was in large part to continue and supplement the work that the Deutscher Werkbund had done before the war, and the latter continued its work alongside the Bauhaus, holding a series of important exhibitions throughout the 1920s. It has sometimes been ignorantly suggested that the Bauhaus was always hostile to the crafts. This was not the case, as can be seen from the manifesto issued by its first director, Walter Gropius:

> Architects, sculptors, painters, we must all turn to the crafts. Art is not a 'profession', there is no essential difference between the artist and the craftsman. The artist is an exalted craftsman. In rare moments of inspiration, moments beyond the control of his

Below left:
Le Corbusier, Pavillon de l'Esprit Nouveau at the Exposition des Arts Décoratifs, Paris, 1925

Below:
'British officer's chair' by Le Corbusier, Pierre Jeanneret and Charlotte Perriand, 1928. Paris, Musée des Arts Décoratifs

William Staite Murray, *Persian Garden,* stoneware vase, *c.* 1929. York City Art Gallery, Milner-White Collection

Bernard Leach, porcelain jar, *c.* 1967. London, Victoria and Albert Museum

will, the grace of heaven may cause his work to blossom into art. But proficiency in his craft is essential to every artist. Therein lies a source of creative imagination.

Let us create a new guild of craftsmen, without the class distinctions which raise an arrogant barrier between craftsman and artist. Together let us conceive and create the new building of the future, which will embrace architecture and sculpture and painting in one unity and which will rise one day towards heaven from the hands of a million workers like the crystal symbol of a new faith.

In its early period the Bauhaus was effectively more craft-oriented than it afterwards became. There was a stained-glass workshop, which occupied men of the calibre of Paul Klee and Josef Albers, until it was incorporated into the mural workshop at the beginning of 1924. Tapestries were woven in the weaving workshop, some particularly distinguished ones being the work of Anni Albers. The windows and tapestries both responded to the new abstract idiom which the Bauhaus itself was pioneering in the art of the time, but this did not affect the fact that they were produced by means of traditional craft processes. In the pottery workshop the situation was different. From the first there was a division between design and execution. Essentially, the Bauhaus potters became, not craftsmen working on their own account, but makers of prototypes for industry. Bauhaus designs were made by a wide variety of different manufacturers, including the State Porcelain Factory in Berlin, founded in the eighteenth century.

This was also the case with Bauhaus designs for furniture, perhaps the most characteristic of its products. When we speak of the Bauhaus today, we probably think first of the famous series of tubular steel chairs, designed by architects such as Marcel Breuer and Mies van der Rohe, and many of them still in production. There was also a successful series of designs for electric table and hanging lamps, successors to those which Behrens had created for AEG before the war. Some of these too are still in production. Discussing the furniture he designed, Breuer said:

Metal furniture is part of a modern room. It is 'styleless', for it is not expected to express any particular styling beyond its purpose and the construction necessary thereto. The new living space should not be a self-portrait of the architect, nor should it immediately convey the individual personality of its occupant ...

All types are constructed from the same standardized, elementary parts which may be taken apart or exchanged at any time. This metal furniture is intended to be nothing but a necessary apparatus for contemporary life.

This, published in January 1928, shows how far Bauhaus philosophy concerning domestic artefacts had moved from their craft-based beginnings.

In a country such as England, where Functionalist philosophy made much less of an impact than it did in Weimar Germany, there

was considerable confusion about the proper role of the craftsman, how he was to be defined, and what he could or could not be expected to undertake. Even in the 1930s, England still preserved considerable remnants of Arts and Crafts philosophy. After all, many of the pioneers, such as C.R. Ashbee, were still very much alive. 'Studio pottery', as it was now called, deliberately stood apart from what commercial firms were producing, choosing instead to reflect rural values or to look for inspiration to the Far East. The two most important artist-potters of the period, Bernard Leach and William Staite Murray, were both heavily influenced by the Orient. Staite Murray thought of pottery as a branch of fine art, on a level with painting and sculpture. He often shared exhibitions with professional painters.

Bernard Leach looked to Japan, whereas Staite Murray looked on the whole to China. 1920 was the year in which Leach, after a long period of study in Japan, returned to England, bringing with him the Japanese potter Shoji Hamada. They set up a pottery in St Ives, where they experimented with pots in the English medieval tradi-

Bernard Leach at work

Marion Dorn,
Cyprus, furnishing
fabric, 1936.
London, Victoria
and Albert
Museum

tion as well as with Japanese techniques. St Ives henceforth became a centre of English craft activity. But the influence of Leach's pottery on commercial wares remained minimal, despite the success of his own enterprise and his growing prestige in the crafts' community. As a result of his travels and experiments, particularly in the 1930s, Leach wrote the craft-classic, *A Potter's Book*, published in 1940, which continues to influence studio potters throughout thc world.

Where British furniture was concerned, there was on the one hand work done directly in the Arts and Crafts tradition, produced by men such as Edward Barnsley and Peter Waals, and on the other passable imitations of the Bauhaus style — pieces in steel tubing produced by PEL (Practical Equipment Ltd). After the advent of Nazism, a number of leading Bauhaus designers emigrated to England, and furniture in plywood by Breuer was produced by the firm of Isokon. There was thus a sharp contrast of possible attitudes — the client who scorned both 'reproduction' and ordinary commercial designs was offered a choice of quite different sorts of furniture, which in turn reflected opposed philosophies and attitudes towards the notion of 'craftsmanship'.

It was only where textiles, and especially woven textiles were concerned, that there was a kind of unity between the best in the crafts and the best products of commercial firms. Marion Dorn, for example, provided designs for hand-knotted rugs, made, not by herself, but in the Wilton Royal Carpet Factory near Salisbury in

Jean Dunand,
lacquer screen,
c. 1925. Private
Collection

Wiltshire; and she also provided designs for Jacquard-woven cottons made by Donald Bros. Ltd, Dundee, and by Warner & Sons Ltd of Braintree. There was in fact a clear distinction between printed and pattern-woven fabrics, the former remaining largely in the hands of designers with some experience of weaving as a craft, the latter being at least sometimes the work of leading fine artists such as the painter Duncan Grant and the sculptor Frank Dobson.

The traditional crafts were by this time thought of in Britain as things to be fostered and protected against contemporary conditions. There was a government-sponsored Rural Industries Bureau, plus a network of craft guilds and societies, among them the Red Rose Guild, the Guild of Spinners, Weavers and Dyers, and the Embroiderers' Guild. These associations, though admirable in themselves, were a proof of the way in which handicraft had been pushed to the margin in little more than a century.

A more successful fusion of craft and industrial attitudes took place in Scandinavia. The movement was pioneered in Sweden, where the First World War, despite the country's neutrality, created a housing shortage and an economic crisis. The Swedish reaction was to take the new theory of Functionalism, and try to humanize it by effecting a marriage with a still strongly surviving craft tradition. One reason for abandoning the view that industry was the only true ally of Functionalism was that Sweden was not as yet a highly industrialized country, and the situation made it seem necessary to use existing skills as well as easily available raw materials. Another factor was the Scandinavian tradition of co-operative living. It showed itself in the influence exercised by the Svenska Slöjdföreningen (Swedish Society of Arts and Crafts and Industrial Design), which bound together designer, manufacturer, retailer and consumer. Swedish design made an impact at the Paris

From left to right: Marcel Breuer, 'Wassily' chair, 1925; tubular steel chairs, 1926; long chair, produced for Isokon Furniture Ltd., London, Victoria and Albert Museum; PEL furniture, 1930s, courtesy PEL Birmingham

The Music-room,
exhibition at Alex,
Reid and Lefevre
Gallery,
December 1932.
Fabrics by
Duncan Grant,
carpets by Vanessa
Bell

Exposition des Arts Décoratifs in 1925, and this was followed by
the Stockholm Exhibition of 1930, which made 'Swedish Modern'
an international rather than a purely national phenomenon, with
strong possibilities for export. Scandinavian design, stark at first
under the influence of the Bauhaus, softened perceptibly in the
thirties, both to accommodate itself to the taste of a broader market,
and to make room for the Scandinavian concept of *'hygge'*, a word
perhaps best translated as cosiness.

One of the pioneers of the new style was the Swedish furniture
designer Carl Malmsten, who first came to prominence in 1916

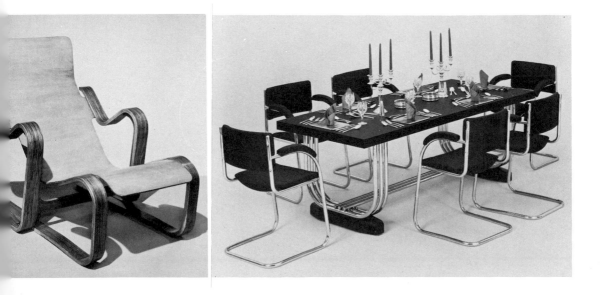

Above:
Edward Hald,
'Grail-Glass' bowl,
made at the
Orrefors
glass-factory,
1927.
Copenhagen,
Museum of
Decorative Art

Above right:
Simon Gate,
engraved glass
vase, made at the
Orrefors
glass-factory,
1936. Copenhagen,
Museum of
Decorative Art

Opposite page:
Bauhaus tapestry
by Gunta
Stadler-Stölzl,
1927–8

when he won a competition for the decoration of the new Stockholm Town Hall. Characteristically, Malmsten's doctrine was that 'moderation lasts. Extremism palls ... ' and in any event he felt there was always a place for some of both, and every conceivable degree of variation in between. Also important were Simon Gate and Edward Hald, two painters who were recruited to work as designers at the Swedish glass-factory at Orrefors. Both had to learn about glass and glass-blowing from the beginning. They started as designers of cheap services of table-glass, but soon branched out into luxury display pieces, some of which seem to have been intended to rival those of Marinot. Their position as artist-designers within a humanized factory system is typical of Scandinavia, and leading Scandinavian designers work in much the same way today.

Essentially what one sees, in Europe and America, in the period from 1920 to 1940 is a constant crossing and recrossing of supposedly fixed demarcation lines. There was industrial design which tried to find an alternative to craft processes; there was similar design which was on the contrary heavily craft-influenced. There was rural craft, seen as something to be preserved (but also as something which was essentially incapable of further development). There was also craft which, standing entirely outside the industrial framework, attempted to rival the fine arts. And finally there was craft exercised within the framework of traditional luxury — things done by hand because quality not quantity was the aim, and because only handwork could produce the results a wealthy and sophisticated elite demanded.

15   The Survival of Craft

It is, however, superficial to see the development of late nineteenth and twentieth-century craft purely in terms of the Arts and Crafts Movement and its consequences.

One weakness of the craft movement was its hostility to the city. It was not only that leading craftsmen, English and American in particular, often moved into the country in order to pursue their chosen occupations in peace. It was also that craft itself often came to be associated with a vanishing rural life. The enthusiast for craft was too often content to be a preservationist and an antiquarian, rejecting the industrial society that surrounded him but not finding anything viable to put in its place.

It is, of course, true that certain craft skills survived in rural communities after they had been lost in urban ones. The daily exercise of these skills was seen to impose a beneficial rhythm on the life of the individual. But the rural crafts were not dynamic — that, indeed, was part of their attraction. One of their chief virtues, in the eyes of many Arts and Crafts enthusiasts, lay in the stubborn conservatism which kept patterns — the precise form of a chair, the shape of a basket, the sequence of stitches in a fisherman's jersey — intact as they were handed down from generation to generation. Some of these inherited patterns were genuine community inventions, eloquent about the society which had produced them. The make of a farm-wagon showed what district it came from, and often its form was dictated by the particular type of agriculture practised in the district where it was built. A countryman's smock, by its form of ornamentation, indicated the wearer's trade. While the rural craft tradition remained intact and unself-consciously healthy, these badges of distinction would be proudly preserved and known for what they were. Even so, and even within that context, other so-called country artefacts had very different origins. They were the fossilization of items which had once been fashionable in town, simplified to match the skills of less expert and sophisticated workmen.

In the second half of the nineteenth century an exploration of the rural crafts began which was necessarily conducted from outside, in the same fashion that traditional folk-songs and country-dances were now being recorded and preserved. Rural skills had come to be thought of as precious relics, just as much so as the actual objects which rural craftsmen produced. This introduced an element of self-consciousness. A particular kind of basket-weaving, practised in the context of a folk-museum, must of course be different in spirit from the same work done to supply a need which has existed,

Traditional
basket-making

Traditional
patterns in a
countryman's
smock

so far as the craftsman knows, from time immemorial, and which
no one has ever thought of questioning.

The enthusiasts for rural craft therefore had to tread a narrow
path. Insofar as their interests were purely antiquarian, they
wanted to keep what they discovered precisely as it was. Development, for them, equalled degeneration. Arguments developed
about 'pure' and 'impure' forms of craft activity. What short cuts
were permissible? What ready-prepared materials could be brought
in from outside? In fact, how far could the rural craftsman adapt his
skills to a changing market and new economic conditions without
losing his identity? Often it seemed as if enthusiasts for rural craft
wanted to put the whole community into aspic.

What the leaders of the Arts and Crafts Movement did think they
found among rural craftsmen was a useful repertoire of skills, simple
and effective ways of handling traditional materials, ways which
were in danger of being forgotten. They also found, as Morris did
in the case of the Sussex chair, patterns which could be adapted
creatively to suit their own, mostly middle class, needs and
circumstances. Some of these adaptations were more sensible than
others. In the 1880s, for example, Mrs Oscar Wilde turned the
labourer's smock into a fashionable form of 'aesthetic' dress.

What the Arts and Crafts Movement tended to ignore was craft
skills still to be discovered in an urban context. For them, there was
a simple opposition of values — rural craft on the one hand, urban
industry on the other. Yet at the same epoch a remarkable
generation of sociological investigators were busy exploring and
mapping every possible variety of urban manufacture, and the
picture they present is very far from simple. One of the best sources
of information for the period is Charles Booth's series of seventeen
volumes, *Life and Labour of the People in London*, published in
1891–1903. Five volumes are devoted to a minute examination of
London's industry. But the word 'industry' is in fact very broadly
defined. There are descriptions of many trades which would now be
thought of as crafts — jewellery-making and silversmithing, book-
binding, the making of saddles and harnesses, cabinet-making and
carriage building. It is clear that the town, as much as the country,
retained a huge reservoir of craft skill, as this description (chosen at
random amongst many) will serve to make plain:

> For carriage-wheels, the utmost nicety of finish is demanded,
> and no little judgement in selecting the wood for each part. The
> best London-made wheel has its outer rim in six or seven pieces
> or 'felloes' (pronounced 'fellies'). Each felloe is connected with
> the hub by two spokes; every hole must be bored true, and every
> spoke fit exactly in its place, and the felloes, as set together, form
> an exact circle ready for the tyre. For the putting on of the tyre
> the wheel is bound down tightly, the hot iron ring is dropped
> over it, and then the whole is slowly immersed, revolving as it
> dips into the cold water. The iron rim contracts as it cools, and,
> in contracting, binds the whole together.

Country craft,
traditional
lacemakers at Le
Puy, France

The world which Booth and his assistants describe is also full of complicated traditional arrangements:

> *Whip-makers* employ stick dressers, stick finishers, riding-whip makers, thong-makers and braiders; these last being women machinists who braid hunting crops. Holly sticks are used for driving whips, and come from the Southern counties, or sometimes from France, but the French stick is not so strong. The sticks are kept by the whip-maker and left two years to season, and are then sent to the whip-dresser, who works at home. The business is confined to a few families, and the art handed down from father to son. The dresser pairs off the bark and chips the knots, and, where required, adds an artificial knot ... The finishers, working on the master's premises, are those who 'quill up', attaching the quill to the top of the stick and the thong with it. They also fix on the handle, and sometimes the metal mounting ... Hunting crops require skilled work. The best are made of whalebone and cane combined, and then braided with gut. Thong-makers' wives often plait the thongs, but the women 'braiders' are not usually the wives of whip-makers.

While division of labour, as in the example I have just given here, was almost the rule, the divisions clearly had the sanction of long-established custom. They take one back to the arrangements enforced by late medieval guild regulations, and are strongly reminiscent, too, of the structure of craft in the late eighteenth century, as described in the publications of the Académie Royale des Sciences and in Diderot's *Encyclopédie*.

It has been customary, perhaps under the influence of Arts and Crafts propagandists, to think of industry as something which broke down long-standing patterns of employment. To some extent this is true, particularly in the textile industry. But even here there are passages in Booth's book which seem to take the reader back to a much earlier epoch, when skill and judgement in handling materials were at a premium. Clothworking, the process of shrinking and finishing woollen cloth once it had left the loom, continued to be carried out largely by hand, an experienced hand working in each case with an apprentice.

What has been insufficiently recognized, in any case, is the way in which certain ideas about craft, which belonged to the age-old heritage of the guilds and which owed nothing to Arts and Crafts theoreticians, were incorporated into the organizational structure of industry as it developed. Despite the triumph of the machine, factory labour developed its own hierarchy. Skilled men were needed, both to make the machines themselves and to provide patterns for things which would afterwards be reproduced in quantity. These skilled men naturally expected to be paid more for their work than those who were unskilled, and they jealously guarded their privileges. Craft unions were formed, to help them resist the pressure of the unskilled mass as much as that of their employers. The printing trade, even in late Victorian times,

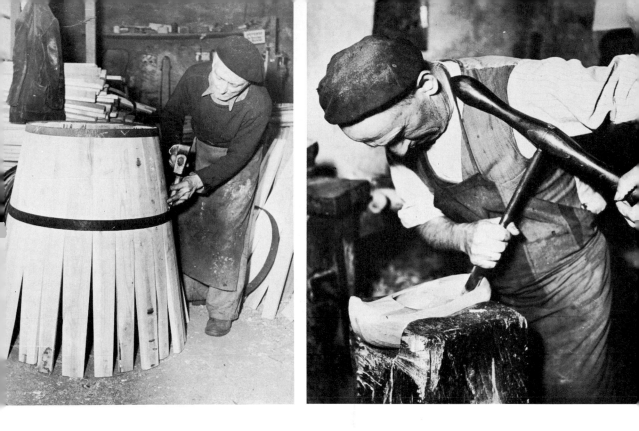

Country craft,
barrel-making
(left) and
sabot-making
(right)

showed lines of demarcation which had existed almost since printing itself was invented. Letterpress printers were still expected to serve a seven-year apprenticeship. In the machine-room a proportional rule was enforced, which allowed only two apprentices to every four journeymen, with one more apprentice for every three additional journeymen. Thus the unions concerned themselves, both here and elsewhere, not only with questions of pay and hours, but also with demarcations between different types of job and different degrees of proficiency. The differentials they insisted upon were a source of friction between one class of worker and another, and sometimes a cause of disruption within industry itself. The situation has, of course, continued until the present day.

The undoubted impetus which the machine gave to production did, however, have another aspect which has been too little examined in its relationship to craft and the idea of craft. This was the question of sweated labour. Sweated labour was the handcraftsman, in this case unprotected by any organization, working in competition with the machine. Nineteenth-century social reformers were generally agreed that it was, of all the social evils of the time, both the greatest and the most difficult to eradicate. Its nature is well described by Clementina Black in her polemical book on the subject, though this was not published until 1907:

> Sweating reduced to its true meaning was not the oppression of the poor in the interests of the poor; but the effort of an uneconomic system to extract from the misery of the unorganised, ill-equipped worker the equivalent of organised, well

paid and well equipped industry. It was the competition of flesh and blood with machinery.

Immigrants, not as yet deeply rooted in the countries to which they had come, were particularly vulnerable to exploitation in sweatshops. Some of the most powerful contemporary descriptions of sweated labour can be found in the pages of Jacob A. Riis's campaigning book about social conditions in New York, *How the Other Half Lives*, which was published in 1891:

Up two flights of dark stairs, three, four, with new smells of cabbages, of onions, of frying fish, on every landing, whirring sewing machines behind closed doors betraying what goes on within, to the door that opens to admit the bundle and the man. A sweater, this, in a small way. Five men and a woman, two young girls, not fifteen, and a boy who says unasked that he is fifteen, and lies in saying it, are at the machines sewing knickerbockers, 'knee-pants' in the Ludlow Street dialect. The floor is littered ankle-deep with half-sewn garments. In the alcove, on a couch of many dozens of 'pants' ready for the finishing, a bare-legged baby with pinched face is asleep. A fence of piled up clothing keeps him from rolling off on to the floor. The faces, hands, and arms to the elbows of everyone in the room are black with the colour of the cloth on which they are

Division of labour in a handicraft environment. The studio at Doulton's factory in Burslem, *c.* 1910

working. The boy and the woman alone look up at our entrance. The girls shoot sidelong glances, but at a warning look from the man with the bundle they treadle their machines more energetically than ever. The men do not appear to be aware even of the presence of a stranger ... They work no longer than to nine o'clock at night, from daybreak. There are ten machines in the room; six are hired at two dollars a month.

The presence of the sewing machines does not make the scene Riis describes here a truly industrial one. Rather, it represents a further degeneration of a situation already familiar in the textile workshops of the sixteenth century. Though sweating was especially typical of the garment trade, and though it was here perhaps that it existed in its most virulent form, it showed itself in many other trades as well. As a result two things happened. One was a decline in standards of workmanship. The other, very often, was a resort to superfluous ornament, like that so often complained of in nineteenth-century furniture. Ornament helped to conceal both defects in construction and shoddiness of materials (if a thing was not to be well made, there was no point in using what was good). And ornament in its own right also helped to sell goods, since handwork (of which it was the visible sign) retained its prestige in the market. We have already seen the same thing happen in the conflict between the illuminated manuscript and the printed book. The Victorians, when they lamented a collapse both in standards of workmanship and in standards of design, were, as often as not, speaking of things made in competition with machines rather than actually by them.

The first industrial designers were well aware of the evils of sweating. They wanted to use the ease and logic of the machine to get rid of it. Those blindly committed to the crafts movement looked in another direction. Sweating was a flat contradiction of their doctrine of the supremacy of the hand and of actual contact with materials, therefore they ignored it. What they feared was not this, but the incursion of the amateur. Though the enthusiasm of amateurs was one of the things that carried the first craft revival along, the leaders often spoke ill of them. Ashbee, for example, thought that 'collectively the output of the amateur, which is in bulk an output of very second rate work . . . has absorbed a large part of the skilled craftsman's market in many directions.'

The man who mounted perhaps the most devastating attack on the whole Arts and Crafts ethos was Lewis Mumford, author of *Technics and Civilization*. Where Ashbee denied that the movement was in any way 'a nursery for luxuries, a hothouse for the production of trivialities and useless things for the rich', Mumford contradicts him without naming him:

> Modern handicraft, which sought to rescue the worker from the slavery of shoddy machine production, merely enabled the well-to-do to enjoy new objects that were as completely divorced from the dominant social milieu as the palaces and monasteries the antique-collector had begun to loot.

In fact, Mumford sees the salvation of handicraft in the involvement of amateurs — the very thing Ashbee detested:

> To survive, handicraft would have to adapt itself to the amateur, and it was bound to call into existence, even in pure handwork, those forces of economy and simplicity which the machine was claiming for its own, and to which it was adapting mind and hand and eye.

In Mumford's view, the amateur craftsman should not oppose the machine, but humbly learn from it. The simplicity the original craft revivalists sought in the country crafts is challenged by a diametrically opposite model. The amateur, with whom the future of handicraft must (he feels) rest, is now likely to be 'liberated by the very simplicity of good machine forms.'

16 Craft Today

Today, when we try to assess the actual state of craft, we see that Mumford's prophecy, made in the 1930s, has in one sense been fulfilled. Amateur interest in the crafts has perhaps never been stronger. On the other hand, his idea that the crafts would begin to model themselves on functional design has not, even in amateur hands, been strikingly accurate.

The Functional tradition, promoted by the Deutscher Werkbund and even more strongly by the Bauhaus designers, is now also seen to have vernacular roots within industry. Not all the items Victorian industry produced were fussy and elaborate. Some were very much the contrary. Some of these unself-consciously 'functional' items were meant not for domestic but for actual industrial use, such as the battery-powered miners' handlamps which were in production by the mid-1880s. Others were made for medical or

An industrial designer advertises his own wares: Raymond Loewy's Bauhaus-influenced office, 1934

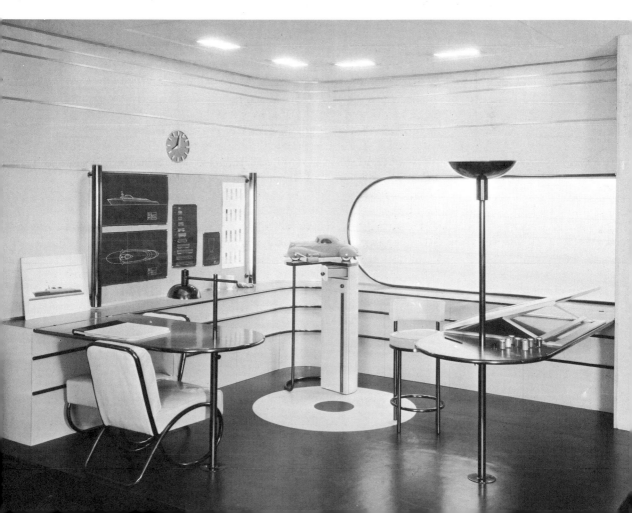

Half-plate
wet-collodion
camera by Horne
and Thornwaite,
c. 1860

scientific purposes, such as laboratory glassware and modern surgical instruments; and others still were forms of packaging, considered important for their contents rather than for their own sake. Into this category fall stoneware inkwells and jars, and glass bottles for patent medicines. To these must be added domestic wares made for use in circumstances where cheapness, utility and durability counted for more than ornament — china and glassware sold for use in taverns and popular restaurants; plain door furniture; brass wardrobe hooks. Technological advance had its own contribution to make — manufacturers were forced to invent forms for items which had no historical precedent. The invention of photography led to the manufacture of cameras of all types; and when a domestic supply of electricity became available there was a call for electric fans, electric heaters and electric tea-kettles. Designing these was one of the jobs Peter Behrens was asked to do by his employers at AEG.

It was important that the machine did not remain in the factory, but gradually penetrated both the home and the office. It also asserted its supremacy on the highroad. These developments gave an enormous boost to industrial design, and did much to divorce the idea of design still further from that of craftsmanship. With the new mechanical artefacts it could not be assumed that their forms arose naturally from the process of making them, though they did spring from the tasks machines were expected to perform. The industrial designer's role was too often that of an editor, rather than that of a creator of forms *ab initio*. He became involved in the design process only after the engineer had done his best or worst. In his autobiographical volume *Industrial Design*, Raymond Loewy recounts how the turning-point in his career came when he was asked to re-style the already well-established Gestetner duplicating machine in 1929. 'The Gestetner', he comments:

> is a classic example of what the profession can contribute to a manufacturer's lasting success. It deserves attention for another reason: it points out the early differences between a straight

engineering approach and the designer's attitude when faced with the same problem — in this case note the four protruding tubular supports. As a consumer-conscious designer, I detected the inherent hazards of the four protruding legs in a busy office. While my client, Sigmund Gestetner, seemed hesitant about giving me the redesign assignment, I quickly sketched a stenographer tripping over a leg, paper flying everywhere. This sold him, and I got the job.

If one looks through Loewy's case-book, one sees that much of his work consisted of providing attractive and serviceable envelopes for existing mechanisms — automobiles, radios, refrigerators — which had come into existence quite independently. Loewy's designs, while certainly intended to make things easier, pleasanter and safer to use, were also meant to promote sales by giving the potential customer the idea that any previous machine of the same type he might possess or have access to was obsolescent. Often this was legitimate enough — manufacturers were making improvements in performance which did not in fact affect the outer envelope of the machine, and Loewy and other designers were asked to find a way to express these improvements by inventing a kind of visual signal or signals. But Loewy's career also brings one face to face with the phenomenon of 'consumerism' — the liberation of the desire to own from the strict claims of necessity.

Long before the Industrial Revolution, this desire had existed at a certain social level. Superfluity was the mark of superior status in the Middle Ages. The ceremonial stepped buffet, covered with gold and silver plate which was never meant for use, is a case in point. Queen Elizabeth I of England left wardrobes full of many hundreds of sumptuous dresses when she died — far more, even, than she

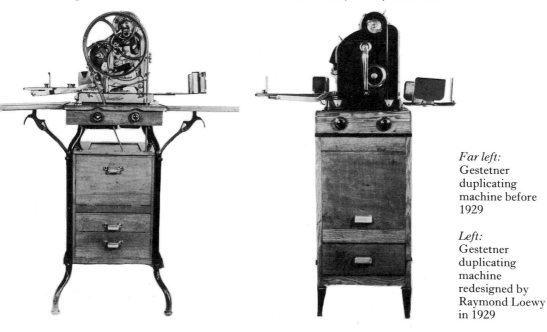

Far left:
Gestetner duplicating machine before 1929

Left:
Gestetner duplicating machine redesigned by Raymond Loewy in 1929

required in order to provide the ceremonial pageantry expected of a monarch. Throughout the seventeenth and eighteenth centuries the pace of change quickened, until following the mode became a kind of mania in the upper strata of society. It was not merely the irregularity and capriciousness of the Rococo, but its insistence on novelty at almost any price, which offended Neoclassical moralists. The Industrial Revolution, however, by making a huge flood of goods available, and by lowering the price of many domestic articles, greatly extended the limits of the market, which was affected by fashion rather than need. At the same time, by loosening the social structure itself, it gave objects additional importance as tangible badges of prestige. But consumerism was nevertheless not the child of the machine, but only its ally. The machine made it possible to implement desires, in particular the desire to accumulate, which had always been present in Western society.

But there was something else as well. The modern movement in the fine arts had not been going for very long before machines began to cast their spell over the imagination of painters and sculptors. The first Futurist Manifesto of 1909 proclaimed, in a famous phrase that 'a racing car ... is more beautiful than the *Victory of Samothrace*.' Picabia made the machine part of his subject-matter, and his lead was followed by the Dadaists with whom he consorted. Marcel Duchamp, mounting a freely-turning bicycle wheel on a stool to create one of his 'readymades', proclaimed the end of traditional sculpture. At the same time, artists started to explore the culture of the mass. The Cubists, in their collages, made use of fragments plundered from a reality which recognized nothing as being permanent.

At the same time, art in general began to move away from the notion of fine craftsmanship. It no longer mattered whether or not a thing was finely painted, it mattered only that it was fiercely original. Refinement of workmanship began to be seen as a sign that this essential originality was lacking, and that the work of art had therefore failed in its primary purpose, which was to express its creator's spirit.

During the interwar years, the crafts survived, though they were often mocked at for being stuffy, unoriginal and nostalgic. They also, as they had done from the beginning, offered a means of escape to those who hated industrialism. To concern oneself with the crafts was to reject the society that surrounded one. Craft, indeed, survived in part because it became identified with a certain kind of middle-class taste. Consumerism became as much the craftsman's ally as his enemy. Craft objects were often prized, not so much for their own sake, but because they implied a fastidious rejection of surrounding vulgarity.

The austerity imposed by the war years seemed to give a second chance to the crafts ethos — the Utility Furniture made in England at this period was certainly lineally descended from the English Arts and Crafts tradition, though neither in materials nor in standards of workmanship did it in any way approach traditional Arts and Crafts ideals. But the post-war period saw an immense upsurge of exuberant popular design, and a fascination, even in the luxury market, with materials which possessed no craft connotations whatsoever, notably various kinds of plastics. Though Scandinavia continued to turn out craft-influenced artefacts which found a ready market all over the world, Italian and American designers promoted a very different style, from which all craft-connotation seemed to have been banished. More and more there seemed to be a shift in focus. A thing was identified, and coveted, not as an object in itself, but for some service it performed, and this service in turn linked the possessor to others participating in the same activity. A television set would be a case in point, fully meaningful only when switched on and displaying an ever-moving flux of images, shared with thousands of other viewers.

The Pop Art of the 1960s was an exuberant, if also ironic, celebration of a culture in which, so it seemed, craft could have only a very minor role. The artist-as-hero appeared in a new guise, as the leader of a fresh revolt against bourgeois standards. The cautious 'beige taste is good taste' attitude of the surviving descendants of the Arts and Crafts movement was especially condemned. Restraint in design, truth to materials, and a preference for what was natural (e.g. wood), as opposed to what was synthetic (e.g. plastic), were all rejected by the avant garde as irrelevant to the new age. But there was more to Pop than simple fascination with mass-culture. Its roots were in Dada, and more especially in the highly esoteric work of Duchamp. Superficially, it might counsel an ironic worship of what was vulgar; more fundamentally, it gave the conception of a work of art — its ruling idea — primacy over the means of its embodiment. It was a comparatively short step from Pop to the

Joe Colombo, 'Chair 4801', 1962, manufactured by Kartell of Milan

Conceptual Art which was one of its successors, despite the fact that Pop Art was often so exuberant, while Conceptual Art took pride in being austere. Richard Long, the leading conceptual artist in England, makes art of words, photographs, unshaped stones and equally unshaped pieces of wood. 'I like sensibility without technique', he said recently — a statement which would be echoed by many other artists of his persuasion.

The result of these developments in the fine arts, apparently so opposed to everything the word craft might be thought to have stood for, has been a paradoxical renaissance. The 1970s saw the

Richard Long, section of his Venice Biennale installation, 1976

upthrust of a second Arts and Crafts movement, which was in some respects very different from its predecessor. There were a number of reasons for this revival. One was the fact that Pop Art's self-identification with mass-consumerism began to seem unattractive, whether or not it was tinged with irony, in a world where the environment was increasingly at risk from industrial processes. At the same time, there began to appear a hunger for physical virtuosity in the handling of materials, something which many artists were no longer happy to provide. The result was a renewed fascination with the figure of the artist-craftsman, who replaced the Pop painter or sculptor as a fashionable culture-hero. There was another, and perhaps adventitious, reason why the crafts once again began to attract the limelight. This was the growth of feminism. Unlike the fine arts, the crafts had never been sexist. While there were craft activities, such as blacksmithing, which were thought of as being primarily a male preserve, the reasons were obvious physiological ones. Others, such as knitting and embroidery, were thought of as largely, though certainly not entirely, the preserve of females, since they belonged to a domestic setting. But sex itself had never been a bar to eminence in the crafts; and from a historical point of view it seemed as if the creative energy women had been unable to use in painting and sculpture had often flowed into other kinds of making, which fell into the category of 'craft'. This, too, made achievement in the crafts a matter of topical interest.

Yet there is more to it than this. It seems to me that what one might call traditional craft has survived in the United States and Western Europe in two basic guises. One is the last remnant of the tradition of making things by hand, which Charles Booth described eighty years ago in *Life and Labour of the People in London* and which stretches far back beyond that to the guilds of the late Middle Ages. Gunsmiths, saddlers, bootmakers, makers of musical instruments — these and others continue to turn out high-quality products by long-established, non-industrial methods. Most commonly these craftsmen work in workshops with others, rather than on their own, and in such workshops the principle of division of labour is accepted without question. So, too, is the idea that the craftsman should serve some kind of formal apprenticeship.

Secondly there is rural craft and craft in the Arts and Crafts tradition, the two things now being almost inextricably combined. Potters, glass-blowers, weavers, wood-turners and furniture-makers provide a whole range of simple, sensible, sturdy domestic goods for a market mid-way between the one for luxuries and the one for things mass-produced by machine. In fact, the two approaches to craft can also be defined in terms of class. In one sort of workshop, often urban, artisans work for an upper-middle and upper class clientele, and there is a sharp division between makers and consumers. In the other sort, often country-based, craftsmen who are essentially middle class work for their peers. Most of the latter have not been born into the trade they practise, but have consciously elected a way of life which seems to them more satisfactory than the possible alternatives.

The effect of two such very different approaches to the idea of hand skill can best be understood by contrasting objects in a field where the machine still has very little importance. 'Real' jewellery, made of precious metals and precious or semi-precious stones, is a case in point. The great urban jewellery houses — Cartier, Boucheron, Van Cleef & Arpels, and their rivals — continue to make up sumptuous jewels in their own workshops, often designing an item to commission. But the designer and the workman are different people, and usually the piece itself passes through diffe-

Above left:
Jewellery by the
English craft
goldsmith Gerda
Flockinger

Above:
Traditional setting
of precious stones.
The Cartier
workshop, Paris

rent sets of hands before it is completed. Diamond-setting is a separate trade in itself, highly skilled and thus requiring a long apprenticeship. The exquisitely finished and perhaps rather cold products of this system make a striking contrast to the products of the so-called 'craft jeweller', generally fashioned by one person from first design to finished article, and with the mark of the hand deliberately left visible. The two kinds of jewel express contrasting attitudes to life as well as addressing themselves to very different markets. But both are craft products, at least in the broad sense in which the word has been used in this book.

Western craft workshops, however organized, are not enough to supply a market which combines an insatiable appetite for the visibly hand-made with a strong degree of price-resistance to what is more expensive than the equivalent machine-product. A modern version of the old East India trade supplies European and American markets with so-called craft products, many of which are made of shoddy materials and under sweated-labour conditions. Yet there is more to it than this. If we look at the situation of the crafts in the countries of the Third World, and sometimes too among ethnic minorities in developed nations such as Canada, New Zealand, Australia and the United States, a complex pattern of activity emerges — the growth of a whole new range of so-called tourist arts, rooted to a greater or lesser degree in traditional culture but differing sharply from it. Mexico offers a whole series of slightly different examples — of the continuation of traditional crafts, but now with a view to selling them outside their communities of origin; and of the actual invention of new art forms for commercial purposes. Craft is promoted by Mexican government agencies for a variety of reasons — because it promotes a favourable image and brings in tourist dollars; because it provides peasants in depressed agricultural areas with an additional source of income; and because it stresses Mexican national identity.

The Seri Indians, inhabiting a coastal strip of desert along the

Gulf of California in the Mexican state of Sonora, are the beneficiaries of a whole new craft industry, which has come into existence since the early 1960s. Today nearly every adult Seri Indian is a wood-carver, though making such carvings has little precedent in traditional Seri culture. One man, an Indian called José Astorga, began experimenting with the dense local ironwood in 1961, producing bowls, spoons and other useful items. In 1963, after a conversation with an American woman who was carving a tortoise in the same material, Astorga began making carvings of animals. Soon half a dozen Indian families had followed his lead. Then American buyers began making regular trips to the region for the purpose of buying the carvings, and at the same time the Seri began to find it more and more difficult to make a living from their traditional industry, fishing, owing to outside competition on the one hand and government restrictions on the other. By the mid-seventies, by now with the financial backing of the Mexican government, carving animal figures in ironwood had become a major local industry. Anthropological research has shown how much of what is produced takes its form from the standards set by distant and alien markets. A researcher reports:

> Many of the first life forms had mouths sawn in, nailheads for eyes, and in general there was an attempt at a more 'realistic' depiction of the animal. Today's pieces are far more stylized, though the carvers often still include lines indicating various anatomical features of the animal. The Seri carvers whom I have questioned attribute this change to two factors. First, they say it saves time to omit, or at least de-emphasize, these details. Second, they point out that the tourists prefer the more stylized forms. Some of the Seri have gone on to say that they themselves prefer the more realistic carvings, that they are better, more attractive.

I have chosen this particular example because it illustrates another, and perhaps even more important aspect of craft activity today — the continual blurring of the line between craft and fine art. Where the new 'ethnic' arts are concerned, a substantial part of what the craftsmen produce is painting or sculpture — but made in series. In Africa, for example, there is now an immense output of sculptures of this type. Many, like the Kamba carvings produced in Kenya, are the work of tribal groups with little or no sculptural tradition of their own. Kamba carvings are a particularly extreme example in another sense as well. Though genuinely hand-made, more often than not they are produced on a kind of assembly line. The same model is repeated with great exactitude many hundreds of times. One carver blocks the figure out, another does the head, a third the ears and feet. A fourth worker adds finishing touches where required, in wire, leather or ivory.

Meanwhile European and American artist-craftsmen have gone to the opposite extreme. What they produce has ambitions to be judged as we would judge art, for formal, emotional and ideological

Seri Indian wood-carving of a tortoise. Tucson, Arizona State Museum

content, though there are still vestigial references to utilitarian forms. The following statement, borrowed from the catalogue of a recent (1980) exhibition of Swedish Craft and Design at the Victoria and Albert Museum, gives a glimpse of the prevailing semantic and indeed intellectual confusion:

> Nils-Gunnar Zander's lead sculpture is art handicraft. Some people would perhaps call it free art. I think it is art handicrafts in the best sense of the word.

The sculpture in question is a series of vase-like forms which are also female torsos, with fluttering flanges of metal upraised in place of arms.

Some of the reasons for this blurring are to be found in the way in which the contemporary fine arts have developed. 'Art handicraft' steps in to supply a market which becomes restless when offered the naked idea in place of the idea embodied in an object. It attracts those who prefer the visibly well executed to the visibly badly executed. But the craftsmen are inevitably drawn towards conceptions which have their roots in avant-garde art. For example, throughout the 1970s, one influential school of artists put stress on the idea of 'process'; that is, they believed that the work of art should make an explicit statement about the way in which it had been created, and that this statement should in fact be its content. Weaving, which is by its very nature the sum of a number of quite distinct actions, analysable from the appearance of the finished work, naturally seemed closely related to a philosophy of this type. Many of the items included in the recent international touring exhibitions of 'Miniature Textiles', put together under the auspices of the British Council, were epigrammatic statements about a process or group of processes, and their makers clearly considered this to be a sufficient reason for producing and showing the work.

Philosophies originating in the world of the fine arts have led craftsmen to strain very visibly against the traditional boundaries of their disciplines. Jewellery, a craft of self-adornment traditionally connected with wealth and the wish to display it, was increasingly wracked with this kind of unease. For example, the avant-garde Dutch jeweller Gijs Bakker describes some of the developments in his thinking as follows:

> In 1973 I made a 'bracelet' from a very thin gold wire. The gold wire was put on the arm as tight as possible until the wire disappeared into the flesh. Only an indication (marking) is visible. In a next step I don't use a wire. I only show the imprint from a wire which has been there before. The imprint has the function of a piece of jewellery. One could call it an organic jewellery piece — organic in the sense that a print is a growing process with a clear course. An imprint appears or grows by an action and wanes after some time, to disappear completely. In another way I tried to make an invisible piece of jewellery by putting something under the clothing . . . .

One characteristic of the fine arts in the years since 1945 has been

to stretch traditional categories to the point of meaninglessness. Thus Richard Long, already quoted in this chapter, can today make what his audience accepts as 'sculpture' by taking a planned and measured walk through a particular bit of countryside and recording his progress in words and with lines drawn on a map. This tendency has shown itself in the crafts as well. On Saturday 28 October 1978, at the Arnolfini Gallery in Bristol, a young jeweller named Tom Saddington exercised his craft before an audience by having himself welded inside a giant steel can and remaining there for two hours before being released with the help of a can opener made on the same scale. A press release issued by the gallery called this 'the logical consummation of his recent work in which he constantly attempts a redefinition of "jewellery" and the verb "to wear".'

Even artist-craftsmen who profess less extreme attitudes find their ambitions turning towards areas which were previously considered the province of the painter or sculptor. Elizabeth Fritsch is currently one of the most admired craft potters in England. She said in a recent statement:

> The work of Piero della Francesca is undoubtedly my highest, if unattainable ideal in respect of colour and clarity; air and light; the unity of geometry and precision in painting. There is also in the frescoes the combination of the stoniness of the materials with the airborne softness of the colours which I find very moving. He used colour in a most musical, rhythmic, atmos-

pheric way, above all the celestial blues, the colour of heaven . . .
I'd say that he above all artists gives the feeling that Space is like
Silence; form like music.

Now that we have accustomed ourselves to purely abstract
painting and sculpture there seems indeed no reason why pots —
clay objects which happen to take the form of vessels — should not
be contemplated with the same kind and degree of attention that we
bring to art-works outside the craft category.

But is the category itself meaningful any longer, when it can be
made to embrace on the one hand a Western artist-craftsman such
as Elizabeth Fritsch and on the other (if we happen to be reading an
anthropological text) the kind of iron-smith who combines with
others with different specialities to repair cars in a West African city
such as Lagos? Forging a hand-made spring to replace an original
made in a factory, the African is still visibly engaged in exercising a
craft. John Houston, a writer of wide experience of the current craft
scene, wrote recently in a catalogue introduction:

> The *artist-craftsman* reunites elements which had been forced
> apart six hundred years ago. Our modern reactions to the words
> *craftsman* and *artist* are the result of innumerable struggles
> about status and expression, marketing and sensibility. In the
> last six hundred years their meanings have been bombarded by
> the words around them, a swarming cluster of meaning perpe-
> tually in motion. This process has inevitably shaped our under-
> standing of the past but it can also distort our approach to
> modern work. The continuing arts-crafts debate is largely about
> historical categories and definitions, but these precedents are
> usually and confusingly expressed as opinions because the
> historical process which formed them has been discounted or
> forgotten.

Gijs Bakker,
Queen Bib.
Collection Gijs
Bakker

This seems to me an excellent summary of the difficulties which
one encounters in trying to tell the story of craft, which becomes as
much the story of man's reactions to a word — a word which
encapsulates a whole intricate complex of ideas — as it is the story
of what man's hands and man's ingenuity have been able to do with
both organic and inorganic materials.

There are, however, some constants. A fundamental part of the
story of mankind's development is the struggle to escape from
drudgery — to find quicker, easier and more efficient ways of
making things. Another struggle, sometimes combined with the
first and sometimes separate from it, is the eternal search for ways
to make things which are better in themselves, which can be
imagined but not known until they have been created. As modern
research has shown, medieval man, like those who came after him,
used machinery for both these purposes whenever it came within
his reach. He would not, for example, have seen the point of doing
laboriously with his own muscles and energy what a water-powered
fulling-mill would do and do better. Similarly, medieval man
regarded division of labour as natural and reasonable, not least

because he experienced society itself as a collective organism. Ruskin's denunciations of the machine, and also of piece-work, were referred by him to an ideal medieval society which never in fact existed, and to that extent at least the first Arts and Crafts Movement was no more than a comedy of misunderstandings. Yet it owed its success to the fact that it answered a deep need. Men were beginning to be frightened of the machine, and to feel that it was dehumanizing. At the same time the nineteenth century saw a great growth in the consciousness of self, and the idea that the maker of objects should be allowed to express his individuality, the separateness and uniqueness of his own existence through the very process of making, was a natural consequence of a profound psychological shift. The emotions that moved Ruskin's contemporaries are just as powerful today.

In fact, the inhabitants of the fully developed industrial countries are enmeshed in contradictions. The machine may be fearful, but it retains its allure. It promises not only that life will be materially easier, but that everyone will have more leisure. Yet it seems to threaten both our sense of individuality and our connection with the life of the instincts. At a purely superficial level, the conflict can be seen in opposing currents of fashion. The suspect passion for the 'ethnic', for whatever seems homespun or handmade (though without too much concern for actual origins), is matched by the equally suspect passion for High Tech — the appearance rather than the reality of the most advanced technology.

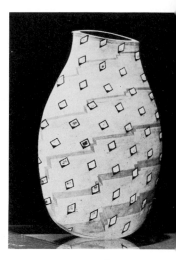

Elizabeth Fritsch, *Optical Pot with Swinging Counterpoint,* 1978. Collection Elizabeth Fritsch

It more and more seems that the craftsman of the future must be not only, as Mumford predicted, the amateur, employing for his own satisfaction great stretches of spare time which only technology can provide, but also the ambiguously labelled artist-craftsman. The role of such a craftsman must be that of a maker of symbols, and his own existence is also symbolic. He takes his place in industrial society as a necessary antonym, a visible reminder of where industry has come from. His products speak of individual fantasy, of the primacy of instinct, of direct relationships to materials. The fine artist, as this book has tried to demonstrate, has a comparatively short history — far shorter certainly than the immense history of craft. Craft seems once again to be taking over a role which not the development of industry but the intellectual categorizations of the Renaissance forced it to abdicate. What industry itself has taken, handcraft will never get back, for industry too is craft, in that word's largest sense.

Bibliography

Adachi, Barbara, *The Living Treasures of Japan*, London 1973

Aitchison, Leslie, *A History of Metals*, 2 vols, London 1960

Amaya, Mario, *Tiffany Glass*, London 1967

Art Nouveau: Belgium/France, catalogue of an exhibition held at the Institute of Fine Arts, Rice University, Houston, Texas, 26 March –27 June 1976; and at the Art Institute of Chicago, 28 August–31 October 1976

The Arts and Crafts Movement in America, catalogue of an exhibition held at the Art Museum, Princeton, 21 October–17 December 1972; the Art Institute of Chicago, 24 February– 22 April 1973; and the Remick Gallery of the National Collection of Fine Arts, Smithsonian Institution, Washington D.C., 1 June–10 September 1973

Banks, Steven, *The Handicrafts of the Sailor*, Newton Abbot and London, 1974

Bayley, Stephen, *In Good Shape: Style in Industrial Products, 1900–1960*, London 1979

Beer, Eileene Harrison, *Scandinavian Design*, New York, 1971

Birmingham Gold and Silver, 1773–1973, catalogue of an exhibition held at the City Museum and Art Gallery, Birmingham, 28 July–16 September 1973

Black, Clementina, *Sweated Industry*, London 1907

Blake, Peter, *Le Corbusier: Architecture and Form*, London 1966

Booth, Charles, *Life and Labour of the People in London*, 17 vols, London 1902–3

Breguet, C., *A.L. Breguet, Horloger*, Enfield, Middlesex n.d.

Brett, Katherine B., *English Embroidery, 16th to 18th centuries*, Toronto n.d.

Burckhardt, Lucius, (ed.) *Werkbund*, Venice 1977

Buxton, L.H. Dudley, *Primitive Labour*, London 1924

Caiger-Smith, Alan, *Tin-glaze Pottery*, London 1973

Camp, Charles W., *The Artisan in Elizabethan Literature*, New York 1974

Carter, Thomas Francis, revised by L. Carrington Goodrich, *The Invention of Printing in China and its Spread Westwards*, 2nd edn., New York 1955

Cellini, Benvenuto, *Memoirs* (trans. Macdonell), London and New York 1906

Colonial Williamsburg, *The Leatherworker in Eighteenth Century Williamsburg*, Williamsburg 1967

Digby, George Wingfield, *Elizabethan Embroidery*, London 1963

Dillon, Edward, *The Arts of Japan*, 3rd edn. London 1911

Christopher Dresser, catalogue of an exhibition held at the Camden Arts Centre, London, 3 October–25 November 1979; and at the Dorman Museum, Middlesbrough, 8 December 1979–19 January 1980

Drexler, Arthur, and Daniel, Greta, *An Introduction to Twentieth Century Design*, from the collection of the Museum of Modern Art, New York, New York 1959

du Colombier, Pierre, *Les Chantiers des cathedrales*, Paris 1953

Durkheim, E., *De la division du travail social*, Paris 1893

Eliade, Mircea, *Forgerons et alchimistes*, Paris 1956

Encyclopaedia of the Social Sciences, New York 1957

50 Years: Bauhaus, catalogue of an exhibition held at the Royal Academy of Arts, London, 21 September–27 October 1968

Geijer, Agnes, *A History of Textile Art*, London 1979

Giedion, Siegfried, *Mechanization Takes Command*, New York 1948

Gimpel, Jean, *The Cathedral Builders*, New York 1961

Gimpel, Jean, *La Révolution industrielle du Moyen Age*, Paris 1975

Glasgow 1900, catalogue of an exhibition held by the Fine Art Society Ltd, Glasgow 16 June–28 July 1979; Edinburgh 18 August–8 September 1979

Gonem, Rivka, *Ancient Pottery*, London 1977

Graburn, Nelson H. (ed.), *Ethnic and Tourist Arts: Cultural Expressions from the Fourth World*, Berkeley, Los Angeles, London 1976

Haedeke, Hans-Ulrich, *Metalwork*, London 1970

Haslam, Jeremy, *Medieval Pottery*, Princes Risborough 1978

Hayward, J.F., *Virtuoso Goldsmiths*, 1540–1620 London 1976

Imperial Ottoman Textiles, catalogue of an exhibition held at Colnaghi, London, 1979

James, George Wharton, *Indian Basketry*, 3rd edn., Pasadena 1908

Jervis, Simon, *High Victorian Design*, catalogue of a travelling exhibition, organized for the National Programme of the National Gallery of Canada, 1974–5

Johnstone, Pauline, *The Byzantine Tradition in Church Embroidery*, London 1967

Joy, Edward T., *English Furniture, 1800–1851*, London 1977

Jugendstil, catalogue of an exhibition held at the Palais des Beaux-Arts, Brussels, 1 October–27 November 1977

Knoop, Douglas, and Jones, G.P., *The Mediaeval Mason*, 3rd edn., Manchester and New York 1967

Knowles, Dom David, *The Monastic Order in England*, 2nd edn., Cambridge 1963

Koll, Michael, *Crafts and Co-operation in Western Nigeria*, Freiburg-im-Breisgau 1969

Kramer, Stella, *The English Craft Guilds*, New York 1967

Levasseur, E., *Histoire des classes ouvrières et de l'industrie en France avant 1789*, 2nd edn., Paris 1901

Loewy, Raymond, *Industrial Design*, London and Boston 1979

Lucie-Smith, Edward, *Furniture: a concise history*, London and New York 1979

Mackmurdo, A.H., (ed.), *Plain Crafts*, London 1892

Madsen, S. Tschudi, *Art Nouveau*, London 1967

Madsen, S. Tschudi, *Sources of Art Nouveau*, 2nd edn., New York 1975

Maine, Sir Henry, *Village Communities in the East and West*, London 1876

Mantoux, Paul, *The Industrial Revolution in the Eighteenth Century*, new and revised edn., London 1961

Mason, Otis T., *The Origins of Invention*, London 1895

Mason, Otis T., *Indian Basketry*, 2 vols, New York 1904

Matson, Frederick R., (ed.), *Ceramics and Man*, Chicago 1965

Mendelsohn, Isaac, *Slavery in the Ancient Near East*, New York 1949

Morris, Barbara, *Victorian Embroidery*, London 1962

Mumford, Lewis, *Technics and Civilization*, London 1934

Naylor, Gillian, *The Arts and Crafts Movement*, London 1971

Oakley, Kenneth P., *Man the Tool-maker*, 6th edn., London 1972

Polak, Ada, *Modern Glass*, London 1962

Pye, David, *The Nature of Design*, London 1964

Pye, David, *The Nature and Art of Workmanship*, Cambridge 1968

Renard, G., and Weulersse, G., *Life and Work in Modern Europe, 15th to 18th centuries*, London 1926

Renard, G., *Life and Work in Prehistoric Times*, London 1929

Riis, Jacob A., *How the Other Half Lives*, New York 1971

Ris-Pacquot, O.F., *Les Petites Occupations manuelles et artistiques d'amateur*, Paris 1894

Robertson, Seconaid Mairi, *Craft and Contemporary Culture*, London 1961

Rossbach, Ed, *Baskets as Textile Art*, London 1974

Salzman, L.F., *English Industry of the Middle Ages*, revised edn., Oxford 1923

Sanders, Barry, (ed.), *The Craftsman: an anthology*, Santa Barbara and Salt Lake City 1978

Sayce, R.U., *Primitive Arts and Crafts*, Cambridge 1933

Schädler, Karl, *Crafts, Small-scale Industries and Industrial Education in Tanzania*,

Munich, London and New York 1968

Schaefer, Herwin, *Nineteenth Century Modern: The Functional Tradition in Victorian Design*, New York and Washington 1970

Schmutzler, Robert, *Art Nouveau*, abridged ed., London 1977

Sèvres Porcelain from the Royal Collection, catalogue of an exhibition held at the Queen's Gallery, London, 1979–80

Singer, Charles, Holmyard, E.J., and Hall, A.R., (eds.), *A History of Technology*, Vol. I, 'From Early Times to the Fall of Ancient Empires', Oxford 1954

Singer, Charles, Holmyard, E.J., and Hall, A.R., (eds.), *A History of Technology*, Vol. II, Oxford 1956

Snook, Barbara, *English Historical Embroidery*, London 1960

Strong, Ronald, and Brown, David, (eds.), *Roman Crafts*, London 1976

The Swedish Institute, *Design in Sweden*, Stockholm 1977

Tait, Hugh, *The Golden Age of Venetian Glass*, London 1979

The Thirties: British Art and Design before the War, catalogue of an exhibition held at the Hayward Gallery, London, 25 October 1979–13 January 1980

Unwin, George, *Industrial Organisation in the Sixteenth and Seventeenth Centuries*, Oxford 1904

Upadhyay, M.N., *Handicrafts of India*, Secunderabad n.d.

Victorian and Edwardian Decorative Art: the Handley-Read Collection, catalogue of an exhibition held at the Royal Academy, London, 4 March–30 April 1972

Vienna: Turn of the Century Art and Design, catalogue of an exhibition held at Fischer Fine Art Ltd, London, November 1979–January 1980

Josiah Wedgwood: The Arts and Sciences United, catalogue of an exhibition held at the Science Museum, London, 21 March–24 September 1978

Acknowledgements

The publishers wish to thank all private owners and museum authorities who have kindly allowed works in their collections to be reproduced; they should also like to acknowledge the help of many photographers and photographic agencies in supplying photographs. Further acknowledgement is made for the following:

By gracious permission of Her Majesty the Queen, 176, 208; AEG Telefunken Archiv, 144, 245 (bottom); Archives d'Architecture Moderne, Brussels, 238, 242 (left); Archivo Mas, 110 (top and bottom left); courtesy Bauhaus Archiv, 259; Biblioteca Ambrosiano, Milan (Codex SP66 f.3r), 9; Bildarchiv Foto Maburg, 40 (left and right), 99 (left and right), 239; courtesy of the Trustees of the British Museum, London, 14, 15, 16 (top left), 17, 20 (top), 21, 26, 36, 47, 50, 56 (top), 60 (top and bottom), 80 (right), 81, 90, 92, 153 (right); Christie's London, 180; Christie's New York 222 (left), 231; Cooper-Bridgeman Library, 154 (bottom right), 155, 166–7, 189, 197, 201 (right), 203, 208, 211, 212 (left), 217, 218 (left and right), 225 (right), 226, 235, 240 (right), 253, 262, 270; Crafts Advisory Committee, 280; Alan Crawford/Victoria and Albert Museum, London, 213; Documentation Photographique de la Réunion des Musées Nationaux, 49 (top right), 136, 148 (top), 183 (right); Philippe Garner, 223, 225 (left), 230–1, 242 (right), 248 (bottom), 255; Gestetner, 271 (left and right); Sonia Halliday, 97 (bottom), 104, 120, 150; Hamlyn Picture Group Library, 19, 24 (left and right), 25, 28, 41 (photo Alex Poignant), 57, 102, 105, 106, 107 (bottom), 112, 117, 140 (left), 141, 156, 160 (left), 171, 175, 177, 198, 227 (left); Bernard Henry/Seuil, 170; Hans Hinz, 174, 188 (right); Hirmer Fotoarchiv, 27 (top), 33, 37, 48; Edward Lucie-Smith, 62, 63 (top); Mallet, London, 69; Metropolitan Museum of Art, New York, 269; Musée des Arts Décoratifs, Paris, 249 (top), 250 (bottom), 250–1; Museum of American Folk Art, New York, 205 (bottom); Museum of London, 56 (bottom), 123; National Trust, 210; National Trust/ John Bethell, 164; Photosources, 101; Josephine Powell, 63 (bottom), 111; Jean Ribière, 263 (top and bottom), 265 (left and right); Ann Ronan Picture Library, 138 (left), 168, 169, 178, 185; Royal Collection, Stockholm, 246; Salvation Army, 267; Philip Sayer/*Crafts*, 260; Scala, 147, 154 (top and bottom left); Sekai Bunka Photo, 85 (bottom), 88, 89 (top and bottom); Ronald Sheridan Photo Library, 29, 49 (top left), 97 (top); Snark International, 131, 138 (right); J. L. Swiners/ Agence Top, 276 (right); Trinity College, Dublin/Green Studio, 129; University College, London, ©Department of Egyptology, 30; Victoria and Albert Museum, London, 205 (top), 279 (left), 281; Visual Arts Library, 20 (bottom), 38 (left), 46, 49 (bottom), 52, 53, 60, 66, 73 (top and bottom), 78 (bottom), 103, 108 (top and bottom), 109, 113, 114, 116 (left and right), 118, 119, 133, 139 (left and right), 151, 159, 161, 186, 215 (left and right), 219, 233, 234, 247, 249 (bottom right), 256 (left and right), 257 (top), 266, 272 (right), 273, 274 276 (left), 279 (right); Visual Arts Library/SPADEM, 272 (left); Werner Forman Archive, 76; Zauho Press, 16 (bottom).

Index